PREACHING
IN MY

Yes
Dress

PREACHING
IN MY
Yes Dress

confessions of a reluctant pastor

JO PAGE

excelsior editions

State University of New York Press
Albany, New York

COLLEEN,
Fellow
yogini!

warm wishes

Published by State University of New York Press, Albany

© 2016 State University of New York

Excelsior Editions is an imprint of State University of New York Press

For information, contact State University of New York Press, Albany, NY
www.sunypress.edu

Production, Eileen Nizer
Marketing, Fran Keneston

Library of Congress Cataloging-in-Publication Data

Names: Page, Jo, 1957–
Title: Preaching in my yes dress : confessions of a reluctant pastor / Jo Page.
Description: Albany : State University of New York Press, 2016. | Series: Excelsior editions
Identifiers: LCCN 2015030795 | ISBN 9781438460833 (hardcover : alk. paper) | ISBN 9781438460840 (e-book)
Subjects: LCSH: Lutheran Church—Clergy—Biography. | Women clergy—United States—Biography.
Classification: LCC BX8080.P195 A3 2016 | DDC 284.1092—dc23
LC record available at http://lccn.loc.gov/2015030795

10 9 8 7 6 5 4 3 2 1

Contents

Acknowledgments

An enormous number of people have influenced this book in a myriad of ways, and a detailed list would try the patience of any reader and still probably be incomplete. This is just a sampling of those for whom I am most, most grateful:

My warmest thanks to the passionate and intelligent people of Grace, Evangelical, and St. John's Lutheran Churches, as well as Emmanuel-Friedens Church, a federated American Baptist/United Church of Christ congregation. It was a joy to serve as your pastor.

I am grateful for the Revs. James H. Slater III and Deborah Steed, early and important mentors; the Rev. Dr. Gordon W. Lathrop, from whom I learned the power of good liturgy; and the Rev. Dr. Timothy Wengert, from whom I learned the richness of Lutheran theology.

I have had exceptional editors in my twenty-five years as a newspaper columnist, and so I give thanks for Shawn Stone at *Metroland* magazine, Jay Jochnowitz at the *Albany Times Union*, and the staff of SUNY Press, who "baby stepped" me through the process of publishing this book.

I have long been sustained and cheered by friends and colleagues who possess both great wisdom and great senses of humor. Fortunately for me, there are too many of you to name, but I must specifically thank Eugene Mirabelli and Karen Hosmer for their tireless love, wonderful conversation, and deep compassion.

My daughters, Madeleine Emma Page and Linnea Hope Page, have given me unsurpassed joy. With their lives, they taught me more about love incarnate than any doctrine ever could.

I dedicate this book to my late parents, Richard James Page Jr. and Norma Jane Gray Page, who brought their daughters, Leslie, Jackie, and Jo, to church.

Preface: Going In

As Sister Luke in *The Nun's Story*, the luminescent Audrey Hepburn makes convent life masochistically chic—all that pious obedience and semi-sexual mortification of the flesh. As a little girl, I wanted to *be* Sister Luke. But I was a preadolescent Lutheran and descended from sturdier stock than waifish, gorgeous Audrey. The death of my father when I was nine left me with a cause-and-effect sense of my own sinfulness. So even though it meant turning my back on the sexiness of Roman Catholic sisterhood, I decided that becoming a Lutheran pastor was an acceptable way to get back on God's good side. The problem: I was a girl, and my childhood branch of the Lutheran church didn't—and still doesn't—ordain women.

By the time I became an adult with a husband, an infant, and a master of fine arts in writing, I discovered that the larger branch of the Lutheran Church in America had long been ordaining them. I joined the ranks in 1993. Fifteen years later, I was in the ecclesiastical trenches: baptizing living babies and dead babies, presiding equally at church members' funerals and those of strangers at funeral homes, marrying couples—straight or gay, young or old, healthy or dying—on mountaintops and in living rooms, in churches and restaurants. And every week I preached compulsory words of hope scraped from my imagination or resignation, with a measure of eloquence that often outstripped my capacity to believe what I was saying.

Meanwhile, our country was turning conservative, xenophobic, paranoiac. Voices were urging that we return to our "Christian" roots. The towers fell, fears grew, wars followed. I didn't see how I could continue to serve this circumscribed role of pastor in an increasingly and restlessly fundamentalist world. Nor did I feel I was able to live as freely and openly in my personal life as I wanted to. I felt that everything I did, from the column I wrote for an alternative newsweekly, to my marital status, to how I raised my children and what clothes I wore, was affected, perhaps distorted, by my very public calling. I thought more and more that I wanted to be simply a woman and not a woman pastor.

But *The Nun's Story* stayed with me.

I learned a lot from that movie. I learned about vocation. Vocation isn't necessarily something you *want* to do; it's what you're called to do—that's how I grew to understand it. After all, everybody who knew her knew that Sister Luke had never been cut out for the convent life. Obedience was a constant struggle. She tries, for the entire length of *The Nun's Story*. She tries to follow the Rule, to practice all the disciplines. *All for Jesus*, she keeps telling herself, *All for Jesus*.

"The life of a nun is a life against nature," her kindhearted father warned her the night before she entered the convent. He took her out for a dinner of oysters and champagne, giving her an actual taste of all she would be giving up.

Instead of discouraging her, his words set Sister Luke a challenge. She spends her years working hard to succeed in leading a life against nature—not that success is a nunlike goal to pursue. But when World War II breaks out and she gets word that her father has been killed by Nazi soldiers, something changes in her. She can't deny the hate she feels. And she will never be able to forgive her father's killers, not ever. Finally she realizes that she must break her vows. She can no longer be a nun.

The whole time that Sister Luke lived the religious life, only a few sisters left. It was shame and failure to go out, her Mother Superior tells her. If she breaks her vows, she will not simply no longer be a nun; she will, in fact, be the unfaithful bride of Christ.

But Sister Luke is resolute. And that's when I learned about the phrase "to go out." It means to leave the religious life. It's a treason of sorts, a kind of spiritual suicide. And yet Sister Luke decides to go out.

My life took a different turn. It took a different turn not only because I wasn't Audrey Hepburn with her famine-sculpted hips and doe eyes, nor because I wasn't really a Catholic, in spite of my RC baptism and my mother's promise to the priest that she would raise her daughters in the one true faith. My life took a different turn because it wasn't a movie. And in becoming a Lutheran pastor, I didn't vow to be chaste, poor, or especially obedient. I didn't cut off my hair or put on a nun's habit.

Indeed, becoming a Lutheran minister is nothing like becoming a nun. But when I decided to go into the ministry, most of my friends and my family seemed to think I was no more cut out for one than the other. I was teaching high school English at a boys' school then, and one day a student asked me if I was going to have to get divorced to become a pastor. No, I told him. I don't have to get divorced. But you won't be able to wear the same kinds of things you wear now, he told me. I think he was thinking about my short skirts. And I figured he was right.

It wasn't only friends and family who had some misgivings about all this. I had a couple of fears myself. The first was that others would think I was a nerd of some sort, a conservative, judgmental Jesus freak in front of whom they could not swear or tell good jokes. The second fear was that I would get fat. Seriously, think about some of the ministers you have seen. Potluck suppers come with the territory, and most ministers are not in possession of bad-ass bodies. Nor am I. But I didn't get fat.

Then, right after graduating from seminary and—in fact—getting divorced, I began to realize a third fear: that even if I were not seen as a conservative, judgmental Jesus freak and even if I were not fat, no one would want to date, much less sleep with, a female pastor.

Well, those fears didn't materialize. Most people don't think I'm a nerd, though some assume I am. Others assume I'm a strident feminist bitch, which is kind of funny because I'm probably more nerd than bitch. But those are the people who don't know me. Once you've got a collar around your throat and a pulpit in which you stand, an awful lot of people are quick to draw conclusions about who you are.

But I *have* been changed in fundamental ways. The longer I have stayed in ministry, the more confident I have become in saying what I have to say about religion—and the less I value, even if I am still troubled by, what many, many other ministers have to say.

I've never shared the certainty of the conservative pastors who seem to have no trouble believing that they knew the mind of God. Psalm 139 says that God has "searched me out and known me." For these pastors, it was as if they had turned the Psalm on its head. "*I* have searched *you* out and known, *you*, God," it seemed they were saying.

And the God they seemed to know was a kind of loudmouthed, self-important, bad-joke–cracking, slightly paunchy, fifty-something white guy. Kind of like themselves.

But I didn't cotton to a lot of more liberal theologies, either. The big theme in twentieth-century liberation theologies is that God suffers with us. But are God's work and will only about suffering? Suffering is tiresome. Sometimes I've felt like Peggy Lee in a clerical collar and little velvet cocktail dress singing, in a smoky voice, "Is that all there is? Is that all there is, my friend? 'Cause if that's all there is, then let's keep dancing."

With my brainy—mostly male—colleagues and fellow seminarians, I shared an appetite for the elegance of Lutheran theology. Truly, it is a beautiful thing—both intricate and passionate, appealing to the mind's rage for order. But the problem with the pure hues of doctrine is that it doesn't really translate into parish life.

And the whole time I've been in ministry, our country has seen a frightening rise in fundamentalism, both Christian and Islamic. But unlike countries whose governments are built around Islamic law, the United States is not supposed to be a theocracy. Nevertheless, more and more voices are swirling ever more loudly, wrapping the United States flag around the cross and defining both faith and good citizenship by a certain code of moral convictions:

That supporting an unjust war is an act of faith. That banning gay marriage and the ordination of openly gay clergy is an act of faith. That opposing abortion as well as birth control and federally funded programs for women and children who live in poverty is an act of faith. That collapsing a domesticated God into a jingoistic patriotism is an act of faith.

There are a lot of Christian voices out there, a cacophony of voices. I speak, too, God's little foot soldier. And over the years, I have felt that I have become more of a voice and less of a person, more of a pastor and less of a woman. What would happen if I did what I had been saying for years that I wanted to do? What would happen if, like Sister Luke, I decided to go out?

I began to fantasize once more about Audrey Hepburn's Sister Luke, only this time it wasn't about the quasi-erotic nature of convent life. It was about what she does at the end of the film:

Unable to forgive—and love—the Nazis who killed her father, Sister Luke breaks her vows. She "goes out." And, unlike every other aspect of convent life, there would be no liturgy to mark her leave-taking.

Instead she enters a small room at the far end of the convent, a room full of shame, reserved for those few nuns who actually leave. And it is empty except for a table on which is laid the outfit she had worn to the convent the day she joined and a small sum of money, so that she is not destitute. And there is also a small mirror—a symbol of vanity, something denied the brides of Christ. But Sister Luke would no longer be a bride of Christ.

She removes her habit, veil, and wimple. She dresses in the outfit laid out for her, and it hangs loosely. Religious life has made her thin.

She looks in the mirror, unable to remember the last time she saw her own face. No longer is she the eager sister of her early years but someone different, older—a stranger.

The door through which she entered this room is different from the one through which she will leave. She is no longer allowed to walk within the convent confines. Instead a second door will open directly onto the streets of postwar Brussels.

There is no one to say good-bye to her, no one to give her a blessing. Instead she counts her money carefully and puts it in her pocket.

Then she reaches for the door latch. Sunlight floods in. And Sister Luke goes out.

Could I do that in my own life?

~

In the summer of 2004 I spent a week in Scotland co-leading a pilgrimage to the Abbey on the Isle of Iona. My teenaged daughters, Madeleine and Linnea, were among the travelers. After flying into Heathrow, our group headed north, spending a rugged week on bleakly lovely Iona—a week of communal living eating simple but delicious meals, sharing in daily worship services and intimacy with nature. When our pilgrimage was over, the others flew home, but my daughters and I took a side trip to Paris. Paris reminded me again of how much I prefer cheese, wine, Bertillon ice cream, and museums to hiking boots, hot-water bottles, and shared dorm rooms.

And now here we were, going through the security check at Heathrow Airport, returning to New York, trying to prove we were not terrorists. The security alert level in the metropolitan New York area had just been upgraded to orange, and we were flying into Newark International Airport. That's as good a time for a Xanax as any.

Making our way through security was time consuming and unnerving. They were checking everyone and everything. I kept thinking, I'm this blond woman without a head scarf with two teenaged daughters in halter tops and jeans. We are not terrorists. We are suburbanites.

Then I felt guilty because I was stereotyping, profiling.

"Can I search her?" the attendant asked me and not my daughter, which seemed a rude intrusion of her privacy. I nodded, and she began to pat down thirteen-year-old Linnea. She stood there very patiently while the woman ran her hands down the outside of her legs, up the insides. Then Linnea stretched out her arms and the woman checked along her ribcage and along each bare arm.

The guard looked in her carry-on. A thirteen-year-old's stash: a notebook, a stuffed animal, a sleeping mask from the flight over, some fruity-flavored lip gloss. Socks.

Then the guard asked Linnea to turn on her portable CD player.

I was surprised. She had personally gone through Linnea's stuff. Why not just open up the CD player too? Then I realized the whole point of asking her to do it was so if there was an explosive device in there, it would go off in Linnea's face and not the guard's.

So my daughter opened the CD player. No explosives. Just a Maroon 5 CD. Nothing else. Not even any rap. We passed into the boarding area and the guard turned her attention to the next passengers. After everyone else had also been checked we finally were allowed to get on the plane and we headed, uneventfully, to Newark.

Back in upstate New York—back in the suburbs—every predictable thing started up again. School began, Sunday School began, band and choir practice began. I was back to feeling the usual vice grip of parish ministry. This was my twelfth year as a Lutheran pastor, eight of them spent at the theologically and socially progressive parish, Grace Lutheran Church in Niskayuna.

Back on the job, I drove from place to place, meeting to meeting, twisting up and down the dial to the various Christian radio stations that I sometimes listened to as a form of mental torture. I am not that kind of Christian. But you'd never know from listening to Christian radio that there are any other kinds. Then I started thinking that maybe I really am *not* a Christian. Not at all. Let *them* have the word. It's been an epithet since it was used in Antioch to describe the rabble-rousing Jesus crew in the first century.

(Except that the rabble-rousing first-century Jesus crew was much more akin to what progressive Christians are today. They stood against the government. They flouted Rome's version of "family values." They had a variety of different Christianities. Nobody was a Bible thumper, because there was no Bible to thump.)

Back on the job, I went to meetings, wrote reports, wrote sermons, preached, and pretended that I had some kind of conventional prayer life. When I wasn't working, I ate breakfast with a friend, played backgammon with my daughters, did the occasional load of laundry, and cooked the occasional nice dinner.

But behind all that activity was this looming fear:

The previous summer, I had completed a novel I had been working on in fits and starts for three years. The novel now sat on my desk in an old shirt box. I didn't know what to do with it. Sit on it, a friend said. Just let it sit for a while. For a year.

That seemed like astonishingly bad advice. Still, I had begun to follow it by default. For one thing, I had no idea how to go about getting it published. For another thing, if it *were* to be published, I was afraid its content would surely jeopardize my job as a parish pastor. They say it is ignorance and fear that make young girls neglect birth control; in the same way—only I was not so young—ignorance and fear were making me neglect the novel.

The really important thing, I told myself, was not to *publish* the novel, but to keep on writing. Write another. Write, write, write, I told myself.

But what was I going to write about? Maybe I was a one non-hit wonder. Maybe I had no more stories to tell, nothing to say.

I began to cast about for plots. The plot's the thing. But everything I dreamed up seemed the stuff of chick-lit. Relationships, troubled girls, and mothers. Self-discovery. No.

But finally I got an idea.

I remembered the look on Linnea's face as she stood there waiting patiently while the security agent patted her down. She looked beatific. She so often does.

What if I wrote a novel about a crazed Christian woman who lets her beatific-looking kid get blown up at the security check in an airport? Blown up like a suicide bomber, except that the kid would not have known what the mother was intending to have happen?

Just like the woman who drowned her kids a few years ago in Texas, my character would be a woman who was mentally unbalanced—nuts, in fact. She would be a fervently fundamentalist Christian who thought that by exploding her child, she was saving her from a corrupt and decaying world. She would believe—against all reason, against all evidence—that her child would be saved by Jesus at the very same time that her child was serving as an example of what Jesus himself had done: be martyred. I mean, this is how a lot of fundamentalists in all the faith traditions think.

This is a great idea, I thought. Why not? I thought.

I figured the novel could revolve around the dovetailing stories of the Christian fanatic and the defense attorney's middle-aged psychologist, Audrey, who would be a lot like me.

I figured this would be a snap. I knew all about Christianity. Plus, I had spent a lot of time researching the far-right fringes of the major religions—to say nothing of the hours I'd spent subjecting myself to Christian radio. I knew enough about fundamentalism to write a book. And that was exactly the point.

But the more I thought about this, the more insistently some little voice in my brain began to whisper to me: if I had so much animosity to so many things Christian that I had to be a turncoat and further pillory and stereotype Christians, then maybe what I really needed to write was another kind of book entirely. Maybe I needed to look at my own feelings about the church and being a Christian minister.

I knew I had a lot to say about that. I also knew writing that kind of book would *not* be a snap. I knew that kind of book would jeopardize my job as parish pastor even more than the handful of sex scenes in last year's novel ever could have.

How had this happened? How had I come to this place? I thought I treasured Christianity, treasured the worship services, hymnody, preaching. I thought I loved the privilege of being allowed to walk with—and sometimes even guide—others. I always said that what I treasured most about Christianity was that, at its heart, it is about loving one another.

And yet over the years I had become more and more reticent to identify myself as a pastor of the church or even a Christian when I was in social situations that were not specifically church related. I discovered that whenever I told someone what I did for a living, something in the conversational flow shifted. It was as if I had said, *I've got early-onset Alzheimer's disease* or *I used to clean house for George and Laura Bush.* People didn't just say, "How nice" and move on to some other topic. There were two main kinds of responses. There was the polite response: *How nice that you're a pastor! You don't look old enough! Do you have a church? Oh, my cousins in the Midwest were Lutherans. You must like Garrison Keillor.*

Or there was the challenging one, which encompassed a spectrum of opinions ranging from the inquisitive (what did I think about religion and politics, religion and sex, religion and religious pluralism?) to the openly derogatory (didn't I realize how simply awful religion is?). I have lost track of how many times I have tried to ignore snide anti-Christian slurs, little pointed barbs no one would ever dare to say about most other religious traditions, except, I suspect, in extreme right-wing circles.

I also began to lose track of where my mouthpiece as a Christian apologist ended and my own convictions began, or where they overlapped. I was always speaking through the filter of my professional identity, no longer simply speaking as me.

If I questioned the wisdom of writing fiction about stereotypical Christian fanatics, I knew even more that I did not want to write nonfiction that explained, defended, excused, or indicted. If I were going to write about Christianity at all, it had to be *my* way, not as a pastor but as a long-silent presence behind the mask. It was not enough to only write nonfiction; it had to be *my* truth.

Throughout my years in ministry, I had had to write so many faith statements for one reason or another that now I couldn't remember what my truth was. Nor could I remember what I had said in any of those faith statements. I had always been writing a story, advancing a case. I had needed faith to get the job. And now had my pursuit of faith left me with only a facsimile of it?

All of my writing had been circumscribed by circumstances for years. I wrote weekly sermons, weekly prayers, monthly newsletters, periodic reports, all with a chatty, personal tone and an eye toward ballasting belief. I wrote biweekly columns on ethics for the local alternative newsweekly, a liberal rag in which I was unafraid to stir up controversy. My progressive political and religious views seemed popular with the readership. Yet even there I wrote as a pastor, a scrim over my most honest thoughts and opinions. I was always a company girl writing in service of the company's goal.

I had no idea what it would be like to write for an unseen audience, an audience of readers for whom the only true requirement was my honesty. Those who heard my sermons or followed my columns were real people, and I tailored my reality to accommodate what they most needed in theirs. But an unseen audience would not expect doctrinal adherence of me. They would not feel either genuinely or habitually compelled to listen to my sermons. I would not feel habitually compelled to please them. I would not have to visit them. I would not have to bury them if they died. I would not know them at all.

If I wanted to write the truth of my life going in and going out of Christian ministry, then I would have to write differently than I have done for all these years of serving Christ's people.

~

Recently I celebrated the twenty-second anniversary of my ordination. I've come to learn that the shape shifting I had previously decried as a warping of my authentic personality has, in fact, become who I am. My "pastoral identity," so often discussed when I was a seminarian and in my internship as a vicar, is no longer a thing apart from myself. And whether I have been warped or shaped by my experience, I can't honestly say.

I was out of parish ministry for four years. When I returned to the parish—on an interim and part-time basis—it was with a different mindset. I no longer cared if I knew exactly what or how I or others believed. I became freely vocal about my progressive theology and politics. I didn't need to portray my children's lives as perfect or them as model daughters (though I find them pretty close to the Platonic ideal of such a thing). Perhaps because I had less at stake—I was more financially secure, had grown children, was in an interim setting—I felt more able to walk with people on their journeys than when I had previously been itching to go off on my own journey away from the church.

I don't know what the future will hold for me as a pastor. I didn't really manage to "go out" the way Sister Luke did. I finally must admit I bear absolutely no similarity to the lovely Audrey Hepburn, who, as that spellbinding nun, symbolized religious life for me as a child and what leaving religious life would be like as an adult.

I remain, for now and in spite of myself, Pastor Jo.

1

Faith of Our Fathers

Faith of our fathers, living still,
In spite of dungeon, fire and sword
Oh, how our hearts beat high with joy
Whene'er we hear that glorious word.
Faith of our fathers, holy faith
We will be true to thee till death.

—"Faith of Our Fathers"
Frederick W. Faber, 1814–1863

The only part of the Latin Mass that I understood was the English part when the congregation said three times, very quickly, "Lord-I-am-not-worthy-that-you-should-come-under-my-roof.-Speak-but-the-word-and-my-soul-shall-be-healed."

"Lord-I-am-not-worthy-that-you-should-come-under-my-roof.-Speak-but-the-word-and-my-soul-shall-be-healed."

"Lord-I-am-not-worthy-that-you-should-come-under-my-roof.-Speak-but-the-word-and-my-soul-shall-be-healed."

My father said it, though I couldn't hear his individual voice. I probably said it, too. I don't remember. Then my father would go up to receive the parchment-papery circle of wafer that was the body of Christ. I didn't go up. I wasn't really a Catholic. I just went to Mass with my father for fun. That's the kind of kid I was.

I liked the holy water in the little holders by the door. It always seemed more slippery than real water, as if its power to bless and to heal were somehow related to my perception of it as having a special viscosity, not that I would have known to describe it that way.

I liked the genuflecting and the kneeling. I liked the marble columns that had pink veins running through them, reminding me of Beech-Nut Fruit Stripe chewing gum. I imagined taking a bite of one.

I loved the incense. And the mysterious sanctus bells that were rung at apparently random moments throughout Mass. Mostly, I guess, I loved the little memorial candles that flickered willy-nilly in their blue or red glass votives. From time to time my father would let me light a memorial candle for Aunt Alice or Grandpa or for his own father, Pop, who had died before I was born.

My father would give me coins to drop into the metal box that sat next to a pile of thin, wax-coated wicks. I would pick up one of those long wicks, light it from another candle, and then choose the votive I wanted. When my candle's flame began to flicker along with its companion candles, I would drop the wick into a metal tray, and its flame would gradually die out.

After my father died, I used to light memorial candles for him whenever I was in a Catholic church. I imagined him watching me as I set a little tongue of flame into a blue or a red votive cup. I imagined that he saw me lighting it for him, and somehow, in a way I didn't understand and could scarcely allow myself to trust, it made me feel closer to him.

I liked the memorial candles best. But I also liked the hollow sound of the priest's voice over the loudspeakers, echoing throughout the walls of the church—first here and then there—like a ventriloquist throwing his voice. I liked the way the ushers swished the offering baskets on their broomstick handles quickly up and down the pews, twice each service.

That's how you could tell it was a Catholic church. Because they took the collection twice.

In our church—my mother and sisters' church, my church—they took it only once, and it was gathered slowly, the shining brass basin passed from hand to hand by every person.

Our Saviour's Lutheran Church was very different from St. Augustine's Roman Catholic church, where my father went and where nearly all of my classmates—Catholics, like my father—went.

Our Saviour's Lutheran Church was a better church, of course, a more godly church. Somehow I had been brought up to believe that. I'm not sure why we thought we were better. Maybe it was because in my mother's church I was so much more terrified of God than I was in my father's church.

For one thing, in her church there was so little to distract you from the fact of God's awful presence. The pastor was a boring preacher who spoke unconvincingly of a loving God. In our hymns we sang of a God who existed only, it seemed, to menace us so that we should know ourselves as sinners, first and last. We sang *"Chief of sinners though I be, Jesus shed his blood for me"* and *"Come to Calvary's holy mountain, sinners ruined by the fall"* and *"Go to dark Gethsemane, All who feel the Tempter's power."*

They didn't sing in the Catholic church. They just murmured responses and kneeled a lot. Maybe the Catholics couldn't carry a tune. I'd never heard my father sing, but my best friend, Denise, was a Catholic, and she was most definitely tone-deaf.

The Catholic kids got to take Communion by fourth grade. I wasn't allowed to take Communion in my father's church because I was a Lutheran.

I wasn't allowed to take Communion in my mother's church either. I wouldn't be able to do that until I was fourteen. This was not only because I wasn't good enough, but also because I wasn't old enough to know just how not good enough I was. I would know a lot more about that by the time I was fourteen.

For some reason I was convinced that the Lutheran church was better than the Catholic church. But maybe that was why: because we *knew* we were poor, miserable sinners and there was no priest or penance to let us off the hook and convince us otherwise.

My two sisters and I had been baptized at St. Augustine's. That had been part of the deal my mother had had to strike with the priest to get married to my father: she had to promise to raise her children as Catholics. But somehow I think it was always understood that she would have the final say about our religious upbringing.

She had grown up a Methodist. I don't think she had been much of a Methodist. The only thing I ever remember her telling me about her girlhood church life was that her pastor had tried to kiss her—and it had not been a holy kiss.

It was after she was married and had children that she started going to Our Saviour's, a Missouri Synod Lutheran Church.

As a child I didn't know much about what it meant to be a Missouri Synod Lutheran. Or why, for a church in upstate New York, it seemed necessary to be identified with such a faraway and clearly backward state as Missouri. The "Show Me State." It wasn't even subtle; they might as well have called it the "Show-off State."

Nevertheless, being Lutheran in a town full of German and Irish Roman Catholics seemed very exotic to me. It was almost as exotic as being Jewish.

"Lutheran." I liked to say the word. And I liked Martin Luther, too, except for his haircut.

Luther seemed to struggle with the same thing I did: ever since I could remember, I had wanted to be good. And I certainly did not think I was.

I was a sinner.

Unlike the Catholics, we didn't tell our sins in secret, as if somehow we could be told to say a few "Hail, Marys" and get off Scot-free. We announced our sins in front of one another. Not the specifics of each sin, of course—that would be rude and would take too long. So rather than bother with individual peccadilloes, we simply announced our general total depravity.

First the pastor would say:

Almighty God, our Maker and Redeemer, we poor sinners confess unto Thee that we are by nature sinful and unclean and that we have sinned against Thee by thought, word, and deed. Wherefore we flee for refuge to

Thine infinite mercy seeking and imploring Thy grace for the sake of our Lord and Saviour, Jesus Christ. Amen.

Then the congregation spoke in unison the scathing admission of our human worthlessness:

O almighty God, merciful Father, I, a poor miserable sinner, confess unto Thee all my sins and iniquities with which I have ever offended Thee and justly deserve Thy temporal and eternal punishment. But I am heartily sorry for them and sincerely repent of them and I pray Thee of Thy boundless mercy and for the holy, innocent, bitter sufferings and death of Thy beloved Son, Jesus Christ, to be gracious and merciful to me, a poor sinful being.

I didn't know what God's grace and mercy would look like or feel like. But what was clear to me was that I was not good and could not be good and if I did manage to do something good, I would soon enough find out I was still not good enough. Nevertheless, I was expected to try to be good because the alternative was my justly deserved temporal and eternal punishment—a.k.a. hell. Hell in life and hell in death.

Hell would be like our basement only much, much worse because most things about our basement I rather liked. My father's woodworking shop was down there. My mother held our Camp Fire Girl meetings down there. All of those things took place in the finished part of the basement.

But there was another part of the basement, the part on the other side of the black sewer pipe.

That part was vast and dank and dark. Hell would be something like that—damp and underground. The stereotypical fiery furnaces of hell never made much sense to me.

I mean, in my favorite Greek story of Orpheus and Eurydice, Eurydice was given that blessed shot at trying to make it out of Hades, relying only on Orpheus's self-control that he not turn around to look at her until they were both once again aboveground.

But Eurydice was not trying to escape *flames*. She was trying to escape a dank prison, an underworld oubliette of bone-rattling chill that never warmed up, never dried out, never saw the sun.

Even though I knew Greek myth was all made up and Lutheran hell was a real place, I still feared it could be like the Greek version, and I really did not want to go there. I needed to keep close track on the number of things I did wrong versus the number of things I did right.

So, in an effort to track my status, I ranked my sins. In this respect it would have been helpful if I could have gone to confession at my father's church. That way I'd have known for sure which were the lesser sins and which were the greater sins. Lacking the priest's advice, I improvised my own ranking system.

For example, disobedience to one's parents was bad, but kind of inevitable. Thinking bad thoughts was bad, but inevitable. These were lesser sins.

Talking about somebody behind their back was very wrong. That was called being deceitful. The French-Canadians who lived across the river were deceitful, my mother always said. Yet she managed to talk behind people's backs quite a lot and somehow we were not supposed to consider it bad when she did it. I never understood how that worked, but I accepted it. She wasn't really being deceitful. She wasn't even French-Canadian!

Lying was definitely a greater sin, maybe the worst of all, except for stealing and killing. Lying was the really bad thing to do. Even though lying was a really bad thing to do, there were lies of lesser and greater consequence.

Little white lies were okay. Like the kind my mother would tell about Christmas presents or birthday presents or letting my Aunt Marion think my mother really liked her even though she couldn't stand her and talked about her all the time behind her back.

White lies were okay. Real lies were bad.

My first lie, the lie that haunted me for years, was about the butter cookies.

They were the round, thin cookies my mother made at Christmas. And apart from the fact that they had little pats of colored sugar on them, they could have passed as thick-cut Communion wafers. They were tiny. And one time before dinner I asked if I could have some cookies and my mother said, yes, just a couple. And I took five.

No, I hadn't lied, per se. I had disobeyed. But I had also omitted to tell her that I was disobeying her, which was, implicitly, a lie.

She had trusted me to do as she had said. To do otherwise was dishonest. I had taken five cookies. So what if they were small—they still counted.

Not that I would have owned up to it if she'd asked (and she wouldn't have; if Mom understood anything, it was a sweet tooth). I just kept quiet about it. For years.

One time I asked her how many "a couple" was. "Oh, maybe two. Or three," she said. I said, "Could it be four, maybe?" And she said, "Yeah, *maybe* it could be four."

Then I said, "Do you think it could be five, even?" And she said, "Well, no. I don't think there is any way that you could say 'a couple' meant five."

She had no clue how guilty I felt. She had no clue because I had never told her what I had done.

I wasn't good at owning up to individual sins, and in that way I was not a real Catholic, in spite of the baptism. Imagine having to tell the priest about the butter cookies. Or the Barbie shoe.

I was five when the Barbie shoe episode happened. And if intention means anything at all, I never intended to *steal* the Barbie shoe. I really only meant to give a stray a home.

I was at the five-and-dime where my mother worked, and there was this table of assorted junk—perfume bottles missing their caps, stockings in ripped boxes, teddy bears missing buttons. And there were some Barbie doll outfits, too, with packages half-opened so that they were missing some of their component pieces. Things had simply fallen out, like a Barbie clutch purse that was supposed to go with the fur-trimmed, red and white satin evening ensemble or a thigh-high boot intended to go with the psychedelic-print skirt and matching Nehru jacket.

I would never, ever have taken one of those half-opened packages. If I had wanted one, I would have asked my father to *buy* it for me and then have been content with his answer.

Nor would I ever have reached inside to take out one of the pieces that belonged to a complete outfit. Either action was unthinkable.

But—fallen like grace from one of the packages was a single red Barbie mule.

Just the one. One was all I needed.

Early Barbies didn't have a lot of different shoe styles. They had those unnaturally shaped feet with their permanently flexed toes that were designed for high heels and high heels only. And the heels Barbie wore were always the same—stilettos with a tiny band of plastic across the instep. Classic Mattel mules. And they came in different colors to match the many different outfits.

I didn't have many different outfits—my family was not one to overwhelm us with toys—so I took great care with those that I had. Only it happened I was missing one red shoe. And here it was, as if provided by the generous hand of Providence: a single red Barbie shoe.

So, making sure nobody saw, I slipped it carefully into my pocket, grateful to God for having seen to my needs. And Barbie's.

I figured I was not so much stealing as I was bringing back the missing, giving a lost shoe a purpose. Who else but I would have the heart to care so much about a little red Barbie shoe?

I brought it home and set it next to the other red shoe in the little wooden wardrobe my father had made for my Barbie clothes.

But I knew, deep down, what I had done: I had stolen.

And I just did not have the guts to bring the shoe back to the store and slip it back onto the sale table of damaged junk. Besides, I needed it more than the store did.

Oh, there were lots of sins I remember, lots of ways in which I was a disobedient kid. I put my feet on the sofa without taking my shoes off. I was noisy and hyper at the Camp Fire Girl meetings held in our basement. I didn't do a good job on my fire prevention booklet because mine was never picked as the winner anyway, so why bother? After a while, Smokey the Bear saying "Only YOU can prevent forest fires" meant very little to me. We didn't even live near any forests.

And there were more sins, as well. The biggest one, though, was clearly a sin of the flesh; I recognized that right away. Even though I had discovered it quite by accident, I knew immediately, as sensations ran through my body that made me want to point my toes just like Barbie's, that what I was doing *had* to be a sin.

~

My father died when I was nine. He died suddenly, though not "suddenly" as in a car wreck or a heart attack. He died over the course of a few weeks. Even so, that's sudden enough: he was healthy and in his forties. And then it was as if the script for his life had been exchanged with someone else's. His dying had no narrative setup to it. It just happened.

It began with stomach pains while we were vacationing in Maine. When we returned home, his doctor told him they needed to do "exploratory surgery." Even then surgery as means of "exploration" must have been a questionable concept. But that's what my mother called it. Exploratory meant that they might not find anything. I had explored beaches and never found beach glass.

They found an intestinal tumor of some sort, removed it, stitched him back up, and were going to send him home. It was getting on toward September, soon time for Daddy to pick all the tomatoes and make chili sauce. It was time for back-to-school preparations. It was time for my sister, Jackie, to start college, the first in our family ever to do so, and for me to start fourth grade.

He was not supposed to get sicker. The stitches were not supposed to break. The bile was not supposed to rush from his intestines and poison his whole body.

But it did. People from the hospital called us and told us to come right down. He had taken a turn for the worse. That was the expression my mother kept using when she would tell people: "Dick has taken a turn for the worse."

For the next three weeks, while Jackie and my mother visited my father, I sat in the lobby of Albany Memorial Hospital. I read a lot of books. Usually somebody—a relative or an adult family friend—sat with me. But I liked it best when I sat there alone.

Often I would go outside to the flagpole in front of the hospital. There were some blue spruce trees out there, like the ones Daddy had planted in our yard. There was a concrete sidewalk that encircled the flagpole and the trees. And there were petunias all around the edges of the sidewalk. White, purple, red, fuchsia petunias. They were pretty and they had a strong smell.

We had lots of things planted in our yard, which was big and well cared for. We had quince bushes and mums and a flaming Japanese maple. We had purple lilacs and white lilacs. We had honeysuckle and forsythia and lily-of-the-valley and some kind of wild cherry tree. We had apple trees and elm trees and lots of pine and juniper. We had tomato plants and Japanese lanterns and tiger lilies and rosebushes. And that year my mother had also planted dahlias. She had been bringing my father little bunches of dahlias as they blossomed.

But we didn't have petunias. And I thought they were the loveliest flowers, exotic and profuse compared with our yard that was so carefully terraced and tastefully landscaped. I almost felt guilty for preferring the riot of petunias to the gardens and lawns my father tended with devotion.

I walked around and around the circle of concrete sidewalk, and I sat in the waiting room every day for a week while upstairs, where I was not allowed to go, my father hung onto life.

Finally, so that she could stay at the hospital all day and night, my mother sent me to stay with my father's sister, Aunt Marion, who apart from her other failings had married a Jewish man only four months after her husband died. We were never supposed to mention that Chuck was Jewish, but surely both Aunt Marion and Chuck knew that. And what was wrong with being a Jew, anyway?

I also didn't understand why there had been this terrible outrage when they got married. And not because Chuck was Jewish but because he and Marion had married so quickly. Four months seemed like a long time to me, but my mother assured me that it was completely improper for her to have married so soon after her first husband's death. She seemed to think that maybe Marion had been seeing Chuck on the side.

The other problem with Aunt Marion and Chuck was that they lived in an apartment, as my best friend, Denise, did. For some reason I didn't fully understand, I knew that it wasn't good to live in an apartment instead of a house. It meant you were lower class.

Of course, technically speaking I suppose you could say we lived in an apartment, though my mother always said we lived in a duplex, meaning, I guess, that there were two apartments side by side, unlike two apartments stacked one on top of the other. Besides, we owned our house; we didn't rent. And it was a new house, not an old flat with speckled linoleum and a sink with a skirt to hide the pipes and metal cabinets.

But I always loved apartments. And I especially loved my Aunt Marion and Uncle Chuck's apartment.

Even though my father was in the hospital, staying at Aunt Marion and Uncle Chuck's was magical. I slept in a bunk bed in my cousin Pammy's room. I slept in the top bunk. It was like being at summer camp, which was something I had never done. I read Trixie Belden books and played with Pammy.

And I played with the wiggly little dachshund, Alfie. I asked the Eight Ball question after question. I ate in the kitchen with the speckled linoleum floor and watched a portable TV that had rabbit's ears on it. This was also supposed to be lower class, somehow—the rabbit's ears, I guess. Our television was an enormous clunky black-and-white console, which meant we had good taste, apparently. But Aunt Marion's was a color TV, and because of that any possible class distinctions were lost on me.

While I was staying at their house, my aunt and Uncle bought me a one-year diary. It was a pink leather book just a little bigger than my hand. It had a latch, as if it could lock, which I don't think it really could. It had lined pages edged in gold, and on the front in gold letters it said "My Diary."

I was excited to have a diary and assumed I would write in it every day, that I would write down everything I did. I soon realized that a diary is a time-consuming undertaking, and I was having fun doing other things, so my entries were shorter than I had intended them to be.

On top of that, I also had to leave lots of time to pray. I prayed for my father. "Lord, please let Daddy get well." "Dearest Lord Jesus, please *make* Daddy get well. Please *make* him."

But maybe I didn't really keep my thoughts enough on him. Maybe I was having too much fun. Because when my mother stopped by sometime during the week I spent at Aunt Marion's, I didn't ask about him right away.

Instead, I told her what I had been doing. I was having a good time. I was excited. But she just looked at me, and in a few minutes I realized I had made a big goof: I had not asked about Daddy first. I had just been going on and on about all the fun I had been having.

I stopped talking. I tried to look serious and concerned. I really *was* concerned. I really *was* worried. And I really *had* been praying.

So I asked, in a calmed-down voice, "How is Daddy doing?"

But she didn't answer. She just looked at me. We were standing in the doorway between the kitchen with the speckled floor and the living room with the portable color TV. She looked at me hard and sarcastically, a way I had never seen her look at me before.

She waited. Her silence hurt like a slap.

"You are such a faker," she said, speaking slowly, each word pregnant with disdain.

I felt my face flush hot and red, my stomach wrenching. I went deaf with shame, hearing only *You. Are. Such. A. Faker.* and nothing else, over and over again. My mother was saying something, but I couldn't hear her. And I was sure my aunt could hear what I did: *You Are Such a Faker.*

I was worthless.

And my mother was right. Still, I just kept on asking my mother about Daddy, pretending to be interested and concerned rather than undone by my shame and worthlessness. I kept up that screen of words until my mother and Aunt Marion got to talking about whatever it is grown women who didn't like each other much talked about. And when it was safe to retreat, I returned, full of self-loathing, to Pammy's bedroom and the shadowy recess of the lower bunk.

After a while my mother came in to say good-bye to me. I was crying, but I didn't know if she believed my tears were real or not. They *were* real. It was *all* real.

I knew I had been a bad daughter. That I had not written Daddy enough notes—not as many as he had written to me when he was still well enough to write them. And now I wasn't concerned enough about him. Why had I ever thought I could leave this all in God's hands? Why had I ever thought that I could pray for him and that would be enough?

∿

Back at home a week later, I found out that it really wasn't enough.

My Aunt Millie had come to stay with me and my oldest sister, Leslie, who was mentally retarded, while my sister Jackie kept our mother company at the hospital. Leslie and I were in our beds one night when my mother and sister came home. I could hear them talking to Aunt Millie in the living room, but I couldn't hear what they were saying, only that their voices were low and sad. What else could it have been but my father's death that made them return home so late and speak so softly? And yet I couldn't imagine that. As long as they stayed in the living room talking to my aunt, it would be just another night when I couldn't get to sleep.

Then my mother came into the bedroom and turned on the light switch. It was the light switch that turned on silently, as if padded with velvet. My father had put it in when he had painted our bedroom. My mother had made new curtains from fabric printed with images of dancers styled after the paintings of Degas's ungainly ballerinas. I had never liked their thick calves and crooked arms.

But I had loved the light switch. It was the light switch that I would turn out each night that my father carried me into bed, pretending I was a princess and he my adoring lord. We would stand at the head of the hallway and I would sing *Dunh-da-da-da-da-da-DAH!*, as if a curtain were opening to reveal the two of us. Then I would curtsey to the imaginary crowd, and he would bow and then he would sweep me up, princess style, and carry me down the hallway.

At the entrance to the bedroom he would pause, bend down a bit, and let me flick out the light using the silent, velvet-padded light switch. And he would carry me across to my bed and tuck me in, along with all of my stuffed animals—Pokey the bear, Casper the ghost, and Flathead the bunny. And I would say three prayers with Daddy—"Jesus, Tender Shepherd"; the Lord's Prayer; and a Hail Mary. I didn't say a Hail Mary when my mother tucked me in. It was a Catholic prayer, and it wouldn't have been right. But I loved it.

Hail, Mary, full of grace, the Lord be with thee. Blessed art thou amongst women and blessed is the fruit of thy womb, Jesus. Holy Mary, mother of God, <u>please</u> pray for our sinners now and at the hour of our death.

"Please" was my own addition. It seemed rude to order the mother of God to do anything.

Then my father would kiss me and tell me he loved me and say, "See you in the morning" (my mother always said "see you in the a.m.") and I would say it back—"see you in the morning" (though with my mother I said "a.m," which I preferred because I thought it was more intellectual sounding).

That night, though—that September night when she and Jackie got back from the hospital—my mother came into the bedroom and turned on the light with the silent switch, woke us up, and said, "Girls, your father passed away tonight."

Passed away is what she said.

I knew then—and it still seems so today—that it was better to say "passed away" than "died."

Girls, your father passed away tonight.

Immediately Leslie burst into a fury of loud wailing and crying. I was astonished. She cried instantaneously, as if she had been cued, as if she had been shocked. I didn't know whether to be jealous or irritated.

I cried second. I cried slowly. I didn't know what any of this meant. A dead father. A father who had passed away. No Daddy anymore?

I couldn't even remember the last time we had walked down the hallway like princess and lord. I hadn't singled out the last time we had done that, thinking, "This could be the last time we will do this," because it never, ever had occurred to me that it *could* be the last time.

I had thought Daddys were forever. Death had never occurred to me.

~

What I remember most clearly is the tolling bell at St. Augustine's on the morning of the funeral. I can never hear a tolling bell without thinking of my father and feeling the heavy sound inside my chest.

We sat in the huge black car that had driven us from the funeral parlor to St. Augustine's church. We waited as they unloaded my father's casket. And all the while I heard the bell—the slowest, deepest, most hollow sound I had ever heard. It made my heart beat like something trapped. It thrummed against my skull.

I didn't learn that it was called "the tolling bell" until I went to seminary. The tolling bell is only used at funerals. But I didn't know anything about that the morning they lifted his casket out of the hearse and rolled him into St. Augustine's. I did know that this was the last Mass we would ever attend together. Though you could scarcely say we were together.

He wasn't with me. He was in that box. I had seen him lying in it. I had touched him lying in it, had kissed his stone-hard forehead. I had put one of my little stuffed animals in it with him. My father had bought me a pair of them, Augie Doggy and Augie Daddy, named after cartoon characters. They were supposed to represent him and me: I kept Augie Doggy with me, but Augie Daddy I sent on with him. Or maybe it was the other way around. I don't remember.

I do remember my grandmother at the funeral parlor, speaking more loudly than she must have realized, "Joey doesn't look too broken up about her Daddy passing away."

It made me wonder what I was doing wrong. I had been crying. I would cry some more. But all of these people kept coming up to see my mother and my sisters and me, and though it was a sad time, there were smiles and laughter too.

I tried, though, to be more appropriately, or at least more visibly, grieving.

But I didn't have to try when I heard the tolling bell. I heaved with sobs I hadn't summoned, sobs I couldn't stop.

The bell made its single, hollow, low sound, more solemn than the September day was bright. It was followed by another single hollow toll, diminishing again into silence. And again. Again, again.

I don't remember anything other than that. Nothing about the Mass—whether it was in Latin or in English. I don't remember whether or not they called him Richard J. Page or Dick Page, though I expect it was Richard. I'm not sure the priests really knew their parishioners.

I don't remember the priest celebrating Communion—which, as Lutherans, we would not have been allowed to take anyway.

I don't remember the trip to the cemetery or the interment there or the priest's words or who stood around the rose-pink granite cross that marked his grave just up the hill from a small and lovely pond.

In sure and certain hope of the resurrection to eternal life through our Lord Jesus Christ, we commend to almighty God our brother, Richard, and we commit his body to the ground; earth to earth, ashes to ashes, dust to dust. The Lord bless him and keep him. The Lord make his face to shine on him and be gracious to him. The Lord look upon him with favor and give him peace. Amen.

The priest must have said these words, standing on the rickety planks that surrounded the grave that had been dug. Maybe he took a ceremonial spoonful of dirt to toss on the coffin. Maybe he sprinkled some holy water. I don't remember.

I don't know what happened as we moved away from my father's grave, either. It just seemed that soon we were back at our house and I was **wondering why there was** a party, for God's sake. There was white-frosted cake that had sprinkles. There were orange and grape soda. Neighbors were bringing casseroles.

I remember hearing laughter and wondering why it was that if I hadn't cried enough at the funeral home, it was now okay for people to seem so lighthearted now. My father remained dead, and now he was buried underground, besides.

This seemed to me no cause for laughter.

2

Baptizing the Dead

Cradling children in his arms, Jesus gave his blessing.
To our babes a welcome warm, he is yet addressing.
Take them, Lord, give life anew in the living waters!
Keep them always near to you, as your sons and daughters!

—"Cradling Children in His Arms"
Nicolai F. S. Gruntvig (1783–1872)

What they teach you in seminary is that you don't baptize the dead.

But the dead children arrived before I had arrived at the hospital. I had never met the parents before. The father had told the staff he'd grown up Lutheran, so the hospital was calling random Lutheran churches looking for a pastor who was in and who could come immediately. When the call came to Grace, the congregation I served, the mother was still in labor. She had already given birth to her dead children by the time I got there, twenty minutes later.

The father stood at her bedside, smiling bravely, tears on his freckled cheeks. The mother, model pretty even minutes after labor, looked shell shocked and betrayed.

The babies were born ten weeks earlier than my own premature daughter, Linnea. She had weighed in at three pounds, a whopper for a twenty nine week-er, and it was her size that helped save her.

These babies never stood a chance of surviving outside their mother's womb. No doctor and no technology could have done anything to save them. They were too small, only about the size of little Cornish hens. But they were magnificently complete. They had perfect tiny arms and legs and translucent eyelids. Their skin was ruddy, almost glowing.

And I baptized them, dipping my finger into a cup of tap water drawn from the sink in the delivery room. I said their names. Sophia. Oliver. I made the sign of the cross. I said the names for God. The babies didn't move, didn't breathe. Their translucent eyelids never fluttered open.

They didn't look dead; they only looked real.

I don't know what happened to the bodies of Oliver and Sophia. I baptized them after they were dead. In my seminary training, I was taught that such a baptism is useless. I have never believed that baptizing the dead is any less useful than baptizing the living.

Death is as much a part of parish ministry as baptism is. In baptism, the pastor says, "Go where you are going." In the funeral, service the pastor says, "Now you are there."

Not in those words, naturally. Particularly for funerals, we cloak the mystery of death in words from the Bible that are supposed to explain loss, comfort the mourners, and promise life after death, in spite of the fact that we have absolutely no idea what that means.

Jesus was never really clear on that. "I am the way, the truth, and the life," John's gospel has him say to Thomas. But Jesus was no cartographer, and his words can't be mistaken for any kind of existential map.

Pastors stand in front of caskets supported by wide fabric tape suspended over open graves. They say, with deep solemnity, that they are committing so-and-so to the ground, earth to earth, ashes to ashes, dust to dust.

And because the pastor is wearing a collar and holding a book and because the pastor is the sentinel at the last checkpoint before mystery sets in, hope gathers thick as a cloud. It is the hope that the pastor knows something about where they are sending the loved one—not to a world of dust and silence but *home*, somehow. Home, where God has lit the lamps and laid the fire and instructed the staff to leave out a plate of cold chicken and a bottle of the good wine.

I was surprised when, a few months later, Oliver and Sophia's parents joined Grace. I never asked them what happened to the babies after their baptisms—whether they were cremated or buried in a special cemetery that the hospital runs for just such body-and-soul heartbreaks. There must be places like that. In any case, their parents hadn't asked me to do a funeral.

But a funeral wasn't necessary, anyway. The baptism did for the parents what a funeral does for mourners. The dying one has already gone to whatever it is that awaits them. That awaits us.

Funny things can happen at funerals. One time I was making my way to the front of the room at the funeral home to start the service when I overheard the dead man's widow say to her daughter—in surely what she thought was a whisper—"Oh, she's got a cute figure." The daughter and I exchanged embarrassed smiles. Mothers!

Yet another time I did a service in a funeral home with a grandfather clock that said *tempus fugit* on the clock face. What funeral director in their right mind would have a clock like that by the front entrance? Maybe he or she hadn't taken high school Latin. Or maybe it was subliminal advertising, a gentle reminder to prearrange your funeral *now* because, you know, *time flies!*

And then there was the time that, just before starting the memorial service of a woman who had committed suicide, one of her mourners whispered in my ear what he'd like to do to me. I don't shock easily, but the comment within this context just seemed outrageous, and I wanted to tell him what he could put up *his* ass. But naturally, I didn't. I just headed on into the columbarium.

However different the circumstances of funerals or however either thick-skulled or insightful the pastor handling the funeral, the language of death is traditional.

In sure and certain hope of the resurrection to eternal life through our Lord Jesus Christ, we commend to almighty God our brother/ sister, _____ , and we commit his/her body to the earth from which it was made/the deep/the elements/its resting place. Earth to earth, ashes to ashes, dust to dust. The Lord bless him/her and keep him/her. The Lord make his face to shine on him/her and be gracious to him/her. The Lord look upon him/her with favor and give him/her peace. Amen.

That's what *Evanglical Lutheran Worship* says in its rite for the Burial of the Dead. It's about the same as other Christian rites of burial. And I have said these words so many times myself, standing on the artificial green turf rolled out around the grave's opening and over which the coffin is poised. The priest who buried my father must have said these same words at his grave, making the sign of the cross over the top of the casket.

"Rest eternal grant him, O Lord, and let light perpetual shine upon him."

Maybe he said it in Latin—*Requiescat pacem et lux perputua luceat eam*—and turned from the grave to address the small circle of us assembled. That is what I do. I look at the family, their faces somber, their cheeks ruddy from wind—it seems it is so often windy at gravesides—and I speak the words of a prayer from the book of Hebrews. It's a prayer that is supposed to inspire those pilgrims still on their earthly journeys to go forth and pursue more good works:

The God of peace—who brought again from the dead our Lord Jesus Christ, the great shepherd of the sheep, through the blood of the everlasting covenant—make you perfect in every good work to do God's will, working in you that which is well-pleasing in God's sight; through Jesus Christ to whom be glory forever and ever. Amen.

"Let us go forth in peace," I say.

And then, because the people don't have order of the service in front of them so they don't know that there is a response for them to say, I say it for them: "In the name of Christ. Amen."

I don't know why I say it. Nobody would miss it if I didn't.

And then there is the awkward leave taking. The funeral director helps the family select a few flowers from the piles of them assembled. Sometimes people cry harder at this point. Other times they seem in a hurry to move away, to get back to where there are sandwiches to make and coffee to brew—the stuff of life, not the strangeness of death.

Other times, if the dead one was a veteran, there will be military honors. Sometimes full, sometimes not.

I'm not sure there is much that is more powerful than military honors. Military honors trump the pathos of the funeral liturgy. And though I rarely have to fight tears at funerals, I struggle not to cry every time I witness them. And hear them.

It may just be the silent, ritualized folding and presentation of the American flag to the widow. Or the parents.

Or there may also be three rifle volleys. This practice is rooted in the old etiquette of fighting—after the dead and wounded were cleared away from the battlefield, the rifle volley indicated that it was safe to commence fighting once more.

I wonder if its symbolic use at funerals is to say that the dead one has been removed from the battlefield of life. The living will resume their struggles, but the dead one is at peace.

The rifle volleys are powerful. First you hear the far-off voice of the officer giving the order to fire. The first volley makes you jump. It's loud, harsh. Your chest and throat tighten; your eyes burn. For a moment you can't breathe, but then comes the second volley and it catches you off-guard, even though you knew it was coming. After the third volley, the silence that follows feels heavy and sorrowful.

But then you hear the sound of a bugler, off to the side of the field. He's beginning to play "Taps." Nobody makes it through "Taps."

The women's shoulders visibly shake. The men try to stand still, but you can see them fidget—a hand drifting toward a pocket or the knot of their tie. They don't want to weep the way the women do. But nobody makes it through the bugler's solemn tribute without tears.

Nobody needs to be told that nothing more will follow. The dead one has been laid to rest.

> *Day is done, gone the sun,*
> *From the lake, from the hills, from the sky.*
> *All is well, safely rest, God is nigh.*
>
> *Then good night, peaceful night,*
> *Till the light of the dawn shineth bright,*
> *God is near, do not fear—Friend, good night.*

And then there is nothing. Everyone begins to return to their cars.

That's often when the funeral director will hand me the envelope that has the death certificate—so that I can record the funeral in the parish register—and the honorarium given to the pastor. By the time I get back to my car, the little suctioned-cup purple flag bearing the word "Funeral" has been removed from my hood. I drive away, slowly, to the cemetery gates.

Then the hearse will be returned to its garage, the funeral director and assistants to their hushed rooms, the family back home for the lunch that follows—platters of cold cuts, foil pans of baked ziti, a tossed salad, and a tray of bakery cookies.

~

When the funeral is in a church, I see everything from the opposite perspective of the grieving family. I am kept entirely apart from the family by the circumstances of architecture and the casket. The casket is wheeled in and placed perpendicular to the aisle. It completely covers the break in the Communion rail. The family and the dead one are in the nave; I am in the chancel, and my boundary is the casket. I am the one on the other side of it.

Everything I see and everything I do is the reverse of what the mourners are seeing and doing. I do not mourn; I comfort. I am not confused;

I reassure. I do not weep; I promise. I do not look up at myself; I look down at tearful faces. I do not follow the casket to the hearse; I lead it.

That is my role. And I don't know whether it brings me closer to an awareness of death or further from it.

Overall, though, I had grown to feel remarkably calm about funerals—until my own mother died. My mother—that complicated, coy, flamboyant former ballroom dance teacher, nightclub chanteuse, and waitress—was being laid to rest. She had been a woman of diverse passions right until the end. In our very last conversation, she stared up the ceiling and said to me—plainly irritated because this wasn't an option at that particular moment—"I want to go out *dancing*."

To honor her, for her funeral I bought a dress that I have since, in other circumstances, worn out dancing.

During the service I sat in the pew with my sisters and my daughters and my ex-husband. I listened while Steve, my mother's pastor, said to her, as I have said, in that strange, coded language of worship, *Now there you are, Norma*," willing her into the sanctuary of God's invisible arms.

At the end of the service, Steve led the casket, guided by pallbearers, out of the sanctuary. We followed, singing "I Want to Walk as a Child of the Light," singing as best we could with tight throats and tearful eyes.

From the church foyer we followed Steve out into the parking lot, and the pallbearers slid my mother's casket into the mouth of the black hearse. But we were not going to follow her any farther than that. Mom was going to be cremated, not interred. There would be no cortege to the cemetery, no leaving her behind as we walked away from the freshly dug grave.

The ceremonial part was over. Mom was in the casket in the hearse and the hearse would soon go to the crematorium. After some hugging and weeping, we left the parking lot and went inside to the fellowship hall to eat sandwiches from a deli platter and to drink predictably weak church coffee. All the while, the hulk of the black hearse was right outside the fellowship hall window. For a long moment I looked at it, trying to absorb the strange knowledge that my mother's body lay inside the smooth wooden casket.

After that I glanced out the window from time to time, but mostly I paid attention to what was happening in the fellowship hall. The ceremony over, the socializing was just another customary part of a funeral. But at some point—midway through a ham-and-cheese sandwich or an awkward chat with cousins I rarely see—my mother was driven away. When I next looked out the window, the hearse was gone.

My mother was gone. I didn't say anything to anybody. I thought it was a detail too small to mention. The body had gone on its way. When I had planned the service I had been glad there would be no grim cortege to the cemetery, no watching as strong men unloaded the burden of the casket over the yawning grave.

But now—and so suddenly—my *mother* was gone. In the twinkling of an eye. She was *gone*, leaving us behind eating sandwiches and coleslaw and pickles. We had not even noticed that she had been taken away from us. Although that's not exactly true—because *I* had noticed, hadn't I? Didn't that count for something? But for what? It counted for nothing. Loss is never partial. Loss doesn't compensate anybody for anything.

∾

The on-call chaplain's suite was the scariest place I'd ever slept. It was tucked away in the oldest part of the hospital directly beneath the belfry, one floor above the psychiatric ward and just across the roof from the hospice unit. It was a dark warren of dusty rooms with an elevator that opened ominously and slowly directly into the living room—a term used here optimistically. And the only way out of the on-call chaplain's suite was if your pager went off. But that only happened if there was a trauma. Or a death.

Clinical Pastoral Education, required of most seminarians, was an eleven-week emotional boot camp. Programs vary, but mine was in a hospital outside Philadelphia, and my supervisor was a robustly demanding Catholic nun, Sister Angela. The five members of our CPE group spent sixty hours a week at the hospital—that included the thirty-two-hour stretch with an overnight in the on-call chaplain's room.

Every morning we checked the patient census to see who had died the night before. Then one of us had to go up to the floor to verify the death. It was important to verify deaths. In the past, condolence letters had been sent to spouses of very much alive former patients. Not good PR for the hospital.

So the first time I ever saw a dead person outside a funeral home was one morning when Sister Angela sent me up to verify the death of a man who, the census indicated, had died during the night.

"You've got twenty minutes or so. Just be sure to get back in time for our group session."

Right. Well, I was sure we'd have to talk about my feelings about death at our group session twenty minutes from now. It made sense to start thinking about it ahead of time—not just the group session, but death as well.

So I went up to the floor and checked in at the unit desk. Yes, Mr. So-and-So was dead. No, Mrs. So-and-So had already gone home. She was old, and her husband had been sick for a very long time, so she didn't stay for very long after he died.

Yes, Mr. So-and-So was still in his room. He hadn't yet been taken by the funeral director or even brought to the morgue.

What room? I wanted to know. I had to make sure that he was dead, but I didn't think I was supposed to tell the nurse that. Actually, I had no idea what I would say if the nurse asked why I wanted to see him. And I didn't really want to see him.

I was afraid to see him. All of the dead bodies I had seen had been pancake-made-up and carefully dressed. They hadn't looked real, which may be why it was considered such a high compliment when someone told a funeral director, "It looks just like her!" That was exactly the point—the body, drained of its own essence and chemically treated to stave off rot, was *not* her any longer. "Just like" was as close as it would ever get to being her.

I did not know what to expect with Mr. So-and-So. I was afraid he would have a slack jaw or sightlessly staring eyes or that his face would wear the rictus of death. It was such a nineteenth-century word, "rictus," and it was only ever used to describe death or its near arrival.

In addition, I wasn't sure about what the sphincters of the human body did when the brain no longer managed them. I was afraid there would be an odor, perhaps a mess. Would his fingertips be blackening, his lips blue?

They told me his room number and down the hall I went. The door to his room was open. I went in.

There was no curtain drawn around him. There was no medical equipment electronically beeping and sighing and buzzing. There was no medical equipment at all. The room was still. Still as death. Just like a cliché.

Mr. So-and-So was on the bed, covered with a sheet. There were no guardrails raised to keep him in the bed. He needed no blanket, even though most patients complained of the hospital's air-conditioned coldness.

I did not need to introduce myself to him the way I introduced myself to every other person whose room I entered.

I stepped closer to him. His face was calm; his eyes were closed; his lips were pale. His hands were the same color as the rest of him, which was the color of the sheet that didn't entirely cover him—parts of his chest, shoulders, feet, shins were exposed. In the morning light filtering through the blind slats, he was colored a soft white, an *antique* white, I thought, like wall paint. He wasn't frightening.

Was I privileged to stand here? Did I have any right to stand here? Was I supposed to be filled with reverent awe? Or was I simply violating the space where somebody's husband and father and grandfather had died? They had a right to be here. I had none.

Then why *was* I here? Mr. So-and-So was dead, most definitely. That was established. But Sister Angela said I had twenty minutes. So what was I supposed to do now?

The question came over the loudspeaker in my brain, breaking the calm silence of the room. It wasn't enough to *be* here; I had to *do* something. But what was I supposed to do?

Pray, I figured. When in doubt, pray.

This is not a prayerful impulse with which to commence praying. And I have never had much faith in my praying skills, anyway. But right then out of the corner of my eye I glimpsed an old black man coming slowly down the hallway, buffing the floors. He looked as though he knew a thing or two more about death than I did. All too quickly the quiet room filled with the worried chatter in my head: I looked lost. I looked stupid. He was the custodian and I was the clueless chaplain. He knew I didn't know what the hell I was doing.

And while I willed my face into some semblance of prayerful blandness, Mr. So-and-So became more of a problem to be dealt with than a body at last at rest. I squeezed my eyes shut and tried out some phrases in my mind. *Let him be at peace, God.* Or was it better to simply quote from the funeral service? I remembered what I could of it: *Into your hands, O merciful Savior, we commit your servant _____. Receive him into the arms of your mercy, into the blessed rest of everlasting peace. . . .* I did this for what must have been a full thirty seconds, hoping the custodian would have buffered his way well down the hallway by the time I opened my eyes.

When I did I noticed two things at once: Mr. So-and-So was as still as before, and the custodian hadn't made any progress with his buffing. He was just standing still outside the doorway. I was standing still at the foot of the dead man's soon-to-be vacant bed. Of the three of us—custodian, chaplain, corpse—it was by far Mr. So-and-So who had the best reason for doing nothing.

I decided it was time for me to leave.

But just as I stepped out into the hall I had a pang of regret. What if I had missed something? What if there had been some gesture or thought or rite that I had failed to perform that Angela would grill me on in twenty—well, now fifteen—minutes? Most importantly, there stood the custodian, only a few feet away. How many student chaplains had he seen make asses of themselves? And here I was, yet another one.

I was sure I saw him smirking as I reentered the room. But I was doing this so that he could see that if I were an ass then at least I was a conscientious ass. I stood again at Mr. So-and-So's bedside, not thinking about *him* at all. No, sir. I kept myself in full sight of the floor buffer, clasped my hands together again, lowered my head 45-degrees and stood there for a full fifteen seconds this time. This time I didn't actually pray. I just faked it.

But when I looked up the custodian was still buffing the same spot. He glanced into the room. I glanced away from him. I didn't want him to think I was aware of his presence. I brought my eyes back to Mr. So-and-So.

I didn't know what else I could do. I couldn't engage the dead man in conversation ("Tell me, Mr. So-and-So, your body language seems so peaceful—had you come to terms with dying?"). I couldn't stand nearby in hopes that he would feel my wordless yet caring presence because, being dead, he surely wouldn't. I couldn't make notes in his chart because it was out at the unit desk. And, as a student chaplain, I wouldn't have been allowed to.

So, feeling that I had to make some gesture of respectful farewell, I nodded to him. And stepped back into the hall. The custodian was shaking his head as he buffed. I was sure he'd seen it all before—student chaplains making asses of themselves every summer. *My Lord, what a morning, when the stars begin to fall!*

I got back to our group session in plenty of time, even accounting for dawdling in the halls. Once everybody was gathered in the conference room we began to go over the hospital census statistics: the new patients, surgeries, deaths the previous night.

I told Sister Angela about going up to check on Mr. So-and-So. I told her what I had done.

"You *what?*" Angela said, bursting out laughing, "You went in and *prayed?* And then went out and went in again and prayed *a second time?*"

"Yes," I said, flushing with embarrassment, "You said I had twenty minutes. I was done at the unit desk in less than five. I figured there was something else I was supposed to do that would kill the rest of the time."

Angela's shoulders shook, "Of course there was. It's called getting a cup of coffee from the cafeteria. All you needed to do was ask at the nurse's station to see if the census was correct. They know better than we do when somebody's dead."

I had to admit she had a point.

"Now go get a cup of coffee and be back in time for ostomy class!"

3

Hiding from the Miracle

"I am not a Christian. Christianity is a faith that betrays its believers!" [*takes off her rosary and throws it down*]. I AM NOT A CHRISTIAN!"

—Sister Theresa
Irving Rapper's 1959 movie *The Miracle*

By the time I was nine, two facts were well established in my life: My father was dead and I was very sinful. Given the possibility of causality, I got nervous a lot. What might God have in store for us next?

Already it seemed the Page family was especially prone to God's heavy-handed corrections. Take my sister Jackie, for example. She was a good girl and beautiful, too. She had long blond hair, blue eyes, a soft voice, and big breasts. The scent of Channel No. 5 wafted along with her when she moved through a room.

She was the first person in our whole extended family to go to college. She had enrolled at the College of Saint Rose in Albany, a Catholic school for women. The nuns were skeptical: she was a Lutheran who wore miniskirts.

In art class she drew dark, disturbing pen-and-ink images and molded wire into anguished, contorted human shapes. In German class she called her teacher "Schwester Chester," though "Chester" wasn't Sister's name.

She also wore elaborate eye makeup—a broad band of white eyeliner edged with another thinner dark line close along the edge of her lashes. She never went to Mass on campus. She probably didn't even make it to every class either, commuting from our house in Lansingburgh in her sharp white Mustang with a red interior.

In spite of her being the rebel Protestant on campus, things were going fairly well until she got a new boyfriend.

Before, all her boyfriends had been decent and clean-cut. Clean-cut at least. Not this one. John Graves had a beard and long hair. He wore boots. He introduced Jackie to the Doors and Jim Morrison's urgent, repeated exhortations to "Touch Me, Babe" and "Light My Fire." For that matter, he cultivated a certain air of Jim Morrison himself. He wrote dark, moody poetry and questioned the existence of God, even though he attended a Catholic college. Jackie was enthralled.

So was I. He wasn't a Lansingburgh boy with a letter jacket. He was a college student, a reader of poetry. A hippie.

Of course, my mother couldn't stand him. The boots and beard alone suggested drug use. She could barely be civil to him when he was around. When he was gone, she and Jackie carped and argued. This was new. My family had never been very argumentative, not that I remember, anyway. And to hear Jackie and my mother go at it was upsetting. I loved both of them. But I felt I had to choose sides. The problem was, I just couldn't make up my mind to pick a side and stay with it.

I could see things from my mother's perspective: She had just lost her husband. She didn't want to lose her daughter to some stoned poet with no prospects.

But Jackie's perspective was more appealing than my mother's. She was in love. After all, it was 1968. She was *supposed* to be in love.

For a while, anyway. Because then the summer of love spilled into another season, and finally Jackie started to come around to my mother's way of seeing things. John was clingy. He was jealous. He was depressed.

Finally she broke up with him. Or tried to. But when she went out with friends to the bars in Troy on Friday nights, John would show up and follow her around. When she still wouldn't go back to him, he threatened her. He sent her the lyrics from the Jimi Hendrix song "Hey Joe" and The Crazy World of Arthur Brown's demon song, "Fire." Jackie was afraid, but not in the fun way she had been before. She stayed home a lot, edgy and sad on weekend nights, disinterested in her classes during the day.

Then one night, after my sisters and I had gone to bed, my mother was dozing on the sofa, as she usually did. Outside it was warm and balmy, a late Indian summer. The wooden shutters were open a little to let in some air. But all night our dog had been restless, sniffing and scratching at the shutters, growling.

Finally my mother got up, went to the window, and peered outside. There in the darkness on our front porch she saw John Graves sitting and staring off into space, his wrists dripping blood.

I heard about all of this the next day, of course. How the police came and took John away. How he hadn't cut his wrists in a way that would have caused him to bleed to death. That he had probably been peering into the windows that entire evening, watching us as we watched TV, watching as Jackie put her hair in curlers, watching as my sister Leslie rocked in her chair.

From then on there was real fear in the house. Jackie stayed home from her part-time job working at Two Guys department store so she wouldn't be walking to her car alone at night. My mother didn't want Leslie walking around the block or even going out to roll down the windows in the car the way she normally liked her to. It had been her special job to make sure the car would not be too hot when it was time to go out in it for errands.

For months afterward, my mother shrouded the windows with heavy blankets at night so that if John came back, there would be no possible way he could see anything. She stayed up late, stirring at the slightest sound. Jackie's social life ground to a halt—my mother didn't want her going to any of the places John Graves might find her.

What had Jackie done to deserve such a lousy turn of fortune's wheel? She had only recently lost her father. Did she have to have a lunatic boyfriend too? Because I'd had it drummed into me that God was good and provided us with good things, the only possible excuse was that Jackie was bad in some way, that she was a sinner being duly punished. So I started paying attention to the lessons God was teaching

Jackie: Don't date bad boys. Don't wear miniskirts, go-go boots, and eyeliner. Don't argue with your mother.

I wasn't at all sure that *Jackie* was learning these lessons. She kept right on dressing like a Carnaby Street model. Then she started going out again on weekends, in spite of my mother's protests. And then she met another boy, a frat boy from Rensselaer Polytechnic Institute who had gotten thrown out of school for fighting but was such a good student and good athlete that the school took him back the following semester.

Within the year, Jackie and Alan made plans to marry.

Nevertheless, I carried on with my mental list of things not to do if you had any hope of staying on God's good side.

As for my mother, she appeared to have learned whatever lesson God had had in store for her to make her a widow at forty-seven with three daughters, one of whom was mentally retarded. That's how it seemed at first, anyway.

For the first few months after my father died, she went—*we* went—to the cemetery almost every day. Even after people started urging her to, she didn't even think about dating. Dick was the only man for her, she'd say. On the one-year anniversary of my father's death, she put a quote in the *Troy Record* in the "In Memoriam" section. It was from I Corinthians, a book in the Bible I hadn't yet really distinguished as being any different from any other part of the Bible:

Love is patient; love is kind; love is not envious or boastful or arrogant or rude. It does not insist on its own way; it is not irritable or resentful; it does not rejoice in wrongdoing, but rejoices in the truth. Love bears all things, believes all things, hopes all things, endures all things.

Love never ends.

Frankly, love sounded difficult and distasteful to me. Love sounded like a sentence we were supposed to fulfill. In fact, it seemed as though if you knew you were working hard and were fairly unsatisfied, you could be pretty sure that what you were doing was being loving.

My mother was sure working hard, and it was plain to see she was unsatisfied. While this made her appear to be the model widow, God must have found some complaint with her, because I couldn't think of any other way to explain what happened next.

She bought a car. And not just any car. She went to a dealership that was run by an old friend of my father's. Warren wasn't in, but Victor—who reminded my mother very much of Harry Belafonte—said he'd help her find a car. He talked her into buying a brand-new, bright-red GTO with a black ragtop that went from zero to whatever in no time at all. It was boss.

But as soon as she brought it home, she feared that people would talk. In fact, she was certain that people would talk. We had never had anything before but Mercury station wagons. Now here she was, a widow, and a fetching, red-haired one at that, with a red GTO parked in front of the house. People would think she was on the prowl for a man. Or maybe just for what a man could do.

Besides the unseemly public appearance of it, there was also the matter of conspicuous consumption and how ungodly that was. I'm not sure my mother had thought of that before she bought the car. But soon after she did, our pastor preached a sermon about conspicuous consumption. He derisively used a phrase from a beer commercial—"Grab for all the gusto you can get." I had always liked that line. I thought it suggested that we should have life and have it abundantly—just like Jesus said. But in our pastor's mouth, "Grab for all the gusto you can get" translated into sinful, greediness, a betrayal of the God who calls us to sacrifice all for Him.

In his sermon he began to cite examples of how Americans are acquisitive and greedy. He used pairs of nouns in a list to illustrate our materialism: *the blah-blah-blah and the blah-blah-blah. The blah-blah-blah and the blah-blah-blah.* I was starting to tune it all out when those *blah-blah-blahs* suddenly got very personal.

"The *Mustang*," he said with emphasis, "and the *GTO*."

You could hear the pauses dripping judgment between the letters.

Collectively we shrank deeply into our pew. Pastor was talking about us, the four Page girls—the widowed one, the mentally retarded one, the rebellious college student, and the guilty eleven-year-old. We hadn't known it, but now we did: We were greedy, acquisitive, grabbing for gusto when what we were supposed to be doing was giving it all up for God.

So what happened next should have come as no big surprise. Driving back from school one day, Jackie was at a red light at a busy intersection. She noticed a big tractor-trailer trying to make a left-hand turn onto the street where she was waiting for the light to change.

Nobody likes to see big tractor-trailers negotiating those tricky right angle turns. But Jackie sat tight. They always cleared with plenty of room, those big tractor-trailers. They train those drivers well. Except that this time the big tractor-trailer *didn't* quite clear the turn with plenty of room. In fact, the driver cut the turn too short, and the tractor-trailer began slowly scraping its undercarriage up the long hood of Jackie's little white Mustang.

All of the distressing and anguished subjects in Jackie's art class projects couldn't hold a candle to the fear she felt as the behemoth truck scraped its way slowly toward her windshield. Her life didn't flash in front of her eyes—the only thing in front of her eyes was the side of the tractor-trailer.

But God is good. God is merciful. The truck stopped. God must have just wanted to scare Jackie, apparently to remind her that she was worth little more than scrap metal if she didn't shape up (Even so, I still never quite understood what was wrong with her, what she had to shape up about that made it okay for this to happen, this tractor-trailer–sized brush with death).

Maybe it was because of the Mustang. Maybe God was saying, *Go ahead, drive a cool car. Then I'll make you pay for it.*

Except that, as it turned out, we still owed more.

Apparently the humiliation of Pastor's sermon and the tractor-trailer incident weren't enough. Apparently we were daft enough, dense enough, *gusto* oriented enough that we needed a really big clue to discover just how sinful we were. The clue came early one summer morning when wedding plans were well under way.

After the wedding, Jackie and Alan were to live in our house. We had tenants in the apartment next door, but my mother said Jackie and Alan could build an apartment in our basement. My father had already made a pretty good start. He had already installed knotty-pine plywood paneling from Grossman's Lumber in what was to be the family "rec room" part of it. He had built a bar, though no one in my family drank except for my father's nightly beer and some New Year's Eve grasshoppers. Behind the bar he had hung his small collection of neon beer signs. There was linoleum brick tiling on the floor and some cast-off furniture my parents had had since they were first married. On one wall my father had hung a huge poster of Albert Einstein, hair disheveled.

All Alan had to do was build a kitchen, a bathroom, install more paneling, and lay more flooring.

All Jackie had to do was figure out how to decorate the apartment. Would the kitchen be done in shades of burnt orange and avocado green? Would the bathroom linens be pastels or a more manly neutral? (Pastels won out.) And the choice of paneling for the still-unfinished rooms—the kitchen, the hallway, and the bathroom—was too important for Jackie to make all by herself, so I accompanied her to Grossman's so that she could benefit from my precocious eleven-year-old design sense.

That's where we were that July morning, picking out paneling at the lumber store. My mother and other sister, Leslie, were at home, Mom, busy with whatever it is that mothers are always busy doing. If anything, it was starting out to be a better day than usual. And I loved Grossman's. I used to go there with my father the way I used to go to Mass with him.

In some ways, the two places shared some common elements. Smells, for one thing. My father's church had been filled with incense from the thurifers the altar boys thrashed up and down around the aisles. The smell of incense at St. Augustine's tightened your chest—or at least made you aware of the effort of breathing.

Grossman's had it own kind of scent. It was of newly cut wood and sawdust, and it reminded me of the scent of my father's workshop in the basement, only exponentially compounded in richness.

Grossman's and St. Augustine's were similar, too, in scale. They were outsized buildings designed to attract people bent on serious pursuits:

building their houses and saving their souls, respectively. It was good to feel small in them. It made you feel that, if need be, you could slip away, unnoticed; it made you feel you could get lost in their stockrooms and sacristies.

But in another way, it made you feel you could never become really lost, never stray too far, because sooner or later the priest in his cassock or the salesman in his carpenter's apron would be striding down your aisle ready to convince you he knew what you needed. Even as a little girl I preferred someone else's decisiveness to my own.

At Grossman's we lingered and dawdled. We chose carefully: sheets of avocado green paneling for the kitchen, silvery birch for the bathroom, and golden maple for the hallway.

And we brought home little rectangles of each kind of paneling to show to our mother, whose opinion meant a lot more to Jackie than Alan's.

Driving home, we listened to the radio. There were so many songs I loved, and I sang them in my head—"I'm into Something Good," "Build Me Up, Buttercup," "Sugar, Sugar," "Hot Fun in the Summertime." I knew them all and who sang them. Herman's Hermits, The Foundations, The Archies, Sly. For the first time in a long time, good things seemed possible. Even the Zombies song, creepy was it was, seemed to offer possibility:

> *What's your name? (What's your name?)*
> *Who's your Daddy? (Who's your daddy?)*
> *(He rich) Is he rich like me?*
> *Has he taken (Has he taken)*
> *Any time (Any time)*
> *(To show) To show you what you need to live?*
> *(Tell it to me slowly) Tell you what*
> *(I really want to know):*
> *It's the time of the season for loving.*

I was singing the Zombies song when we turned onto our street.

But, as we drove closer to our house, we saw that there was a commotion on our street (*Tell it to me slowly*). We saw our neighbors milling about—the Dowds, the Fogartys, the Cruickshanks. Even the Crandells, who never mingled (*Tell you what*). All these neighbors had not come outside just because an ice cream man had driven down our block. There was never an ice cream man driving down our block anyway. Something was *wrong (I really want to know).*

Jackie braked, stunned at what we saw. There was a massive red metal wreath wrapping the telephone pole between our house and the Fogarty's house. It was a smashed car. A smashed car with a windshield shattered to bits. With broken strips of metal and broken headlights. It was *our* car. Our mother's red GTO.

(It's the time of the season for loving.)

I thought first of what I feared most.

My mother wasn't there. Had I lost my mother, too?

I could only think of my mother. All I had. My beautiful mother. With her red hair and that peculiar smell of coffee, cigarettes, and silver fillings. Was my mother dead?

The neighbors were maddeningly calm, examining the car. It was a total wreck.

What happened? we kept asking. What happened?

It took them forever to tell us that nothing had happened. (How could nothing have happened?) Or at least that no one had been hurt—not seriously hurt, just a lot of blood. From Leslie's nose. From Leslie's nose? Yes, from Leslie's. But she's okay. What about our mother? She had been in the house. Leslie was in the car. Your mother is safe. She's okay. Go to the hospital. Don't worry.

Don't worry? I would never stop worrying again.

But my mother was safe. That was all that mattered. That washed away enough of my worry for those moments. Let every thing else fall apart. Let noses be broken. Let blood be shed. Let cars be wrecks. Only let my mother be safe.

So Jackie and I drove to the Leonard Hospital, where it was just as my neighbors said it would be: my mother was safe. She hadn't seen the accident happen, only heard it. And when she rushed outside and ran to the car, she found Leslie bleeding, her head smashed against the steering wheel (Leslie had been at the wheel? Nothing made sense—Leslie didn't drive), and our tenant in the passenger seat, trying to open the jammed-shut door.

I was coming to believe that things didn't need to make sense to be what we call true. Or at least they didn't need to make sense for us to find ourselves having to experience them. Because this is what happened:

My mother had sent Leslie out to open the windows in the car. She especially loved opening the windows in the new car because they were power windows and she needed a key—critical to all exercises of power—to open them.

That particular morning, our tenant saw Leslie going to open the car windows.

"Hey, Leslie," he said. "Come on, I'll teach you to drive."

Leslie laughed. He was joking. Of course. But he had her get into the driver's seat and put the keys in the ignition. He told her that they were going to start the engine, and to do that she would need to put her to put her foot on the gas pedal and press down. When she did that, the car purred to life.

Our tenant was going to put the car in drive and steer for her, he'd told my mother afterward. They'd just cruise down to the end of the block.

But he hadn't told Leslie to take her foot off the gas pedal. He hadn't realized her motor skills were not as subtle as most people's and that she had pressed the pedal to the floor. He hadn't known that when he shifted the car into drive, the GTO would do what it was best known for—go right from zero to whatever in a nanosecond. And by that time, the GTO was wrapped around the telephone pole, Leslie's nose was broken and bleeding, and our tenant had whiplash.

But that was all. It could have been so much worse, the hospital staff kept telling us. It could have been so much worse. But we already knew that.

~

Weeks passed. The whiplash went away and Leslie's nose healed. Jackie drove especially carefully everywhere she went.

I began to think that it had been, like the tractor-trailer incident, a sign of God's great mercy. He could have made it be so much worse, just like the hospital staff said. He could have taken my mother away or made Leslie a cripple or blinded one of them. But broken noses heal. Bruises fade. And I figured that finally God had gotten through to my mother: a widow with three daughters is just not supposed to drive a red, convertible GTO sports car.

Meanwhile, my mother and sister went on planning for a modest wedding at our little gothic Lutheran church. Pastor's wife gave Jackie a small shower at the parsonage. The church ladies came, older women with white hair and good manners. They gave her tea towels and serving dishes, and I think some of them may have wondered if Jackie was pregnant. (She wasn't.)

For lunch, Pastor's wife served lots of delicate sandwiches with cucumbers sliced thin and little slivers of ham, and date nut bread spread with cream cheese. There were tomatoes that had been cut into budding flowers and stuffed with the best tuna fish salad I had ever eaten.

But it was the dessert that floored me. What Pastor's wife set down in front of me looked just like a cloud fallen onto a plate. On top of that cloud were raspberries and strawberries, a fat dollop of pale *pink* whipped cream topped with lovely red juice that spilled in streams down its sides. The cloud itself was crispy and light.

This was a pavlova, I learned—like the famous ballet dancer Anna Pavlova.

Between decorating her brand-new apartment and having such a wonderful wedding shower, I figured Jackie must be on cloud nine. I was.

Which was part of the reason why my mother's undertone of worry seemed so distressing. She was still upset about the car, I knew. But on the other hand, didn't she realize that God had shown great mercy?

Leslie's bruises were fading. And we had a new car—a much more suitable car. That's because when my mother went back up to the dealership where she had bought the GTO from the smooth-talking man who looked like Harry Belafonte, she requested to speak to her old friend who ran the dealership, Warren.

As an old friend, Warren was all too happy to help my mother out. For starters, he blamed Victor, the salesman. He was mulatto, Warren said, and that explained some of his irresponsible salesmanship, but he still should have known better than to sell a GTO to a beautiful young widow with a family. It's too much car for you, Warren explained. He said he himself would help her pick out something appropriate, something reliable, wholesome, and affordable.

My mother drove home in a brown Pontiac Custom S sedan.

It was a dull car, and not only because it was brown. It didn't have power windows. It didn't have a ragtop. No pastor was ever likely to use it as a sermon illustration. But it was still an honest-to-goodness *new* car, something we never had when my father was alive. And dull was far, far better than sinful. My mother should have been grateful for Warren's help and pleased to have found a car that matched her lifestyle.

Instead, she seemed discontented, distracted. She didn't even seem all that interested in Jackie and Alan's wedding. I couldn't think of anything other than the wedding, so how could she? I was going to be a bridesmaid. I was going to wear heels for the first time. I would get to wear pantyhose. My mother had made me a prim A-line dress of mint-green satin. She made a petal-pink one for Leslie. Using the same Simplicity pattern, she made Jackie's dress of some kind of fabric that looked like a brocade tablecloth. Our bridesmaid's dresses were sleeveless, but for Jackie's dress my mother used see-through white fabric to make billowy puffed sleeves that tapered into cuffs.

For her headpiece, my mother made a big, flat white brocade bow. It sat squat on the top of Jackie's head, holding back her little veil. Jackie protested that it made her look like Minnie Mouse. But I thought she looked like a dream.

The wedding day dawned sunny and warm. Inside the church the dark woodwork and stucco walls were splashed with color from the stained glass windows. Everything about the day felt significant and purposeful. And when I walked down the aisle I felt the proudest I ever had in my life. I was a *bridesmaid*. With a bouquet of flowers. Once again, things seemed to be looking better. It was about time, I thought.

Not that there weren't little clues of potential trouble. My mother's distraction, for instance, which for now I was trying to ignore.

Alan's family, as another instance. They had threatened not to come because it wasn't going to be a Roman Catholic ceremony, but at the last moment his mother and his older sister had driven over from a suburb outside Boston. They stood around awkwardly at the reception, disapproval evident behind their pursed lips and New England reserve. Jackie was a sexy little blond number who belonged to the church whose founder had called the Pope the Antichrist. It may have been centuries ago, but for Alan's family it seemed as though the Reformation had happened only yesterday. What good could come of this union?

But even their grim faces couldn't dull the sense of joy that had been building in me all day—building in me for weeks. And after the ceremony, when we drove around Lansingburgh honking horns the way people did after weddings, I thought I would burst with joy. Then we went back to the church hall where there were confetti and presents and punch and salads and wedding cake and, for some odd reason, buckets of Kentucky Fried Chicken. I felt happier than I had felt since before my father died.

Even so, I wasn't really sure I wanted to be happy. It scared me. Because we all knew what was coming next—*un*happiness. It just remained to be seen what form it would take.

~

Then for a long time things seemed okay. Jackie got pregnant and gave birth to a son the following June. That made me an aunt at twelve, which I thought was just about the neatest thing in the world.

I liked being an aunt a lot more than having a nephew. It seemed that Jeffrey practically lived with us. In a way he did—my mother baby-sat while my sister, who'd left Saint Rose, worked in a bank. There was always baby stuff around, and Jeff was noisy, or we had to be quiet because he was sleeping, or we had to fuss over some apparently terrific baby thing he had just done. I pretended to like it all well enough, but privately I thought babies were more trouble than they really needed to be. I thought God could have come up with a more self-reliant model.

Plus, I was jealous of Jeff. My mother had never been one to play games with me or anything like that. But she and I used to talk all the time. She would take me with her when she went grocery shopping. She would listen while I read her the stories I was always writing.

Now that Jeffrey was here, all that changed. We didn't go out as often because it was a lot of trouble to get him in and out of the car to go to the grocery store or the Dairy Queen. She never had time for my stories. And even though I knew I shouldn't feel this way, I hated it that she thought Jeff was so cute. *I* was used to being the cute one. But as bad as it was having to share my mother with a charming baby whose constant needs trumped everybody else's, my mother's attention was soon to be further subdivided. I would have still less of her. A lot less.

Because she fell in love.

And of all the men in the world, she fell in love with Warren, the old friend and car dealership owner who had sold her the cheaper, duller car.

It shouldn't have come as surprise to find out he wasn't only inter-ested in helping out a widow destined to live on her dead husband's modest Social Security and pension. He was interested in her.

It all began when he started dropping by now and then to make sure the car was running right. The car was always running right. It was a brand-new car, still spiffy from the dealership. So it struck my mother as very conscientious of him to make house calls.

I thought it was conscientious, too. Only the Fuller Brush man and the family doctor did that—and Mom was on the outs with Dr. Albright. He had tried, without success, to get her to begin birth control pills. He had told her this could help to stabilize her hormones during menopause.

But my mother didn't buy any of that. She thought he wanted to bed her, the old fool. He was nearly old enough for retirement and married to a pleasant woman with prematurely blue hair. How could he think for a moment that she would have been interested in *him*?

But my mother welcomed Warren's house calls. She usually had a pineapple upside down cake or a fresh blueberry pie—he loved blueberry pie, he had told her—waiting when he came. And they would sit at the table, smoking, drinking coffee, eating pie for an hour or two—two old friends.

There was nothing wrong with that that I could see.

For reasons of her own, though, my mother soon made it clear to me that she and Warren were, in fact, a lot more than friends. She told me she was in love with him and that he was in love with her. She also made it clear that she and my father had not had such a happy marriage. That he had never once told her he loved her. Not once in more than twenty years.

Warren loved her.

But he's married, I said.

Yes, he's married to a fat wife who keeps a sloppy house and can't cook worth a damn, she told me. She told me that Olive didn't understand Warren the way my mother did. That he had only married her because that was the right thing to do when he had got her pregnant at age sixteen. He'd done the right thing since day one, she said. But now his son was grown up and married himself. Warren even had three grandkids—apparently they all married young in that family. He'd spent his life "doing for other people," she said ("doing for other people" was not a phrase I'd ever heard my mother use before, and the lack of a direct object truly bothered me). Now it was time for him to find some joy for himself, she said. So someday, when he could work it all out so as not to hurt Olive too much, Warren was going to leave her. And then he would marry my mother.

It sounded like a plan to me. A fat wife and a sloppy house really did seem like a raw deal. And besides, didn't my mother herself deserve a shot at joy? She had been so unhappy for so long: the loveless marriage, the birth of a mentally retarded daughter, young widowhood. And even though she hadn't loved my father in *that* way, she still wanted a husband.

Which now, of course, she had. Without any of the duller of the wifely duties.

Warren and my mother would take his big Pontiac Bonneville with the air conditioning and the leather upholstery and go on long afternoon drives. They'd drive to Vermont or Massachusetts or up to Lake George. One time Warren bought her two little porcelain figurines that were supposed to represent the two of them, an Indian and his squaw. Warren liked to say he was part Indian. (Maybe he was; we would never know.) But that was enough to make my mother sentimental about the Indian head on the Pontiac insignia.

She kept her little squaw and chief duo on the knick-knack shelf and told me that I shouldn't dust them when I was doing the rest of the living room. She preferred to dust them herself. Maybe she feared I would knock them down and break them, and she already had enough broken things in her life. Or maybe it was because she liked to position them face to face with one another, as if kissing, and she knew I was intentionally inexact in how I replaced them after dusting the shelf.

Truth was, I didn't like Warren at all. I didn't like the way I was expected to kiss him hello and good-bye when he came and left—lip kisses, and his lips were always wet. I didn't like the princess phone with the separate number that my mother had installed by her bedside. Only Warren had the number—and us girls, but to be used in case of emergency only.

I didn't like Warren, but I tried hard to, especially because Jackie and Alan made no secret of how much they disliked him and how much they disapproved of what my mother was doing.

Try as I might, though, Warren made my skin crawl.

I knew, of course, that what my mother was doing was very, very wrong. Worse than what she had done when she had bought the GTO. Worse than what Jackie had done in falling for John Graves. I tried to believe that although my mother was an adulteress, God somehow didn't mind. That in this case and under these circumstances, it was okay that Warren was cheating on his wife with my mother. Because, after all, hadn't he told her that he was going to leave his wife and *marry* her? In God's eyes that must have meant *something*. For everybody's sakes'— except maybe poor Olive's. I hoped so.

But God, apparently, will not be mocked.

Because one day, when Warren was supposed to stop by, he just didn't show up. No word of explanation, no phone call on the private princess phone line. My mother was confused. Things come up, though. So she took it in stride. But he didn't come the next day or the next. And he didn't call. Not just for a day or two or even for a few days, but for a good long while. A week or two, at least.

All during that time, my mother moped around the house, not wanting to leave in case the phone rang. She didn't even try to hide the fact.

Was my mother getting her comeuppance? Had Warren found someone else to take on afternoon drives?

Finally my mother couldn't take the silence anymore. She got out his business card and called the dealership. Victor answered. No, Warren wasn't in, he said. My mother asked Victor to have him call her as soon as he could—there was some trouble with her car. But he knew better than to believe that. She wasn't the first of Warren's lady friends.

So in view of the fact that she wasn't just some disgruntled customer, Victor told her the whole story: Warren had had a massive heart attack. He had almost died and had spent a week in the intensive care unit. He had managed to pull through—he was a man as strong as an ox. But right now he was frail, feeble, home bound.

Warren had almost died! (And I wished he had—it would have made things so much more simple.)

Warren had almost died, and my mother went into a deeper mourning than when her own husband actually *had* died.

She intensified her moping. She grew weepier. She stopped being any fun at all. Worst of all, from my point of view, she stopped wearing the hot pink paisley polyester bell-bottom jumpsuit that I had given her for her birthday. That jumpsuit had been the first real present I had ever bought anybody, the first *grown-up* present. At eight dollars, it was also the most expensive present I had ever bought. You might think, given its bold design (pink!—paisley!—polyester!—bell-bottomed *and* with a zipper up the front!), that she would have found excuses for retiring this groovy bit of loungewear long before this. But she was too loving to offend me in that way.

I guess she was more superstitious than loving, though. Because when I asked her why she never wore the jumpsuit anymore, she told me that it was because that was what she was wearing the day she called Victor at the dealership and found out about Warren's heart attack. Now that jumpsuit meant nothing more to her than pain.

And rather than resent her superstition, rather than resent her for being blind to a child's attempt—and need—to please, I just felt guilty. The jumpsuit hadn't caused the heart attack. But my gift had become an anguished symbol, a concrete reminder that pain is never really an abstraction; it's as real as the clothes we wear.

So I watched my mother mourn again—this time for someone else's husband. More and more I began to think that this God we were bound to worship, this God we were bound to please—or at least appease—was determined to take away everything that she had ever really wanted.

But then, after another week of anguish, something changed. My mother may have been in the throes of love, but she was a practical woman, determined to hoist herself back into the existential saddle: in a fit of domestic inspiration, she wagered that all could be made right with a tactful house call and a plate of freshly beaten homemade fudge.

Few women would have come up with such a plan. Fewer still would have had the guts to follow through with it. And whether she was being foolish or cruel, I couldn't tell you. But she had decided that the best course of action was to go right on up to visit Olive and Warren in their red brick ranch house with the automatic garage door opener and snowmobiles parked just inside.

I knew that the New Testament book of Ephesians told people to put on the whole armor of God so that you might be able to stand against the wiles of the devil. But there had been nothing in Ephesians about how to arm yourself against a wily redhead with a hand-beaten pan of fudge.

So it came as no surprise when Olive opened the door and my mother introduced herself as one of Warren's friends. Not the first of Warren's "friends," I'm sure. But I am also sure she was the only one brazen enough, crazy-mad-in-love enough to march right up and expect Olive to welcome her into the living room.

That's just exactly what Olive did, though. She swung wide the door and let my mother into their lives.

~

Somewhere in the midst of all this came *The Miracle*, and my fate was sealed.

For a while now I had already been nursing the dream of becoming a nun à la Audrey Hepburn as Sister Luke in *The Nun's Story*. She made convent life quasi-erotic. Several times we see her in a state of dishabille: when the lunatic patient nicknamed the Archangel attacks and presumably tries to rape her and again when she is in the Congo being diagnosed with TB by a rather saucy Peter Finch playing Dr. Fortunati. I aspired to such a combination of discipline and disobedience as she seemed to embody. Being Lutheran rather than Catholic never struck me as any kind of problem. The only real problem, as I saw it, were my looks. Unlike the semi-emaciated Hepburn, I was from sturdily built Scandinavian stock. Nevertheless, I kept hope alive and imagined ways I might transform myself into a placid, dewy-eyed, drop-dead gorgeous, chaste yet sexually realized Catholic sister who spoke in dulcet tones, charmed Dr. Fortunati, and still managed to walk away from the convent young enough to bear offspring similarly genetically endowed.

Jesus had said, "with God all things are possible." Who was I to argue?

Becoming a nun appealed to me. From what I had observed from my friends who went to Catholic schools, the nuns seemed to me to live very uncluttered lives, lives free of emotional messiness, as if such a thing could be hacked off in the same way their hair was hacked off before they took the veil.

I was all for losing the emotional messes in my life. I wasn't crazy about the idea of losing my hair.

I didn't much like the poverty-chastity-obedience trinity either. I wanted love, love, love. If I was going to be obedient, I wanted to be obedient to a firm-but-gentle husband: I wanted marriage. I suspected I wanted sex too. And poverty had absolutely no appeal.

Still, Sister Luke made convent life look pretty decent. And in fact if there had been any chance that convent life could somehow shape my eyebrows and cultivate my speech so that I looked like—or even just sounded like—Audrey Hepburn, God could have gotten the whole ball of wax: Chastity. Obedience. Even poverty. He could have had my red fuck-me Barbie shoe. And my confession about the five lousy butter cookies. Anything so long as I got to be just like Audrey Hepburn as Sister Luke.

But I was no fool. I knew that wasn't going to happen. And in a way I guess it was a relief. If I wasn't going to look like Audrey Hepburn, I also didn't have to give it all up for God.

That's what I thought, anyway. And then I saw *The Miracle*.

After my father died, my mother became more of an insomniac than ever before. Every night she dozed on the couch for a few hours, then woke up to climb into bed around 3:00 a.m. She seemed frail on the couch, with thin skin starting to wrinkle from years of sunshine and heavy smoking. She was subject to fits of coughing and was diagnosed with diverticulosis. She needed watching. So I became a night owl, crawling out of bed to prowl the house, making sure we were all present and accounted for.

I would watch late-night TV lying on the floor, chin in hands. But I wasn't only watching TV; I was also guarding my mother's life. On commercial breaks I would observe the continued rise and fall of her chest to make sure she was still alive. After "The Star Spangled Banner" was finished and the color bar came on, I listened closely for the whispery sound of her breathing. I needed to make sure she was still there with *me*. The only way to do that was to be there with *her*.

It was on my night watch that I saw *The Miracle*.

A schlocky film by any standards, *The Miracle* was filmed in early Technicolor with a haunting score by Elmer Bernstein and a story that couldn't have been more histrionic. Carol Baker was badly miscast as the beautiful young nun Theresa. A particularly effeminate Roger Moore fawns all over himself as Captain Michael Stuart. The film is set in a small convent tucked into a remote Spanish village during the War of 1812. It was probably a Pyrenees village because it sat in the middle of a big patch of bad soil and lousy weather. The valley's meager prosperity was wholly dependent on the statue of the Virgin Mary, whose presence loomed darkly from her own dais in the convent chapel.

And it was into that very convent that a wounded English officer, Captain Michael Stuart, was carried from a battleground on which Spanish and English armies fought to stave off the invading French. Of all the sisters in the convent, only the beautiful young postulant Theresa can help him heal. We discover right away that Theresa doesn't seem cut out to be a nun, though she claims to want to be one. We sense from the very first that just beneath her starched white wimple, Theresa is a woman of deep and seething passion.

So to no one's surprise, Theresa and Michael fall in love. Michael wants her to marry him. Theresa, in the throes of a vocational crisis, goes into the chapel to beg the statue of the Virgin Mary for a sign: should she remain in the convent, devoted to good works and the dark mysteries of Christ, or should she go off with Michael to the sunny new Jerusalem of Britain to be his bride? Anyone might think that was a question worthy of an answer, but no answer is forthcoming. All Theresa hears is the silence of the convent chapel. Silence. How can she serve a God whose will is absolutely shrouded in silence? Her will—her desire—has a shape and a name. And so she vows to leave the convent and marry Michael.

She throws down her habit and runs, half-naked, into town just as any love-struck nun without a clothing allowance would do. But in town she finds only chaos. The French have invaded. Death is everywhere. People are fleeing, soldiers are killing, bandits are pillaging. And that's how Theresa discovers that Michael has been killed—she sees Michael's distinctive boots on what she assumes to be his dead body.

Almost naked and entirely alone, Theresa stumbles aimlessly. What can she do? She is lost. She has no marketable skills—at least none that the viewer knows about yet. So when a wise old Gypsy woman offers to help her, how can she refuse? The old Gypsy woman brings Theresa to her camp. She feeds Theresa. She gives her a dress that is warmer than the scanty shift she'd fled the convent in, yet far more fetching than her chaste, white postulant's habit. This dress is black. It shows shoulder. It shows leg.

What red-blooded Gypsy male wouldn't fall in love with an ex-nun in an eye-popping, breast-sculpting little black dress, who, it turns out, can also sing and dance like, well, a Gypsy?

Not just one, but *two* Gypsy males do. They are brothers. One of them is the good brother. And the other is as bad as they come. Theresa chooses the good brother, and they make plans for a wedding. But as the couple dances at the wedding reception—the standard Hollywood Gypsy version of foreplay—the bad brother sneaks up and drives a knife into the back of the good brother, killing him instantly.

And now Theresa, twice a widow, yet never a bride, is shattered. Mad with grief, she flees the Gypsy camp. Where will she go?

We have to wait to find out because, meanwhile, a backstory is going on. We discover that Captain Michael Stuart has not been killed at all. A thief had stolen his boots, and it was that very thief whom Theresa had seen lying dead, not Michael at all. He had escaped.

And now we see him returning to the valley, stopping in at the convent for the Mass at which Theresa will profess her vow—but how can that be? It doesn't make a whole lot of sense to the viewer, but we watch him watching Theresa as she makes her slow way down the aisle in the convent church. She is dressed like a bride—a bride of Christ. She is so lovely.

And there is nothing hesitant, nothing hurried or uncertain about the way she prostrates herself before the priest, before Christ, before those who have assembled to watch her transformation from woman to nun. Her lover is convinced: this calm and beautiful being has a religious calling. She was never meant to be his wife. The only home she will know is the convent where she will live with all the other brides of Christ.

But the convent has fallen on hard times, as has the entire village. A vice grip of drought chokes the valley. Nothing will grow. And little wonder. Several planting seasons ago, the statue of the Virgin Mary in the convent chapel disappeared. Someone stole her. The inhabitants of the valley believe that the drought is their punishment. They are all being made to suffer for the sin of the one who stole her.

At this point, the story shifts back to Theresa. She has long since fled the Gypsy camp. She has long since stopped suffering over her lover's murder. She has drowned her grief in concupiscence and fame. An impresario has discovered that this former nun and erstwhile Gypsy has a great flair for the stage. Her calls her "Miraflores, the Gypsy." Soon she is dancing and singing in theaters all over Europe. Her life as a nun is behind her now; she travels, drinks champagne, and enchants a matador, an aging aristocrat, and her public.

And then one day Captain Michael Stuart goes to see "Miraflores, the Gypsy" and discovers that she is none other than his Theresa. And yet how can that be? How can this woman be the lovely novice he saw professing her vows to Christ?

He meets with her backstage. And as they talk it's clear that the love they share has never diminished. And it is not too late, Michael assures her. They can still marry; they can still find bliss in each other's arms!

He tells her of his journey to find her, how he went to the convent to seek her there. And then he tells her of the drought, of the sufferings in the valley of the convent. He tells her that the statue of the Blessed Mother had been stolen, and the people live in fear of God's unyielding wrath.

And as he tells her all this, something stirs within her. She sees now. She understands. It is the will of God. All those she loves—Michael, her Gypsy lover, the people of the valley, her sisters in the convent—all of them are doomed to suffer as long as Theresa continues to ignore what God has called her to do: give her entire life to God.

There is no compromise. There is no middle way. Theresa must leave Michael—for his own safety. She must leave her singing career and worldly pleasures. She must return. She must don the habit and bow to the will of the One who will never leave her alone, the One from whom there is no escape!

And so once again she flees. But this time she flees to the drought-stricken valley and to the convent, weeping and penitent. The wind tears at her skirts. Tree branches scratch her face. Lightning splits the Technicolor sky.

She races into the convent chapel and throws herself to the stone-cold floor. Guilty, tormented by her sins, she begs for forgiveness. And as she lies there, praying and weeping, the viewer sees what Theresa will never see: the shadow of a tall, graceful woman moving across the chapel floor. The shadow falls across Theresa's prone figure and then enters into the booth of the Blessed Mother, the booth that has stood empty for four years. The Blessed Mother—the sublimely blissful nun Michael had seen professing her vows—remains no longer the living, breathing substitute for Sister Theresa, but a statue once again. The real Theresa has returned. She has learned her lesson. She had never, ever really been free.

Only Theresa—and the viewer—will ever know of the Miracle of the Statue. Only Theresa—and the viewer—will fully comprehend that it had always only been a matter of time until Theresa would feel the irresistible force of God's will. It was only a matter of time until, worn down by sin, she would return, in full and beautiful submission, to Him.

It was then, as the Bernstein score crescendoed to its close and Theresa lay pristine and obedient on the floor, that I knew I was done for. At twelve years old, I knew God had me in His sights. Just like Theresa, my life could never, ever really be my own. End of sorry story.

God had me. And God was always *here*. God was always *there*. God saw everything, knew everything. He knew my sinful thoughts, my terror of Him, my vanity. God knew what I feared and what I loved, and God knew how to hurt me.

And more and more I believed that if hurting me was what it took to make me give my life to God, He wouldn't hesitate.

I knew those words of St. Paul's in Romans too well:

For I am convinced that neither death, nor life, nor angels, nor rulers, nor things present, nor things to come, nor powers nor height nor depth nor anything else in all creation will be able to separate us from the love of God in Christ Jesus, our Lord.

—I Corinthians 8:39–39

I used to think those words had been meant to console us, to assure us we were never alone. But now I understood. *The God I feared was with me all of the time!*

And I would never, ever be able to get away.

4

Breaking Silence

Servants striving for the Lord,
prophets burning with the word,
those to whom the arts belong
add their voices to the song.
Pow'rs of knowledge and of law
to the glorious circle draw;
all who work and all who wait,
sing, "The Lord is good and great."

—"Let the Whole Creation Cry"
Stopford A. Brooke (1832–1916)

I'm up there in the pulpit in the middle of the sermon when the first car alarm goes off. It belongs to the woman sitting toward the front, but she doesn't like to wear her hearing aids so she doesn't notice it. I pretend not to. For some reason, one of the tenors in the choir thinks it's his car, and he makes his way out of the choir stall, treading over the other choristers' feet, then across the uncarpeted side aisle, out of the sanctuary, and into the parking lot.

Now another car alarm begins to go off. A second choir member decides it must be *his* car. He makes his way out to the parking lot too.

Then both alarms stop. Both men come back into the sanctuary, down the side aisle, and noisily back into the choir loft. Mission accomplished. And I've only got a few more pages to go.

But then the first car alarm goes off again, and now the tenor realizes that it hadn't been *his* alarm that had gone off before. Somehow he's figured out that it's the car belonging to the woman who doesn't like to wear her hearing aids.

So he decides it's a good idea to go tell her about it. But just as he is stepping down from the choir loft again, the second car alarm starts up once more. And this time a third car alarm goes off. It's like a parking lot full of wailing toddlers—it only takes one to set them all off.

I see the tenor walking toward the woman who doesn't like her hearing aids. Then a man in a red tie gets up from about halfway back in the pews. He thinks one of those alarms is his. He makes his way out of the sanctuary to the door into the church foyer. Then I see a woman sitting toward the front. She's been holding her baby, but now she hands the baby off to her husband and sprints after the man going to the back of the sanctuary. Suddenly it all seems like a football play, the two of them setting up an offensive formation. I expect the husband to lob the baby into the choir loft. Whatever happens, I hope it's a completed pass.

Meanwhile, the tenor has made it over to the pew where the woman who doesn't like her hearing aids is sitting. She is looking up at me with a rapt smile and doesn't hear him coming. So she jumps in surprise when he speaks to her. She looks confused and he talks. I find out later she hadn't even realized she *had* a security system in her car. So naturally she would have had no idea how to turn it off even if she had heard it.

She gets up slowly, a little stiffly, and she and the tenor join the others going into the parking lot. After a bit we hear the car alarms turn off, one by one. Then the man in the red tie, the tenor, the young mother, and the woman who hates her hearing aids, all of them holding their car keys, come back to their pews. Not knowing what else to do, I've just kept right on preaching and am now just a half a page away from the "Amen."

"Rabbi, what can we learn from the sound of a car alarm?"

"That what you need to hear is not always what you are listening for."

If you can't have a religious experience when you enter the upper chamber of the Sainte-Chapelle in Paris, you must have your eyes squeezed shut.

Floor to ceiling, on all sides, blood-red, azure-blue, and citrine-gold stained glass tells the story of characters from the Bible in scenes stacked one on top of the other like Chinese ideographs.

But the religious experience doesn't come from the stories portrayed—I've been to Sainte-Chapelle twice and can't remember a thing about the narratives in the glass. The religious experience is in the light pouring *through* the glass. It's as if you are inside a jewel, walking through the nearly liquid, shifting, simmering colors. It's synesthetic: you *are* the colors. You move within the essence of the thing, and suddenly it seem as though being and seeing are the same experience—except that you don't need to think about it or talk about it the way I am trying to. You just know it in a kind of wordless, numinous way. When I look at and through the brilliant colors at the Sainte-Chapelle, I feel as though I am seeing alchemy at work.

For me, designing a worship service is, in its way, the practice of alchemy. We were never told that in seminary, of course. We were taught that alchemy is a fake science, the science of pagans, a vestige of magic, a medieval trifle. Alchemy is the stuff of a Donovan song—summoning Atlantis and her twelve exiled gods: the poet and the physician, the farmer and the magician and all the rest. We weren't supposed to take alchemy seriously.

Yet in spite of my seminary's low regard for the term, for me, designing a worship service is practicing alchemy. Because there is no way to measure someone's experience of God, no way to guarantee or persuade them that they even *will* experience God's presence, the crafter of a worship service can't rely on the barometer of reason. At their best, worship services are made to appeal to something in addition to our conscious minds: the senses—the aroma of candles and wine, the taste of the bread, the sound of the organ and the people singing, the closeness at the Communion rail. A good worship service incorporates and heightens all five senses, even as it follows an ancient and largely unvarying order:

First we gather, singing. I don't know who actually said that the one who sings prays twice. Augustine gets the credit, but apparently it appears nowhere in his writings. What he does do is compare the sound of singing on earth with the sound of singing in heaven:

> *O happy is the alleluia sung in heaven! O alleluia of peace and security! There no one will be an enemy, there we will never lose any friend. There the praises of God will resound. Certainly, they resound here on earth too. Here though with anxiousness, while up there in tranquility. Here we sing as dying ones, there as immortals. Here in hope, there in reality. Here as exiles and pilgrims, there in our homeland. Here we sing not so much to enjoy repose, as much as to relieve ourselves from fatigue. We sing as travelers. We sing but we walk. . . .*

And that is how many liturgies begin, with singing and walking, a procession that may include the pastor and servers and a choir. And it's a journey that's repeated at the end of the service as well, with the processional cross at the head of the train and the pastor bringing up the rear, everyone singing and everyone walking their journey of life.

After everybody has taken their places, then we read passages from the Bible, always one from the Hebrew scriptures—the *Old* Testament, as Christians persist in calling it. Then comes the Psalm—sung or chanted. After that comes a reading from the letters that make up the bulk of the New Testament. These letters tend to be problem specific, written to address particular concerns that had arisen in the house-churches of early Christendom. Personally, I don't think using first-century advice to figure out solutions to twenty-first-century problems is directly applicable, but that doesn't stop people—among them our politicians—from trying.

Then comes a reading from one of the four gospels, each of them different versions of the same events in Jesus's life. I think of the gospels as accident reports written for the insurance company—one driver sees it this way, and another driver sees the same event slightly differently. What's true? In the end, whatever the insurance company says is true.

After the readings and the sermon come the Prayers of the People.

Different kinds of prayers are sprinkled throughout the service, and most of them are based on ancient forms. Only the Prayers of the People, successive snippets to which the congregation responds with something like "Hear our prayer," address our specific, current realities.

These prayers cover everything—social justice concerns, the state of the world, personal anguishes and hopes. They are a laundry list of our hopes that God will make us stronger, better people in a stronger, better world.

But the most heartfelt parts come when the petitions deal with personal trials. It's here that we end up pleading with God to heal the sick and comfort the sorrowing and to help those who are addicted or in bad relationships or feeling alienated or depressed or any number of the awful things we experience as humans. It's in these parts of the prayer that we're asking God to intercede and give us a break from the pain we, or those for whom we pray, are experiencing.

It saddens me that so much of prayer centers on asking for a respite from life.

People will tell you that the brilliant thing about Christianity was that, in Jesus, God became human, *just the same as all of us*, and was able to feel all human suffering, *just the same as all of us*. And isn't that great, they'll say? It means God knows just what it is like when we suffer.

But personally, sometimes I think that is the coldest, saddest kind of comfort. Yes, it's good to have a God who suffers with us—shared sorrow is halved sorrow and all that, as my Danish maiden aunt assured me. But I don't think we really want God to share our suffering; I think we want God to inoculate us against suffering, to vanquish the power of suffering each and every time it finds us.

But we know full well that that does not happen. So sometimes as we pray I think the *real* Prayers of the People are the ones not being said aloud, when words really do fail us. Sometimes as I look out at the faces of the people of Grace, my congregation—I know so much of their heartache—I wonder how they can stand to say, as we do each week in the Lord's Prayer, "Thy will be done." Who can really tell what God's will for us is anyway? Or if there really is such a thing as God's will? Is it the will of God that we suffer? I just don't believe that. But we do suffer. Sometimes it seems as though God is strangely distant, strangely silent. That's when we end up making excuses for God for allowing the world to be as it truly is.

These are things I never say to the people of Grace, or any of the churches I've served, things I believe I should never say. My call to this community is about upholding faith in a merciful and benevolent God. I was not called here in order to be a rationalist, a realist, a pessimist, an atheist, an agnostic. I was not called here to break down the paper walls of hope we raise against the winds of misery. We hang a picture of Jesus on those paper walls. We hang a cross. What priest or shaman has a right to ransack hope? I don't. And in fact, I talk of hope all the time. Because I, too, hang a palm-leaf cross on my paper walls of hope. I, too, want a magic God who will make my house of cards a mansion of stone.

And so we stand together, "beggars before God," as Luther called human beings.

What follows next is the heart of every service: Holy Communion. The sharing of bread—usually Styrofoam-style wafers—and wine is bracketed with prayers. But it is that act of eating and drinking together that is so powerful. And even after all these years and with all my disillusionment about the church, this is one of the most intense experiences I regularly have in my life.

When I hand out the papery discs of mystery and hope we call the body of Christ, I touch each hand. I look into each eye. It is as intimate as anything I know. At that moment it feels as if I am able to love genuinely and without a filter almost everyone who reaches out their hand and lets me touch it with the scrap of processed parchment we call flesh. It is my flesh and their flesh that are touching. The wafer is a kind of intermediary, maybe, the excuse that lets us touch, the reason that gives us permission to kneel, to nod "Amen." Because when I put the wafer into upturned, uplifted hands I also get to look into the faces of those receiving it.

Here is humanity gathered, kneeling—old and young, infirm and whole. Everyone is close together, so close together their shoulders touch. They are reaching out their hands. Their faces give their hearts away. Sometimes they smile. Other times their eyes glaze with tears. Sometimes they bow their heads and only notice that they have received the wafer when they feel my hands place it into theirs.

Who could really describe what is happening?

It's not about me. Or them. It's about us—the three of us: me, the person I touch, and that which is unseen between us, somehow dissolving the particularity of failings and sins and grudges, replacing all that with something invisible and unspoken, even as I speak the words we barely know how to understand: *This is the body of Christ.*

~

Seven months after September 11, 2001, a friend and I went to New York to attend the annual conference at Trinity Institute on Wall Street. The Trinity Institute conferences draw huge crowds because they feature nationally known speakers, each addressing the theme chosen for that year. This year's theme was *How Then Shall We Live?* It's a quote from Ezekiel, "Our transgressions and our sins weigh upon us, and we waste away because of them; how then, can we live?"

It was a good question to be asking. The speakers were to address how we might move forward as people of faith in a nation heartbroken by the events of September 11, hungry for vengeance and frightened by what was to come. It was poignant question, too, made even more so because Trinity Parish on Wall Street is just a few footsteps away from the World Trade Center. It had been both a staging ground for recovery efforts and a memorial site to the thousands who had died.

How Then Shall We Live turned out to be a strange conference, though. Famous theologians and speakers addressed the throngs of conference attendees and wrestled with a question that seemed to give no ready answers. Lots of us could only see them on the video monitors placed throughout the sanctuary and in additional gathering spaces. My friend and I sat in the back of the sanctuary, squinting to see the actual speakers, wanting their corporeal presence to somehow provide answers.

We were both preachers, after all. And we were liberals. And when a preacher is a liberal, as so many are, you've got to watch what you say from the pulpit. There's an old saw that says a sermon is supposed to comfort the afflicted and afflict the comfortable. It's risky business inflicting affliction. And self-righteous besides, not that that necessarily stops anybody.

We were preachers, and add to that the fact that we were a little in love. This conference, *How Then Shall We Live?*, was sort of a romantic getaway. You wouldn't believe what pastors find romantic. We had arrived late the night before, parked my friend's beat up VW on the street in front of our hotel, and tried to check into our rooms. But there had been a flood at the Holiday Inn where conference attendees were staying. We were redirected to the Ritz-Carlton, assured that first thing in the morning our original rooms would be ready. We got back in the car and drove the limping VW the few blocks to the Ritz-Carlton porte cochere. The valet glanced at the well-rusted car, wordlessly took my friend's car keys, and drove into the parking garage.

The hotel lobby was thickly carpeted, elegantly furnished, and glimmering with lights from the enormous chandeliers. At the front desk, the concierge welcomed us warmly. He said he hoped we would feel right at home. It only took a heartbeat's time for me to decide I'd have no trouble feeling right at home in such a swell place. Still, the concierge assured us we would be back at the Holiday Inn tomorrow—it was so much more convenient a location for us.

But why would we ever want to leave the Ritz-Carlton? The rooms were little playgrounds of luxe: feather beds and stacks of pillow, Bose radios and boxes of chocolate truffles. And there was a telescope for looking out at New York Harbor, its night-black surface laced with lights from boats and bridges. In the bathrooms were expensive toiletries, double marble showers, and bathtubs big enough for full-immersion baptisms.

How then shall we live?

In our case, apparently with an astonishing sense of duty and punctuality. Because early the next day, before the conference was to begin, we skipped breakfast. We packed up our bags, had the valet fetch the VW, and moved back up West Street to the Holiday Inn.

"You're on the 39th floor. You've got some nice views," the man at the check-in desk told us, "Good views of the harbor."

But not like the ones at the Ritz-Carlton, I thought as we stepped into the elevator and pressed the button for the 39th floor. It wouldn't be anything like the Ritz-Carlton at all. Why hadn't we just skipped the morning session and had room service? I thought of the deep bathtub and the long soak I was missing, the fancy little bottles of bath products I had not even had the presence of mind to steal—I am certain that the commandment against stealing was never intended to include even the higher-priced hotel toiletries.

Then the elevator doors opened, and we stepped onto the 39th floor. I did what I guess most people do when they step off the elevator in a tall building. I went to the window right beside it, and I took a look outside.

There was a wide path of blue sky in front of me, as if the buildings on either side of it had parted to admit the early morning daylight. It was lovely the way the sun flooded the space with so much unimpeded radiance. I looked to my right and saw a nondescript skyscraper. On my left was a gorgeous older building. It was dignified and weather worn, with ornate quoins and carved pediments. But, like a woman wearing hijab, it was veiled behind black nylon netting that blew in the breeze, shrouding the building from its rooftop to as far down as I could see. On tiptoe, I pressed farther into the window well, my forehead to the glass, trying to see where the netting ended. For a few seconds I stared without seeing, and then my throat suddenly tightened and I got so dizzy I braced myself with palms against the window: immediately below me was the maw, the bodiless grave of Ground Zero.

I hadn't known.

I hadn't realized the Holiday Inn had once been in the towers' vanished shadows. All I had thought, when I first looked out the window, was how pretty it was to see so much sunshine pouring in. But it was only pouring in because the towers had crumbled one by one while thousands of lives had turned to ashes and dust. Sun and sky were all that was left to fill the gaping cavity. Seven months after September 11, the site had been scraped clean of all debris, as empty and open as a gargantuan drilled tooth.

"Come here," I said to my friend who had walked on ahead of me down the hall, "Look."

He came back to stand beside me. But what was there to say? We stood looking down 39 floors into the void, into the tragedy. There were no buildings to see. There were no words for us to say. We stared into a stony acre of death, speechless.

How then shall we live?

I wish I could say the conference was powerful and meaningful, but I can't. No one could answer the question the conference had proposed as its theme. We wanted to know what to say when you come to the end of speech and then you gaze, slack jawed, at all that lies beyond.

On the last day of the conference, we walked over to the plywood platform built to allow visitors a grim glimpse onto the World Trade Center site. We stood there with a crowd of people. There was graffiti on the plywood walls, prayers and blessings mostly. We saw a set of venetian blinds that were tangled in the branches of a leafless tree like a comb sticking out of a drunken woman's hairdo. We heard a couple arguing about whether or not to take a picture. They spoke English with thick German accents.

"But why do you want to take a picture? There is nothing there," the man asked the woman.

"There is *not* nothing there," she replied angrily.

We heard a little girl ask her father if many people had died when the buildings had fallen. We could hear his helpless silence. No parent wants to be the one who teaches his or her children about the senselessness of death or—still worse—about its endlessness.

So we walked on, leaving the World Trade Center site, making our way up Broadway into a bitter wind as far as we could stand it. We had been planning to visit some galleries, do a little shopping in Soho. But this was the wrong time for shopping. We let the wind turn us around and we walked, hand in hand, hunched over, back to the Holiday Inn, stopping to buy take-out clam chowder to eat in the safe blandness of our rooms. New York was cold. There didn't seem to be any answers forthcoming. We had a view of New York harbor, it's true. And we didn't look out of the window by the elevator when we got off on our floor.

~

How then shall we preach?

It doesn't matter if a pastor says that faith doesn't necessarily offer answers but rather raises more questions; there is still the expectation that in the sermon, some kind of meaning or message will be forthcoming. If you believe St. Paul, writing in Romans, faith is supposed to come from what's heard.

So there's an agenda in sermon writing—to try to find words to make audible the mystical interface between the mortal and the immortal: Moses and the blazing bush, Elijah and the chariot of fire, Mary Magdalene and the empty tomb, or the two disciples and the unrecognized walker on the Emmaus road.

The pastor is supposed to preach the vision. And the vision is always supposed to be redemptive. Even after Columbine. Even after 9-11. Even after the Virginia Tech shootings. And the Aurora shootings. And Newtown. And so many other catastrophes, natural or otherwise. The vision is always supposed to be redemptive. It's always supposed to be good news. That's what "gospel" means. It's from the Old English "godspell" or good message, which is from the Latin "bona annuntiatio" or the

Latinized version—"evangelium"—of the original Greek, "euangelion," meaning good ("eu") message ("angelion").

So when the text for any given Sunday says, "Abraham, take your son, your only son, Isaac, whom you love, and go to the land of Moriah, and offer him there as a burnt offering on one of the mountains I will show you," (Genesis 22:2), it is the pastor's job to find the good news in that.

If the text for any given Sunday says, "Do you think that I have come to bring peace to the earth? No, I tell you, but rather division" (Luke 12:51), it's the pastor's job to find the good news.

And when the text says, with a glaring anti-Judaic bias, "Since then, we have such a hope, we act with great boldness, not like Moses who put a veil over his face. . . . Indeed, to this very day when they [Jews] hear the reading of the old covenant, the same veil is still there, since only in Christ is it set aside" (2 Corinthians 3:12–14), it is the pastor's job to extract good news and to somehow try to persuade the people that Paul was not a *real* anti-Semite, evidence to the contrary.

I don't expect visions when I write my sermons. I don't expect inspiration. I know too much to expect any of that. There are times, of course, when my fingers fly on the keys. But mostly I resonate with the verse of an old hymn, "Spirit of God, Descend Upon My Heart":

> *I ask no dream, no prophet ecstasies,*
> *No sudden rending of the veil of clay.*
> *No angel visitant, no opening skies;*
> *But take the dimness of my soul away.*

That's pretty much my position. *Just take the dimness of my soul away.* Just let me get this out there and out of me. Whatever it is. And let it be good enough.

And often it is good, or good enough. From time to time as I'm coming down from the pulpit I think, "Well, I preached the piss out of *that* one." It's a prayer of thanksgiving in the purest sense. At that moment, all I want is a big pull on my tall glass of water and a moment of heart's ease: "Please, God, do not let me have screwed up. Please, God, do not let me have overstepped my boundaries. Please let it be okay that I am a girl and I am talking as if I know what I am talking about." (Yes, self-doubt about my gender and my vocation remain.)

But the preaching and the writing are not the same thing. The moments of speaking and the hours of writing are different not only in duration, but in process, too.

There is a grapefruit spoon in my flatware drawer. Just the one. I don't know where it came from, and I don't know that I've ever used it on a grapefruit—because wouldn't those serrated edges feel nasty on your tongue? But usually by the fourth or fifth Sunday of the seven-week liturgical season of Easter—in other words, when we are still too far away from summer, when everything will be warmer, better, easier—I start to feel that writing a sermon is like taking a grapefruit spoon to the soft tissue of my soul.

It's gotten so I can somewhat anticipate those coming weeks of heart-heavy sermon writing. Still, there is no respite. I am still supposed to be delivering the gospel. Wringing out of the onion-skin pages of my favorite little Bible something that can pass as existential comfort and meaning.

But all I feel is tetchiness, exhaustion. What now? What next? Why are the disciples such suck-ups? Why can't Paul have had an editor? Why does the damn lectionary of biblical readings only give us snippets from the book of Job? Why are the Psalms so violent? And why is their language so crusted over with male pronouns for God? Why in the world does anybody think the Bible has something to say to them? And what can I dream up for this Sunday to help them continue to believe that it does?

Those are the dark weeks, the weeks that I scrape my soul with the grapefruit spoon to get a sermon to take to the pulpit.

Because the burning bush is no longer on fire. The clouds have forever swallowed Elijah's chariot. And the unrecognized walker on the Emmaus road has long since walked on.

Frederick Buechner, writing in *The Alphabet of Grace*, says, "it is the silence encircling the sound that is itself most holy."

Still, silence was not part of the deal I struck at my ordination. The deal I struck was that I would use words to summon faith in the unseen and unknowable. It's a fool's errand. And I do it every Sunday. I break the silence. I don't have any choice.

5

Steward of the Mysteries

Think of us in this way, as servants of Christ and stewards of God's mysteries.

—1 Corinthians 4:1

I hadn't yet read *The Art of War* when I was thirteen, but I must have had some instinctive grasp of what it was all about: Confront your opponent ahead of time. Learn his game. Further his ends. Ape his style. But none of that was my intention.

All I consciously intended was to serve the God whose good side I wanted to be on, having been on the bad side long enough.

Not that I thought I regarded God as my opponent. I had been taught better than that. I had been taught that God was a loving Father, in spite of the fact that my experience with fathers suggested some had shorter shelf lives than others.

I had been taught that God was like my brother, a brother who had gone so far as to die for all of my sins. But I wouldn't have wanted my brother to die for my sins. I would have wanted my brother to play with me.

I had certainly been taught that God was male. All the pronouns ever used to describe God were masculine, and I was still almost two decades away from eschewing all the male language that actually ends up being pretty limiting ways to describe an ultimate being.

I had also been taught, of course, that God was a Holy Ghost. But apart from Casper, the Friendly Ghost—hardly a representative example—ghosts scared me. As much as I wanted to see my father again, I always feared that if I did see him, he would be a ghost. Just to imagine my father as an ectoplasmic apparition of paternity—his hazel eyes glowing from their spectral sockets, the wedding ring he wore encircling glowing bone—was terrifying. I didn't want a ghost father.

The thought of a ghost *God* was even worse. It was bad enough that God knew my every thought and movement, bad enough that His divine calculator tracked my diverse sins. Ghosting around in my life seemed excessive and hardly the image of the Comforter that Jesus in the Gospel of John had said the Holy Ghost would be.

Still, I would never have seen God as my opponent. While it sometimes seemed that a kindly uncle might have done a better job of shielding me from my short life's sundry misfortunes, I wasn't one to blame God. If you think your life is difficult now and you decide to blame God for that, God knows *what* will happen next.

No, I had to find a way to work with God. I was trapped without an inch of wiggle room. I simply needed to capitulate to God's will up front. Maybe a suitable plan of escape would emerge later. Or maybe I, like Sister Theresa, would be molded into compliance, scared into submission.

Because the convent was not an option, I decided that the next-best proactive approach was to become a pastor. I was thirteen now, already confirmed, and clearly a church geek. I knew full well that Missouri Synod Lutheran girls were not allowed to be pastors. For some strange reason I felt they would make an exception for me. I felt that somehow I was different. *Most girls* couldn't become pastors. But it seemed a genuine injustice that I could go neither into the convent nor into the ministry. There had to be some way around the problem.

So I made an appointment to talk to my pastor. Pastor was a red-faced, smiley man who kept himself well groomed, as men of God are supposed to. He was courtly and friendly in spite of being a deadly boring preacher and an only slightly more animated confirmation class teacher. I thought he might be pleased that I wanted to become a pastor like he was. I felt very grown up as we met in his office to talk it over.

His response was reasonably gentle but definitely firm. I couldn't become a pastor. I was the wrong gender. And because I was apparently not the first girl to have asked this question, the Missouri Synod publishing house had thoughtfully prepared a little pamphlet—which Pastor was quick to give me. This pamphlet quoted chapter and verse about what role women could play and couldn't play in church life. Such as this, from 1 Corinthians:

As in all the churches of the saints, women should be silent in the churches. For they are not permitted to speak, but should be subordinate, as the law also says. For it is shameful for a woman to speak in church.

—1 Corinthians 14:34–35

Or this, from 1 Timothy:

Let a woman learn in silence with full submission. I permit no woman to teach or have authority over a man; she is to keep silent. For Adam was formed first, then Eve, and Adam was not deceived but the woman was deceived and became a transgressor. Yet she will be saved through childbearing, provided they continue in faith and love and holiness, with modesty.

—1 Timothy 2:8–14

Becoming a pastor was not an option. But, Pastor said, I could become a deaconess.

I didn't know much about deaconesses beyond that they were expected to remain celibate, unmarried, childless, and live in community.

Deaconess, I thought. It was like being a nun, but without the interesting habit and headgear. It seemed decidedly less glamorous. Had Ingrid Bergman ever played the part of a Lutheran deaconess? Had Audrey Hepburn, Rosalind Russell, Carol Baker, Deborah Kerr, Jean

Simmons, Debbie Reynolds, Sally Field? Just try and imagine a TV show called *The Flying Deaconess*.

If I couldn't become a pastor, I would do the only other logical thing: I would become a pastor's wife!

That made sense to me. I liked Pastor's wife. She was a wonderful cook with a quick wit. She had a great job, she spoke several languages, and she earned more money than her husband. I wanted to be a pastor's wife. Just like my pastor's wife—only thinner.

The problem was that the few Lutheran boys I knew were truly nerds. I did try to flirt with one of them for a while. But he showed absolutely no inclination of going into the ministry, and I certainly wasn't going to waste my time on him if he wasn't going to be a pastor! The rest of the boys I knew were Catholic, and it would have done me absolutely no good if any of them became priests.

God had a way with roadblocks. I couldn't be a *pastor*. And *I* couldn't be a deaconess. And based on the sheer lack of available talent, I couldn't be a pastor's *wife*.

Eventually I realized—and why was I surprised?—that something was wrong with me. Why did I want to do what only a man was able to do? Why was I unwilling to consider the celibate life of a deaconess? Why couldn't I even find a decent seminarian for whom I could cook and clean and bear children? Something was wrong with *me*.

❧

By the time I was midway through college, I was convinced that, quite apart from the Missouri Synod Lutheran Church's prohibition against female pastors, I wouldn't have made a good one, anyway. I had left the church—not a formal leave taking, just more of a retreat from judgment.

I was no longer the chaste Lutheran girl dreaming of bearing the pastor's children. By now I was drinking cheap Alsatian wines, smoking pot, dating Jewish boys, and participating in women's consciousness-raising groups. My copy of *Our Bodies, Ourselves* was dog-eared. And I had my very own plastic speculum. With that and the aid of a hand mirror, I had seen my own cervix. Lots of girls at left-leaning East coast universities in the 1970s had seen their own cervixes.

Regardless of all that, I still knew that now, more than ever, the church didn't want me. I was damaged goods.

But John Coltrane, D. H. Lawrence, and Fyodor Dostoyevsky didn't pass such judgment. True, they were all dead. But it was equally true that they had lived out some version of Christianity, one that clearly didn't depend on chastity, poverty, or obedience.

Ingmar Bergman's movies became my passion. Gerard Manley Hopkins's poetry spoke to my soul. John Donne's holy sonnets made me cry. I wasn't a very original lapsed Lutheran, heading straight for all those semi-Christian iconoclasts, but I was able to live a churchless but richly spiritual life for seven years.

Still, I thought I was doing something slightly heretical and definitely sinful in embracing the joys and pleasures of food, men, wine, books, music, and art. Nor could I be happy with anything less than all the life I had. Why would anyone choose to live otherwise? I remember my astonishment in discovering that George Bernard Shaw had made a celibate marriage. That explained why his expression seemed so pickle-ish and tense in all his photographs. Celibacy—as well as his vegetarianism—was written all over his penuriously bearded face.

For reasons that remain unclear to me, I returned to church when I moved to Charlottesville, Virginia, for graduate school. I was up early one Sunday morning making pancakes when I heard church bells chiming. Suddenly I was crying, longing for church, longing to sing hymns, to pray, to feel I had a place in a church. And fortunately, in the American South, it's not considered weird to go to church, even if my graduate school roommates, both Northeasterners, thought I had taken leave of my senses.

Charlottesville, of course, is full of Episcopal and Baptist churches, but I'd always nursed a soft spot for Luther. So I checked the one Lutheran church in town—near enough that I could walk to it—and simply started going regularly. St. Mark was (and is) a progressive Lutheran church that at the time had three pastors, one of them a woman. After a few months,

I joined the church, and during the hour I spent in worship on Sunday morning, I tried to forget about what I was doing with the rest of my life.

The man I was seeing—my former early American literature professor—had been separated from his wife for two years. Shortly after we became involved, he mentioned—*mentioned*—that his wife, A., had recently moved back into the house.

It was entirely sexless, he assured me, separate bedrooms and all that. The whole thing was a sham, he said. But obviously he and I wouldn't be spending any more time at his lovely country home. And although Chip and A. did divorce eventually—long after I was out of the picture—I began to feel like my mother, making her tasty treats for Warren because Olive was a mess in the kitchen. And—if you believed what either Chip or Warren said about their wives—in the bedroom as well.

I hated to compare Chip to Warren. But it was impossible not to. They both saw themselves as fetching blends of romance and machismo. Chip wasn't *just* a scholar, of course. He also kept cattle on a farm outside Charlottesville. He wore old jeans and scuffed boots to school, though the unspoken dress code at the University of Virginia was a lot tidier than that—this was Mr. Jefferson's Academical Village, after all. He drove a truck with a gun rack across the rear windshield. Once, as we were picnicking along Skyline Drive, a state trooper pulled over and told Chip to stow his rifle.

Mostly we spent time at my house, a little stucco bungalow sublet from a professor on sabbatical. My roommates knew Chip, but we were graduate students—lots of things happened in English departments. One of my roommates appeared to be carrying on some kind of mysterious affair with the professor whose office she shared.

Chip and I, talking it over in the intimacy of an already long lunch, thought it was disgusting. My roommate's professor's wife was the Dickinson scholar in the department. She seemed such a trusting soul. How sad to have her husband bedding the fetching graduate student nearly underneath her nose.

Were we all that different, I wondered? I knew he feared his wife finding out about us. He cared about what people might think—and, more importantly, what they might say. I'll never forget our one genuinely public date. We had gone to see the ballet. That wasn't Chip's thing, but he wanted to please me.

But as we talked in the lobby during intermission, me with a champagne flute and Chip with a Scotch, he became suddenly edgy and stammering. I thought he was having heartburn—because he was fifteen years older than I was I figured I had to expect such things—but when he suddenly ducked behind a column in the theater lobby I understood completely: he was hiding, plain and simple.

As I discovered after the second curtain, he had seen a colleague. That colleague also happened to be my medieval literary theory professor—a fine man from West Texas—and Chip feared that he had been caught fraternizing with a graduate student.

"Caught," I thought. Wow.

After the performance he made an exaggerated show of walking out proudly with me on his arm. But it was too late for all that. I felt raw and cheap and wanted to get to the car as quickly as possible.

More and more I felt I couldn't have—and didn't deserve—a place at St. Mark's. I was an anomaly, a fornicating Northerner whose whiteness seemed to be the only thing I had in common with all these married-with-children, wealthy worshippers of God.

So I when I heard these words one Sunday in church, my world was pretty much turned upside down:

> *For the promise that Abraham would inherit the world did not come to him or to his descendants through the law but through the righteousness of faith. If it is the adherents of the law who are to be heirs faith is null and the promise is void. For the law brings wrath, but where there is no law there is no violation. For this reason it depends on grace, in order that the promise may rest on faith and be guaranteed to all his descendants, not only to the adherents of the law but also to those who share the faith of Abraham . . .*

> —Romans 4:13–16

I didn't believe what I had just heard read: For the law brings wrath, but where there is no law there is no violation.

I understood right away that St. Paul wasn't talking about civil law. Of course we needed consequences for violations that damaged the common good—time-out chairs for naughty toddlers, traffic tickets for speeders, prison sentences for rapists. Instead, St. Paul was talking about some kind of existential law, one that shouldn't exist—"where there is no law, there is no violation." Without such a human-made law, nothing was without value. Without such a law, there was hope.

If I understood what I had just heard, then God's grace trumped the law that set the impossible standard I had been trying—and failing—to meet my entire life. If grace was real, then I was not without value.

Grace was the most subversive, insane thing I had ever heard of.

If this was true—and why shouldn't it be, if St. Paul wrote it and Luther jump-started the Reformation with it?—I didn't have to be good. I had already been declared good. "Forensic justification by grace through faith" is what, I would learn in seminary, it was called.

I had grown up a Christian and never even had a whiff of grace. Discovering it now—however much it unsettled and thwarted my previous sense of who God was and what God wanted from me—I wanted to spread the news of that grace. I wanted to spread it profligately and selflessly.

And what better way was there to do that than to become a pastor? I was right back where I had started.

I was back where I started in some ways, but not in others. I had joined a branch of the Lutheran church that ordained women. Over the next few years, I completed a master's degree in writing and began to teach and write for local newspapers. I married Joe, a brilliant though emotionally quiescent man, and we had had our first daughter, Madeleine. Eventually I was given the okay by my candidacy committee to attend seminary, for which I was awarded a full scholarship. When Madeleine was two, Joe and I moved to Philadelphia, living in seminary housing and hoping Joe would be able to find a job. He hadn't finished college, and though he would go on, long after we divorced, to become a self-taught and gifted code writer, at the time of our move, we wondered how we would be able to get by with me as a full-time student and mother of a toddler and Joe as our breadwinner.

Grace may have been a terrific theological concept. But I found out right away that you didn't just go to seminary and get your God degree. It turned out that there was a committee tasked with verifying the value and potential worth of any candidates wanting to become Lutheran pastors. This "candidacy committee" had a lot of practical value, helping to keep at least some of the nut jobs out of parishes and pulpits. But for me it was a reversion to my childhood compulsion to try to be good. Maybe God thought I had some intrinsic worth. When it came to the candidacy committee, I would have to prove it.

The committee met with students yearly for a two-day retreat consisting chiefly of group and individual therapy sessions run not by psychologists, but by pastors and laypeople. And though I do believe my own committee in upstate New York worked with the best of intentions, it telegraphed terrifically mixed messages. We were supposed to be honest and revealing. But honesty and self-revelation resulted, inevitably, in knitted eyebrows and continued probing that ran the risk of derailing the seminarian's plans for ministry entirely.

In short order, I learned to keep the more problematic truths to myself. My marriage had long been troubled, not simply by our precarious financial circumstances, but by emotional upheaval as well. In my first year with the candidacy committee, I had hinted as much. Then I learned that this was a bad strategy, one that drew attention to my potential unfitness as a pastor. So in the following year I was more discreet and less truthful. Yes, Joe and I had seen a counselor. We'd addressed a lot of our problems. Yes, our marriage had improved.

It hadn't, of course. But I recognized I could not be without both a marriage and a career. I was a mother now and, based on all probabilities, was priming myself to be the main breadwinner. I simply couldn't risk jeopardizing the path to ministry. I would be whomever they needed me to be to get where I needed to go.

The fact was that it was hard to be authentically oneself while at the same time convincing a candidacy committee that you would make a good pastor. Intentionally or not, candidacy committees expected their seminarians to fit a certain mold. Individuality was welcomed, but only as long as it wasn't too noticeable.

A good candidate was playful, but never coarse in his or her sense of humor. He or she was devoted to the faith, but never self-righteous.

Strong theological convictions were good. But it was less good to be outspoken about how these convictions affected one's political outlook.

Divorce was frowned upon. So there was a lot of pressure to have a good marriage or sure make it look as though you did.

It was expected that a pastor be willing to relocate his or her family as needed to serve the needs of the larger church.

Celibacy was never explicitly discussed, but it went without saying that single pastors—and pastoral candidates—were to remain officially "chaste" until married (though, as I found out when I was in seminary, many of my fellow students defined "chaste" conveniently loosely, as I myself would after I was divorced).

When it came to gay clergy and candidates for the clergy, celibacy was an explicit requirement. In those pre–gay marriage days, there were no provisions made for committed same-sex couples. It was expected that if you self-identified as homosexual and wanted to be a pastor, you would be celibate.

So gay classmates either lied and proceeded toward ordination or told the truth and didn't. I had a classmate who, with her partner, was a foster parent of two babies born cocaine addicted. It was not an easy job, and because they were lesbians, they had not been able to legally adopt these children. Nor did they have any money to speak of: V. had been four years in seminary, and her partner had had the primary responsibility for the kids.

But when it came time to discuss her future with her candidacy committee, V. couldn't have lied if she had wanted to. She had never made any secret of who she was. And while the seminary had been happy to have her as a tuition-paying student, the larger church rejected her as a pastor. Those were (until 2009) the rules of the game.

It went without saying that if you were young, male, hard working—ideally with a wife and/or kids and perhaps with some military service behind you—you were golden. So there was always tremendous pressure to aspire to an acceptable status quo. If a marriage was sour on the inside but pretty on the outside, that was preferable than having to admit to a divorce.

Also, it was best not to be too encumbered with family. If you wanted to move back to the part of the country you had left to go to seminary or if you had a spouse's career needs to accommodate that would limit your mobility, it made you a trickier candidate. That had the potential to raise the question of just how serious you were about serving Christ. After all, the disciples hadn't needed to go home every night and help the kids with their homework. They had important things to do.

I tried not to be, but managed to be a problem case. During my last year of seminary I gave birth to my second daughter. Linnea was born in February, almost eleven weeks before her due date. It was a dizzying and terrifying time. Joe and I moved through our days like children lost in a city where all the streets signs are backward and all the adults speak different languages.

I was afraid to withdraw from classes because I didn't know if we would be allowed to stay in our well-subsidized seminary housing. I was afraid to be seen as a stereotypical female whose family's needs trump her vocation. So I carried on with a full load of classes, doing as much as I could independently while I sat by Linnea's warmer bed in the Neonatal Intensive Care Unit half an hour away from the seminary in Bryn Mawr Hospital. She stayed there for seven weeks.

Though in many respects her size had spared her the greatest dangers of premature birth, Linnea had not been in utero long enough to have developed a sucking reflex. For the first month, her nurses poured the breast milk I expressed five times a day into the nasogastric tube that went from her nostril straight into her sunken tummy.

Though she was able to breathe on her own, she often forgot to. The alarm on her warmer bed would sound, and the nurses or her father or I would jiggle her feet, the noise and stimulation shocking her into breathing again. She couldn't lift her head to turn it from side to side, so we had to do it for her to prevent her skull from becoming permanently misshapen. We made a bittersweet joke that our Linnea was going to have a "flounder head" if we weren't careful to regularly reposition her.

Her heartbeat was erratic, her immune system not fully developed. She had a difficult time learning to suckle a bottle or a pacifier—though after the first month or so she took enthusiastically to breastfeeding. Once she was finally allowed to come home, she wore a heart monitor for the next nine months. Madeleine, memorably inventing an imaginary friend I hadn't previously heard of, claimed that "Little Johnny wants to put the baby out in the trash."

For the rest of the semester and the year of full-time parish internship to follow, my life was split between the unceasing demands of ministry and caring for my museum-fragile premature baby.

~

After my internship year drew to its close, I told my candidacy committee that I wanted to remain in upstate New York. I had my extended family there and I had two small children, one with special needs. And I told them that my marriage was ending.

To some extent, I still regret making the decision to leave the marriage—it was my idea. But this was long before people were given appropriate antidepressants; long before people had labels that, however limiting they may be on one level, can also provide help and a framework for understanding different personalities and pathologies. I also think, though, that in some ways I made a very selfish decision in wanting to divorce, acting out a kind of early midlife crisis. I didn't want a staid life as a wife, mother, and Lutheran pastor. I still nursed hope for romance, and my life seemed to be the antithesis of romantic.

Of course, it wasn't enough to tell my candidacy committee about the impending divorce. I was required to talk to my bishop about it. In person. So on a rainy October night, two months into unemployment, I sat opposite him in a brightly lit Friendly's restaurant and nervously broke the news.

He was sympathetic. But he had never been divorced, of course.

He did tell me he would pray for me. And for Joe and our daughters.

That was something, I thought. I had been so grateful for the prayers of the seminary community when Linnea was in the NICU. But I needed more than prayers now. I was a newly single mother of two small children. I was geographically restricted to an area so my daughters could remain near their father.

I needed more than prayers. I needed a church. I needed ordination. I needed a job.

~

Some of my seminary classmates had gotten calls to pretty country churches or to beautiful downtown behemoths with stained glass windows and vaulted ceilings. Some were members of staff ministries in thriving suburban parishes.

I got a call to a former chicken restaurant converted into a church on a down-at-the-heels street in a "suburb" of Schenectady, one pockmarked with fast-food joints, drugstores, gas stations, and a falling-down bowling alley. The church sat just opposite the Roller-Rama.

Before its incarnation as a chicken restaurant, it had been a chicken farm. And indeed, there was something cooplike about the physical plant with its narrow rooms and low ceilings. Once or twice I tried to joke that we had the best potluck suppers because the spirit of chicken still hung in the air, but nobody laughed. This was a no-joking kind of place.

As it turned out, I had been called to serve a dying congregation, not merely a declining one. And it is a genuine testament to the protective power of denial that it took years for me to realize just how tough St. Tough Spot—my pet name for it—had been.

Well after I'd done my time there, colleagues confided that they'd thought the bishop's office never should have sent a newly ordained pastor to such a troubled church. But it wasn't really the bishop's fault. I had wanted to go there. I was eager, pea brained, idealistic. And I had needed the job. I had needed the money. And I had wanted, more than anything, to be ordained. It was like wanting to get married more than caring who you marry. At last I would have the red stole of ordination around my shoulders and an income—meager—with which to support my kids.

St. Tough Spot was a case study of how, in a dwindling congregation, a few angry souls can wield power disproportionate to their numbers. Some of those still active in the church were warm, caring people. But others were not. Stubborn, stiff necked, possessive of their property, they made the climate so inhospitable that newcomers, those few who visited, never wanted to stay for long. After a while, that's how I came to feel, too. But I wasn't free to leave.

Congregational members would voice their desire to bring some new blood into the congregation. But the not-so-subliminal message they conveyed was, "What can you do for us? Teach Sunday School? Join the Altar Guild? Sit on the Church Council?"

Though they didn't really mean that either. Ossified in patterns that were no longer working, the congregation had lost all sense of how to share their ministry. Any type of innovation was threatening. I was too new at the job to understand that in a climate of it's-broke,-but-don't-fix-it, change was impossible

I knew next to nothing about congregational dynamics. What I knew—and what I knew they knew—was that I was a newcomer and I was a woman. The odds of success were not in my favor. They didn't trust me—and why should they? I didn't trust me, either.

And then, after only a few months at St. Tough Spot, I committed an act the congregation found just side of treason and heresy. What did I do? Sleep with the sexton? Share the Communion wine with the confirmation students? Steal from the collection plate?

No. What I did was, *I moved the flags.*

Any damn fool pastor knows that, at least for the first few years, *you don't touch the flags.*

And what's worse, I hid them. Just not very well.

It happened one night after a church council meeting. I was talking to the Council president, a feisty younger woman—meaning, in her fifties—and I mentioned that having the flags in the chancel area was really a theological no-no. It's not God-and-country we come to worship, I said. We're not in Texas, I said, thinking I was being funny, then hoping she didn't have relatives there.

I like to think it was her idea and not mine, but I don't remember. All I know is that we took down the dusty stars-and-stripes and the New York State "Excelsior" flag, and we hid them back behind the altar in a little-known storage space, where I hoped they would remain hidden. It didn't occur to me that anyone would notice their absence.

I should have known better. The Altar Guild ladies know every nook and cranny in every church. And when they noticed the missing flags, they scoured the building for them. And first thing on Sunday morning, the president of the Altar Guild ladies asked me why the flags had been rolled up and put in with the collection of musty felt processional banners that hadn't been used in decades.

Why hadn't I realized that you shouldn't try to keep secrets from the Altar Guild ladies?

Nor should you lie to them. Not because lying is wrong, but because they will see through you, so it isn't even worth it to try.

Nevertheless, that's what I did. I lied. I told Altar Guild president that the Council president and I had taken them down because we noticed they needed a good cleaning. That didn't explain why we'd hidden them, of course. Nor did I try to explain the theological incorrectness of flags in church. No, I was too scared to do that. So I simply lied.

The Altar Guild president did not buy my story. She didn't say so, but I could tell. She just told me, tartly, that she would take care of the flags.

By the very next Sunday, the flags were back in place and it was all over the congregation that the young lady pastor had hidden the American flag. And if she could do something as heinous as that, who in hell knew what diabolical acts might follow?

~

Not surprisingly, we continued to lose members. Toward the end of my second year at St. Tough Spot, it became clear that within six months the building would have to be put on the market and the congregation would need to merge with another church nearby.

In reality, this was the best possible thing that could have happened to them. It was a chance for revitalization when all other resources had been exhausted. But it also meant loss. And because it is easier to lay blame than it is to grieve loss, I became the logical target. I was the the greenhorn who had closed "their" church, just too uppity to have done what it would have taken to turn the church around. Not that anyone had any idea what that would have taken. But it had been my job to save the church, and instead I had lost it.

At the congregational meeting where the details of the inevitable sale and merger were to be worked out, one of the members suggested that for the remaining six months my salary be brought up to meet minimum compensation level set by the Bishop's office. I had gone to St. Tough Spot knowing that my salary was below the minimum compensation level, but I had been desperate to find a church and had accepted what they had offered me.

I was touched that the woman would suggest the increase. But, as she pointed out, it wasn't as if the extra money they would pay me for six months was anywhere near enough to save the church. Compensating me fairly was not going to hasten the death of the church, and everyone in the room knew that.

Then Will Johnson stood up. Will was what used to be known as "a real churchman," the respected figure who worked hard as a leader both within an individual congregation and also in the larger church body. He was also one of the only male authority figures left at St. Tough Spot, and the members looked to him for guidance. He had a stern demeanor and could be difficult to read, but I thought he respected me. And I expected he would speak in support of the woman's proposal.

He said nothing at first, and the silence seemed portentous. He just stood there, gripping the back of the pew in front of him, his heavily jowled face flushing with anger. Then he leaned forward and raised a scolding finger at us.

"I think it is simply obscene," he bellowed in the bellicose voice of a fire-and-brimstone preacher, "I think it is absolutely *obscene* to suggest we raise *her* salary when *our* church is going to close!"

And then he sat down again, the portentous silence returning. And my first thought, as my intestines began tying knots not found on bondage Web sites, was that of course he was correct: the congregation was closing and merging with another. The building was being sold. All of this was happening on my watch. But, paradoxically, I had never felt either less adequate in doing my job nor more deserving of a raise.

Silence deepened. No one spoke up to oppose Will. It would have taken considerable courage to disagree with a person who spoke with such conviction and authority. But I believe that the hint of misogyny in the way he had spoken—his claim that paying me more was "obscene"—struck the congregation as fundamentally unfair. And when the proposal to increase my salary went to a vote, it passed unanimously—except, presumably, for Will's vote.

The meeting ended soon after that. There was an air of sadness as members gathered up their coats and purses and quietly left the church building. The last person to leave was the Sunday School superintendent, a kind-hearted powerhouse of scattered creative energies. Of all the people at St. Tough Spot's, I liked her best. She came over and hugged me wordlessly, her eyes brimming. My throat ached with tears I held back. I didn't want to cry. I understood the pain these people, my parishioners, were feeling. They were losing their church building and its comfortable familiarity.

But I was losing my livelihood, my health insurance, and my mission. They knew what church they were going to go to. I had no idea where I was going. None at all.

～

Naturally, the closing of St. Tough Spot made me feel like a total failure as a pastor. All the time I had spent trying to prove myself worthy of being one had gotten me nowhere. On the other hand, no one had a claim on me any longer. I felt oddly liberated. I was broke, but I was nobody's. And that was fine by me.

For a while I crawled back to safety on the shores of journalism, returning as a freelancer to the local daily. I continued to write my biweekly column, "Reckonings," for the area's alternative newsweekly, which I had been doing since I became pregnant with Linnea. I preached every Sunday, filling in where there were vacancies or where pastors were on vacation, so I was pretty much guaranteed a weekly taste of ministry, as well as a check for seventy-five dollars plus mileage.

I understood that I would have to reenter active ministry at some point. I hadn't even been ordained for three years, so quitting was unthinkable. I wasn't ready to admit defeat. And I longed to have the title "pastor" mean something real and particular to me. One day after the closing of St. Tough Spot, my daughter Madeleine, aged six, asked me whether or not she was still a pastor's kid. She had liked being a "PK." Yes, I told her, you still are.

Madeleine was a pastor's kid, but I wasn't sure yet what a "pastor" was. Sometimes I felt a burning need to be respected as a pastor. Other times I felt the word unsexed me, stripped me of all that I loved about being a woman. I *wasn't* androgynous, but feminine to a fault. Other times, the word suggested order and wisdom; it was a male word that carried with it male authority. Applied to me, it made me feel fraudulent. I was a *woman*, for Christ's sake. I didn't have what it took to be a pastor. I'd been raised knowing that, hadn't I? I could never forget the brochure my own childhood pastor had given me to read. I had not forgotten that when I was ordained, he didn't come to the service or even send a word of congratulations.

Those relentless contradictory feelings chased each other around in my brain like the tigers in *Little Brave Sambo* whirling around the palm tree. Yet all this tiger-chasing-tiger ruminating was finally beside the point. I needed money. I had a household to feed. And pride was no small factor: I was much more concerned about saving face than saving souls. And that was just as well. Because when I got a three-year contract as the part-time Protestant chaplain at the local university, I didn't really need to worry about saving souls. Because there wasn't even a congregation.

This wasn't exactly the truth, but it was close to it. For the first year, and on a weekly basis, I postered Protestant campus ministry flyers all over the wind-scoured campus, a campus known for its own special kind of upstate New York Mistral—the wind in the south of France so mind-numbingly strong it has been used as a murder defense—only in upstate New York we also had snow. I hated postering; it was hard work on a big campus, and it was made all the more annoying because our acronym, PSA (for Protestant Student Association), was the same as the one for the Pagan Student Association. The overlap between a Protestant and a Pagan sensibility probably depends a lot on who is doing the name calling. In any case, we didn't draw in any pagans. And very few Protestants.

Each year would start with a handful of students showing up for the Sunday afternoon service. But in most cases they were in search of more conservative Christian groups. After a few weeks they would find their way into InterVarsity Christian Fellowship, Campus Ambassadors, or BASIC (Brothers and Sisters in Christ). By my last year at the university there was only one student who came regularly to the Sunday services. Just the one.

Cristobel was Haitian, and her English was very poor. And in the place of both right and left hands she wore prosthetic hooks. These were grotesque-looking metal hooks, straight out of Peter Pan, except they split in the middle in order that she could, with difficulty, hold things. It was painful to watch her as she slowly took off or put on her coat or as she searched around in her book bag for something. But she did it with such dignity—or obdurate persistency—that I never thought it appropriate to offer to help her. I feared offending her. And I had no idea how she had come to have hooks instead of hands, whether it had been a birth defect of some kind of accident. She never explained to me what had happened to her. With another person I might have asked, because it was impossible to overlook her disability. But she was so shy and formal that a personal question of any kind beyond social pleasantries seemed inappropriate, as if somehow it would offend her. So I kept the talking short. In fact, I kept the whole service short.

We didn't sing any hymns—there were just the two of us. There was no sermon. I tried to have "discussions" in place of them, but her English wasn't very good. This led me to wonder how she did her course work. Her reticence and her poor English were challenges enough. But Christobel also had a curious habit: she was narcoleptic. She fell asleep, sound asleep, nearly every week.

The first time it happened, I figured either she was exhausted or I was boring. Both seemed real possibilities. In the following weeks I tried to both punch up and shorten the already skimpy order of worship. It made no difference. She kept falling asleep. It was strange to continue reading or praying or talking while the only other person in the room lapsed into a polite though unmistakable snore. And it wasn't as if I could just sit there in silence when she fell asleep because she was also given to waking up at random moments.

Perhaps it should have been the perfect arrangement for me. I had come to think of myself as a people-wary pastor. So what could be better than having only one parishioner, and her off in Dreamy-Dreamland half of the time? The situation was comical enough. Comical, but troubling, too. Each week when I made that long, quiet walk from the deserted classroom building back to my office, a great loneliness would take hold of me.

Did it matter what I did? Was the whole thing a sham? Who were these people whom other people called "pastor," and why was I one of them?

"Dear Abby" was always advising people to "talk to their clergyman," but did anyone really believe a clergyman had anything worthwhile to say? We had no holy Ouija boards or never-fail Magic 8 Balls to guide us.

On those long walks back to my office I felt lonely and fraudulent. I had led a sham of a service. The silent woman with no hands had fallen asleep. And I was as spiritually empty as the vacant corridors of the classroom building on a Sunday afternoon.

~

While I was finishing up my last year as the Protestant campus chaplain, I found out about a small congregation in Raymertown, out by the Vermont border, that the Bishop's office had in mind to link to another small congregation. Neither congregation was keen on the prospect of becoming linked. But while the Bishop's office worked with the two churches to help them realize they needed each other, the plan was to send a part-time interim pastor to Evangelical, Raymertown, for about a year.

Our local dean contacted me about it. He wasn't familiar with Evangelical. He only knew that it was an old church, a pre–Civil War building out in the country surrounded by its own graveyard. The dean also knew that a lot of the families were related and the pay would be really low since the membership was very small. But my part-time campus chaplain salary wasn't enough for me to support my children, even with Joe's generous child support. Furthermore, both the dean and I knew that if I ever wanted the bishop to send my name to a decently-sized and decently-paying church, I needed to get more parish ministry experience under my belt. I could refuse to serve Evangelical only at peril to my future ministerial options.

So on a rainy spring night the dean and I went to meet with the Church Council. It was a long drive out to Raymertown, well east of Troy and along a stretch of Route 7. The town center, what there was of it, consisted of a pizza parlor on one side and a funeral home on the other. I turned off the main road by the funeral home and climbed a short hill. The church sat at the top amid a stand of fir trees. It was a small white clapboard building with stained glass windows and a cement-block basement.

The meeting was held in the basement, which seemed very dimly lit, or perhaps that was just a reflection of my state of mind. About eight people sat at a long table. They were country people, I thought. Country people with serious, doubting faces. One was introduced as

Jeff, the director of the funeral home just down the hill. He was the son-in-law of its founder, who lived just across the street. He was also the Council president. He was polite, but I knew the congregation had had a rocky relationship with a female pastor once before, and I wasn't sure he had a particularly rosy view of women as pastors. There was no way I would have believed, on that dreary spring night, that Jeff would be the funeral director who would handle my mother's funeral just a few years later and that of my brother-in-law, Alan, a dozen years after that.

I was introduced to a gentle-faced young man named Matt, who didn't say anything but just nodded at me with what seemed like resignation. At one end of the table was a woman with multiple ear piercings and blonde hair shaved close to her head. Sue was the church organist. She smiled at me. Mostly everybody smiled—politely but not happily.

At the other end of the table there was not even a polite smile. The older woman sitting there was wearing a zippered nylon jacket with the name of the local motorcycle shop on it. She looked put out by the dean and me in our black-and-white collars. She's going to be trouble, I thought. She probably doesn't think women should be pastors. Already I could tell people were looking to her for her opinion. She was the matriarch. She was Martha.

The dean began his spiel. He explained how, until Evangelical could link with another congregation, I would be their fill-in pastor. I'd lead worship, I'd attend council meetings, I'd teach confirmation classes. I'd visit the sick, conduct funerals, baptize babies, and perform marriages. Did anybody have questions?

The dean's question met with silence. No one asked any questions about my previous experience, my strengths or weaknesses, my understanding of Lutheran theology, my views on giving children's sermons, my thoughts on the frequency of Communion. Finally the old woman at the end of the table broke the silence. She had some teeth missing, and she didn't even try to hide her annoyance.

"Well, what difference does it make if we have questions? We don't have any choice but to take her, do we?"

The dean shifted uncomfortably and mumbled some phrases that basically amounted to "No."

Then old woman turned to me abruptly.

"What'd you say your name was again?" she asked me. If they had to take me, she at least wanted to know what to call me.

"Jo Page," I said.

"Jo Page?" she responded with force. "Jo *Page*? Are you the one that writes that column in that weekly newspaper?"

That newspaper. That *tabloid*. The one with the left-wing spin and the pull-out porn section. The paper had been a deal breaker before. When the bishop had sent my dossier to two other area churches, they informed her that if they were going to consider me as their pastor I would have to stop writing for that newspaper with the left-wing spin and the pull-out porn section. I told my Bishop to inform them that if I were to consider being their pastor it would have to be understood that I would *not* stop writing for that newspaper. After all, what are a salary, housing allowance, pension, and benefits compared to seventy-five dollars biweekly? Just call me the Free Speech Fool.

That newspaper? Oh, no, not again. I couldn't turn a third church down because of "Reckonings." I would have to stop writing it. Already I was hating these people.

"Gram loves your column!" the young guy with the gentle face spoke up, suddenly.

I looked at him. For real? "She likes my column?" I asked, not sure this wasn't some kind of trick.

"Yeah," Matt went on, "she makes me bring her home the paper every Thursday so she can read it. She never misses it."

"*You're* Jo Page?" Martha said, "Really?"

Was I thinner / fatter / older / younger than she had thought I'd be? People had said such things to me before.

"Yes," I said, "Really." No point in denying the truth.

"Well," she said, gently, "Matt's right. I do love your column."

And she gave me a big, tooth-missing grin.

It was the blessing of the matriarch. It was the breaking of the Tough Spot spell. It was the Holy Spirit tickling me in my ribs: *Come on, now. Just be yourself.*

~

I served Evangelical in Raymertown for two years. It was not a thriving congregation and never had been if "thriving" meant lots of people and lots of money.

But I don't think I ever had an unhappy Sunday there. The building was small and old and beautiful, more so it seemed to me because real beauty outlasts the efforts to enhance it. And the people were relaxed, mostly all related to each other in one way or another, as is often the case in small country churches.

And if Evangelical had its matriarch in Martha, it had its patriarch, too, in Hayner. He was not Martha's husband, but he was a cousin. Practically everybody there was somebody's cousin. Just to make things more confusing, Hayner's first name was the same as several families' last names. It was also the name of the next town over, Haynersville. Eventually I learned everybody's names and rough family connections, but I'm glad I never had to map out a family tree.

Hayner always sat in the back of the church and took attendance on an old service bulletin that he left beneath the cushion on the pew each week. He never smiled, and for a long time I thought he was measuring my value by the fluctuations in people attending. But the numbers didn't fluctuate much. And eventually I discovered that Hayner didn't bother too much with smiling—he went straight for the laughter. There was a lot of that at Evangelical.

The organist, Sue, with the brush cut and the piercings, was a spunky woman with a belly laugh and the ability to play the organ, sing a descant, and hold a lit candle all at the same time during the Christmas Eve services. In her mouth, the *Kyrie Eleison*—"Lord, have mercy"—wasn't the plea of a timid supplicant, but more a bit of advice sent heavenward: *Look, God, give us sinners all a little break. It's hell being human.*

Jeff, the funeral director, gave the children's sermon each week. His kids and my kids were among the only ones there, but each week he had something to say that connected with them. His wife, Donna, blond, petite, and spirited, would say, "Sunday mornings we leave the house to walk to church, and Jeff tells me he has no idea what to say to the kids. Then, by the time we get here, he does."

And they only lived right next door.

It's simplistic but not untrue to say that the people at Evangelical taught me how to be a pastor. For the first time since my ordination four years earlier, I began to feel more free in ministry than I had ever been. I would find myself laughing without having to double check whether this was an appropriate moment for laughter. If I felt tears well up during a moving hymn, I didn't feel embarrassed. All the congregation wanted was an ardent pastor to love and care for them. And I did. Because they made it easy. And they loved and cared for me and my two daughters right back.

Of course, I knew I couldn't stay there. It was part time, the pay was meager, and the distance from my home was considerable. Besides, the Bishop's office had a plan for Evangelical. Nevertheless, in the years after leaving Evangelical I have continued to be both friend and chaplain to several of the families there. Even after I was no longer officially serving as their pastor, I came back to the church for Hayner's funeral, for Jeff and Donna's daughters' weddings, and for various Christmas and Easter services. Some of my most faith-filled moments along with some of my most laughter-filled ones were spent leading worship at Evangelical Lutheran Church in Raymertown.

If the Bishop had a plan for that congregation, they also had a plan for me. My name was submitted to the Call Committee of Grace Lutheran Church in Niskayuna, just a mile or so away from the General Electric Research and Development Center and Knowles Atomic Power Laboratory. It was a desirable parish I'd long known and admired. There was everything to recommend it. The congregation was bright and inquisitive, most of them scientists and their families drawn to the area because of their work at GE R&D or KAPL. They were driven people, unafraid to question and demand results. The church was known for its social justice work and progressive theology.

The physical plant was in good shape despite having been built in the early 1960s, when church design took a real turn toward the goofy. Back then, church architects were regularly churning out oddities—buildings that looked like upended Easter lilies, their eaves drooping toward the ground like petals, or ones that looked like little heaven-bound space pods, fueled up and Rapture ready. Grace had been spared that exterior goofiness. And its interior was all wood and warmth and golden light, as if the architect had been trying to appeal to the Scandinavian preferences of its then mostly Swedish congregation.

I would stay at Grace for ten years, loving the people there, grateful always that I learned at Evangelical that it could be safe to love the people. Much of the work I did at Grace I valued and enjoyed.

Nevertheless, having fought so hard to become a pastor, I was also recognizing in myself a profound disappointment with the institutional church, with my denomination, with the rise of right-wing religious fundamentalism. So much of what was being called "Christian" left me feeling spiritually stranded and angry—then and now. I believe that for much of the ten years I stayed at Grace, surrounded by smart, caring, and progressive people I loved and genuinely enjoyed serving as their pastor, I also wanted deeply to do as Sister Luke in *The Nun's Story* had done. I wanted to go out.

~

It's the day after Easter, and I'm driving back from a grueling Stewardship Committee meeting. I'm exhausted—Holy Week always packs an emotional punch. In Europe, the Monday after Easter is a holiday, but not here. Here, everybody is back on the job.

In addition to the Stewardship Committee meeting, my job tonight includes dealing with the not-uncommon anger of L., one of the women on the committee. She was livid that her Easter plant, the azalea she had ordered and paid for, had been given away at the evening service last night.

Last night one of the Alter Guild women, in her ardor to tidy up the church, gave away all of the leftover Easter plants that hadn't been claimed after the morning service. Katherine gave them away randomly to anyone who would take them. She gave them away without regard to the fact that these plants had been paid for by people expecting to bring them back to their houses, if not this Sunday, then next.

I don't blame L. for wanting her plant—Katherine acted in haste and without reason. But I am worn down and fed up with L.'s predictable complaints and cutting comments. She's unkind. And though she's a devoted member, her nostalgia for days old-long-since makes it hard for her to find much good in the here-and-now. Older members of the congregation are used to her and pretty much shrug their collective shoulder—that's just the way she is.

But her negativity gets to me—as it does to newer members who are not used to her belligerence. The fact that she doesn't like me bothers me. The fact that I still try to please her bothers me. The fact that I know she will successfully find fault with something, anything, bothers me. As far as I'm concerned, L. is just plain coldhearted and mean-spirited.

I decide to drive home from the Stewardship Committee meeting by way of the liquor store. But the liquor store is closed. I guess the Monday after Easter is a holiday for some Americans.

"I can't stand it," I say aloud to no one else in the car. "I've got to find an exit strategy. I'd rather be on welfare than be doing this!"

That's not true, of course, but I *do* feel stuck. There are times when I think this job is bad for my health: the conflicts between people over stupid things; the gossip that I know goes on, but I only catch in snippets; the criticisms over completely ridiculous things; the perception that because I am a woman and creative, it is a de facto truth that I am also not organized. Which simply is not true.

I'm tired of having my stomach tie in knots, my heart thump heavily in my chest. I'm tired of waking up too early revisiting a meeting I was at or an e-mail I'd written and wondering if someone could find fault with something that I said.

I'm tired of chuckling and nodding like a trained seal when someone makes the standard and ubiquitous joke: "You've got such a good job; you only have to work one day a week."

The unspoken code for people in my profession goes something like this: pastors are not supposed to be angry with parishioners, even when parishioners are behaving badly. Pastors are not supposed to be grumpy, even when they are having a shitty day. Pastors are not supposed to speak without thinking or be vulgar or be distracted by their own health, family responsibilities, or personal lives. Pastors are not supposed to become emotional during meetings or worship services unless it's a kind of prophetic, righteous indignation about the sorry state of the fallen world. Pastors are not supposed to have children who get drunk, have sex, or shoplift. They are not supposed to have spouses who are uninvolved in the church. They are not supposed to have lovers if they are single. They are not supposed to get divorced, though a good many of them do.

There are other careers somewhat like this, of course—those of politicians. But I think the difference is that most people accept as fact that politicians are insincere at least a good part of the time. For the pastor, earnestness and sincerity, patience and moral rectitude are expected at all times.

So it doesn't need to be said that I was not supposed to show my disgust when, at the Stewardship Committee meeting tonight where we are deciding which children to photograph for the church brochure, L. chooses the little girl who is one of only two white kids in the pre-K Sunday School class.

"She's cute," someone says.

Indeed she is. Cute as a button, cuddly, talkative, spirited. At three, she already has a good sense of humor. But she is one of only two white kids out of eight kids. Two are adopted Chinese girls. One is Latino. The other three are biracial. Two of these three are my great-nephew and -niece.

I'm annoyed. I want to say, "Don't be ridiculous! We have all these minority kids in our church and you want to use the little white girl?"

But I must not say that. I *may* smile and gently point out the value in having such diversity. I *may* suggest that we feature that diversity prominently in our brochure. And I do. Nevertheless, I sit out the rest of the meeting, stewing. And hoping my smile doesn't look too awfully much like Laura Bush's.

Sitting and stewing is a pastoral skill. Sometimes you sit and stew. Sometimes you just sit. You sit at meetings; you sit in counseling sessions; you sit at potluck suppers. You listen. And most often you really *are* listening. Sometimes, though, your mind is racing with all the many things you need to do. Still, you must convey the sense that your time is *their* time and that nothing is more important to you than giving them your full and undistracted attention.

Sometimes I wish Lutherans followed the old-fashioned observance of the holy office as I understood it to be practiced by monks and nuns in the earlier years of the church. Bells rang eight times a day for the prayers of *lauds, matins, nones, terce, prime, terce, vespers,* and *compline,* each spaced at three-hour intervals from one another. So within a twenty-four hour day, no more than three hours ever passed without having your attention taken away from whatever you were doing so you could stop and remember God.

Remembering God meant, for a blessed moment, forgetting all about people. Nowadays, when you're supposed to see the face of Christ in every person you come across, you just can't catch a break.

Except that a good pastor—at least a sane pastor—has to figure out a way to catch a break. It's called "self-care," that euphemistic-sounding antidote to the standard pastoral malaise, "burnout," which is to be avoided at all cost. But unfortunately, the system of ministry is set up almost to insure that burnout happens.

When I was first ordained, a new pastor was informed that, apart from being on twenty-four-hour call for emergencies, it was expected that the pastor put in sixty hours a week. *Only* sixty hours. This was down from the previous seventy-hour-per-week expectation. We were also to designate one day—not two—off per week. Reducing the number of hours and designating a day off was supposed to help ease the growing problem of burnout.

I knew pastors who bragged about how many hours they worked each week. No one would own up to working only forty hours, even if that's what they did. There was a sense that unless you were out most nights at meetings or in the hospitals part or most of every day, you weren't really doing your job.

The fortunate part of being a single mother was that I simply couldn't be away from home that much. And the people of Grace were fine with that. Their pastor of the previous thirty years had worked a lot from home. So nobody expected that I be in my office all the time, though I *was* there a lot—a little haven, with a deep, soft couch, lots of books, my own bathroom (which for a time sported a cushioned toilet seat), and a little porch. I really enjoyed working there. But no one was bothered if I worked at home.

It took a little more doing to get the congregation used to the idea that I wouldn't be attending every single meeting of every church committee, though. Certainly I had attended all of the meetings at St. Tough Spot, fully aware that my presence was entirely superfluous most of the time. But in many churches it had been a longstanding practice that the pastor show up at all the meetings of the church. At Stewardship Committee meetings, Evangelism Committee meetings, Christian education, social ministry, finance, property, worship-and-music, Altar Guild meetings. In addition, it was expected a pastor would serve in some community organizations as well, which necessitated even more meetings.

Going to meetings is a great way to whittle away at that sixty-hour-per-week expectation. People see you. You're *doing* something. You're involved, even if all you are really doing is sitting on your tired ass at still another meeting.

Of course, in the rush to attend meetings, plan worship, visit the sick, teach confirmation classes and adult studies, write sermons, and serve in the community, other things tend to get lost. Like spending time with your family. And taking care of your health.

The divorce rate among clergy is high—it's hard to have a home life. Chubby clergy are common—it's hard to justify going to the gym. Stressed-out clergy are a dime a dozen—if you're not doing *something*, you're doing something *wrong*.

The other casualty of the overscheduled life is the spirit. Why would a pastor make time for meditation, reading, and spiritual renewal when these are activities that nobody can see, nobody can measure? Whether or not they might be vital to the strength and elasticity of the pastor's soul, it's just easier to run around and be perceived as productive than it is to be still and perceived as lazy.

All of us want to avoid any version of burnout. But the creeping toxins of exhaustion, fear, and resentment are subtle, and when they don't undermine the health of the congregation, they too often undermine the health of the pastor. Parish life is a petri dish of self-doubt and second-guessing.

Therefore, it feels almost like an involuntary action for me to allow one unreasonable member to affect my feelings toward the entire congregation. And my feelings swing from pole to pole, from wide-sweeping and unnecessary guilt to wide-sweeping and disproportionate anger. I have to take the time and make the effort to remind myself it's just one person acting like a jackass, not every single member. Even if there are several jackasses all at once, that does not represent the whole congregation. Of course, keeping that in perspective comes about as naturally to me as solving algebraic word problems comes to a stuffed teddy bear.

Yet congregations need non-anxious leadership. My own struggle to be as non-anxious as as I can be is a difficult, ongoing, and flawed one. Just as I will never run the Boston marathon, I will never be a cool customer. I credit this handicap to having grown up in a family in which expansive personalities were the norm and moderation in emotion was downright suspicious.

For example, my mentally retarded sister is prone to crying excessively at unexpected times. The counselors in her group home have worked on this with her for years. But sometimes I think this is simply evidence of a family proclivity, unrelated to her disability. All three of us sisters are profligate weepers, and our mother was no stoic either. But several years ago, one of my sister's counselors tried to help Leslie develop what she calls her "coping skills."

I have taken a page from her book. After a few years in ministry, I stumbled on a few "coping skills" of my own.

Shortly after arriving at Grace, I had a relatively minor conflict during a phone call with an older woman who was a pillar of the congregation. She insisted I should be attending a certain community service meeting each month. But I had chosen not to and had explained my reasons calmly: other members of the parish already attended. My presence wasn't necessary. Nor did I want to add another weeknight obligation when I had children at home and no one to look after them.

I sounded composed during the phone call, but as we spoke my intestines twisted up like wrung-out dishcloths. And when I hung up the phone I was crying. I didn't know what I felt—guilt over my supposed negligence of duty or anger over the woman's presumptive expectations of my time. I looked at my daughter Madeleine sitting across the dining room table from me doing her homework. She saw my tears. I was sure she was about to say something comforting. But she just shook her head.

"Mom, get *over* it!" she snapped, "You made a decision not to go to that meeting—stick by it. *You're* the pastor. She's not!"

I didn't like this twelve-year-old, know-it-all attitude. And who was she to pass judgment or give me advice? But I didn't snap back at her; it would have turned ugly. And I was too weepy to deal with ugly. So I simply strode into my bedroom and managed to only slam the door a little bit.

After all, who the hell did she think she was? Wasn't I doing this full-time ministry gig and living in a suburb beyond our economic means so that she and her sister would be in the same superior school district as the children of Indian doctors, Russian physicists, and crack Asian mathematicians? *We* were the economic diversity in our voting district.

And hadn't I just gotten into a tangle with a member—a member I respected for her commitment to all I was also committed to—so that I would be able to have an extra night home with her and her sister? It was I and nobody else who would be carving the goddamn pumpkins and coloring the goddamn Easter eggs with her.

But I knew she was right.

I sat on my bed, annoyed with her, annoyed with myself, and annoyed with the woman from church. Screw it, I thought. I'm forty-one. I'm very bright. I can get my MBA and be earning the big bucks by the time I'm fifty.

It was in that moment I discovered the lifesaving usefulness of having a coping skill.

"Screw it; I'll just go get my MBA" became my new, silent mantra. "Screw it; I'll just go get my MBA" was the coping skill I began to use to get through long meetings, complaining parishioners, problems blown out of proportion, and the general unfortunate reality that full-time ministry meant dealing with people. Full time.

I once asked a colleague how her ministry she was going, and she answered curtly, "Great. Except for the people."

Possibly because I knew I'd never get my MBA, I eventually I found another coping skill, one that didn't involve screwing ministry or fantasizing about my untapped acumen as a business woman. And, suitable to my vocation, I discovered it in 2 Corinthians, which just goes to show that I do read the Bible from time to time.

For what we preach is not ourselves . . . but we have this treasure in earthen vessels, to show that the transcendent power belongs to God and not to us.

It was a familiar passage. And I had never liked it much. To me, it always smacked of the expendability and insignificance of human effort. We were just breakable crockery, nothing enduring, nothing of worth. Only what was inside the vessel had worth.

I understood the Corinthians passage to mean we were all supposed to toil selflessly for the sake of the gospel, and if we broke beneath the weight of it, well, *tant pis pour nous*: too bad for us. There were other pottery vessels for God to burden with the water of life.

But then one day when I came across the passage I read it differently. The sense of the words turned topsy-turvy in my mind. Words that had always imprisoned me now freed me. And though Paul probably hadn't meant for his words to be understood in this way, this is what the passage suddenly meant to me:

I was worth plenty and I was necessary. And if I was an earthen vessel, it wasn't meant to suggest weakness, but rather that the earthen vessel is not responsible for the effects of what it holds. We don't blame the pitcher if what's inside makes a man a drunkard. It's not the pitcher's doing.

Simply, I was not responsible. I could not be held responsible. If I was and if ministers truly are vessels, then anything inside the vessel is God's doing.

I had to care for the vessel. I was responsible for keeping the vessel functional. But I had neither responsibility for nor power over what was in it. None of my apologies for God, excuses for God, defenses of God mattered. All I had to do was pour out what had been poured in.

And some days this was a comfort. And some days it was a cross.

6

Making Love

Hasten as a bride to meet him,
Eagerly and gladly greet him.
There he stands, already knocking;
Quickly now your gate unlocking,
Open wide the fast-closed portal,
Saying to the Lord immortal
"Come and leave your loved one never;
Dwell within my heart forever."

—"Soul, Adorn Yourself with Gladness"
Johann Franck (1618–1677)

East of Utica, I leave the mind-numbingly flat terrain of central New York. From here, the Thruway begins its languid descent from the snowbelt to the Mohawk Valley. Soon the straight road begins to gently oxbow. I round a bend and see fields whitened by a sifting of late-winter snow. Soon there is the Mohawk River, now high up its banks because the dense snow pack has already begun to melt. Soon I pass the old mill towns, mostly run-down, but still running: Fort Plain, Fonda, Canajoharie.

I am glad to be out of central New York, where the Thruway is spine straight and much of the radio dial is devoted to Christian broadcasting. By now it's late afternoon and the sun is low in the west. Ahead, the sky is still blue.

I had left the conference a day early. This was because my boy-friend—also a pastor—and I were going to spend our first night together.

The conference topic was the Evangelical Lutheran Church in America's three-year Human Sexuality Task Force. And the newly appointed chair of the task force was to be the conference speaker, who appeared committed to making sex talk absolutely no fun at all.

As I drive, I wonder what it would be like to spend *years* on the task force. Perhaps the new chair was already sick of thinking about human sexuality, and that was why he appeared so humorless in discussing it. As it was, the members of the task force were to convene regularly, through-out the three years, flying in from wherever they lived to meet together. Once gathered, they would then spend hours and hours in tedious stud-ies of what the Bible, theologians, scientists, psychologists, sociologists, and social historians all had to say about sexuality. They would pour over tens of thousands of responses to the task force's national survey of Lutherans and their views on sexuality. I imagine them having to read and consider what Betty Button from Ogden, Utah, and Jane Plane from Kutztown, Pennsylvania, and Harry Nickers from Belchertown, Massachusetts, all had to say about sex. It had the potential to be har-rowingly uninspired reading, no competition for "Savage Love."

I wonder if all this research will make the task force members sick of sex. Or, conversely, might it cause them to their upgrade their lovemak-ing methods, to make a trip to the adult store for films that tastefully—or not—explore the lure of BDSM or water sports? Will they begin to look at people of their own gender in a new way, wondering what it would be like to do this and that with someone plumbed thus and suchly?

The actual issues they faced were clear. In spite of its wide-sweeping title, the Human Sexuality Task Force, the somewhat veiled focus of the study group was the issue of blessing same-sex unions and ordaining pastors who are in committed same-sex relationships. (Churches have been ordaining closeted—which isn't the same as celibate—pastors for centuries.)

The current church-wide policy mandated fidelity in marriage—and indeed I know of pastors who lost their ordination status, thus their livelihoods, because they were unfaithful to their spouses. My own opinion is that this is a draconian policy, punishing both the offending spouse and the offended one—who wants to lose either half or all of the family income because your spouse cheated on you?

Church-wide policy also mandated "chastity" when single, meaning, of course, that single pastors were expected to refrain from sexual relationships until they were married. According to the logic of the church-wide policy, because there was no option for gay marriage, non-celibate homosexuals were, by definition, in violation of it and could not be ordained.

Being a single, straight pastor who had never envisioned a life of celibacy, I couldn't help but notice the unspoken double standard: no one was scrutinizing either my sex life or lack thereof. My congregation, I believe, trusted me to be prudent, wise, and loving in how I lived my life. Those were my personal goals as well. So if I had the latitude and the privilege—if not officially, then in practice—of a probably-more-discreet-than-most, but still private life, why were the sex lives of gay and lesbian pastors under the spotlight? I knew I benefited from this double standard. And I knew that it wasn't fair.

∽

I reach the outskirts of Albany at twilight and pull into the outlet shopping center where M. and I have arranged to meet. We hug and kiss. Then he takes my overnight bag and I take my satchel of papers from the conference and we load them into the back of his car.

We get into the front seat and kiss again.

"I got some champagne," he says. "But I thought we could stop in Bennington for some stuff to make a picnic."

"Good idea," I say. "What time are we supposed to get to the bed and breakfast?"

"I said we'd try to get there by eight."

We pull out onto Route 7 and make the steep descent into Troy. The lights of the city gleam and flicker. The Hudson River picks them up and shines them back at us. I'm excited. I'm nervous. I remind myself that I have known M. for a few years. He's single. I'm single. Of course, in the back of my mind, I worry: my congregation thinks I'm out at church camp for another night of sex talk. If there's a death in the parish and they try to find me, they'll think I've gone missing somewhere. I try to suppress an image of state troopers and sniffing dogs on the trail of the missing Pastor Jo.

"Where did you tell your congregation you were going?" I ask, because certainly M. must have the same concerns.

"Nowhere," he says, "They won't miss me."

"But your car won't be in the manse driveway."

Manse. M. is a Presbyterian. They call their parsonages that. It sounds so very Hawthorne and dour. I like saying it.

"They won't notice. Or if they do, they'll be happy for me." He reaches over, squeezes my knee.

"What about your son?"

He laughs. "Oh, he's going to a sleepover. Just like me."

~

The night before, I had gotten lost on the back roads around Lake Verona trying to find the rustic church camp where the conference was meeting. I missed dinner, and when I got there I had to make do with some lumpy yellow pudding and Hydrox cookies, remnants of what had probably been an uninspiring meal.

At our opening session, the task force chair spent what seemed an unnatural amount of time talking about natural theology and Thomas Aquinas and reason and Luther and sin. Even allowing for the fact that he was an academic and therefore allowed to be didactic and—frankly—boring, I was surprised. We had all driven a long way, and if the leftovers were any indication, supper had been lackluster. Was some early-evening sex talk too much to hope for? Or, more seriously, was the task force going to take such a dryly academic approach to it all?

By the time the session ended, people seemed both tired and agitated, hankering for a beer or a glass or two of boxed wine. But nobody had thought to bring any. So we made our way upstairs to our rooms, each sensibly furnished with a metal-framed single bed and some scratchy blankets, a bit more like prison than camp, I thought, but then I knew little about either. There weren't many bathrooms, so we stood in the hallway taking turns to brush our teeth, trading war stories. One pastor had recently left a church and gone to work in a hospice. He said that one night a few months ago a dying woman had told him that she was seeing a bright light.

"I thought to myself, 'Great!'" he said, "Isn't that what dying people are supposed to see? A bright light? A white one? Whatever. So I told her, 'Walk toward the light, Mrs. Schumacher. Walk toward the light.' Suddenly she gasped. 'I see Jesus in the light. Pastor! It's Jesus.'

"At this point I thought I was home free. Hospice was going to be a cakewalk compared to parish ministry. So I encouraged her some more: That's beautiful, Mrs. Schumacher. Walk toward Jesus. Jesus wants you.'

"'Jesus is coming toward *me*,' she said. And I said, 'Great, great! Jesus is coming for you, Mrs. Schumacher.' Then," he paused—preachers, politicians, and stand-up comedians know the value of a well-timed pause, "then she said, 'Pastor, Jesus *just walked right by me!*'"

We all laughed. This is what comes of seeing visions of Jesus. You think he's coming for you, but he's just on his way to pick up a roast beef sandwich at the deli.

What did you do then, we wanted to know.

"I don't remember exactly. I guess I said, 'Maybe he'll come back' or something. You know, 'catch ya later, kid.'" He shrugged and laughed. "I thought it was going to be so easy, hospice work, but it's turning out to be more than I was expecting."

"Did she die that night?" I asked.

"No, she didn't even die," he said, and there was an awkward pause.

"Wow," somebody else said, to fill in the silence.

"But mostly it's good to work with the dying," he went on. "I think it's really important to keep your ego out of it."

"Like it's okay to have an ego in the parish," somebody quipped.

"Right," he chuckled.

"What do you think we're going to talk about tomorrow?" somebody else asked.

"Not more Aquinas, I hope," somebody else said, "At some point we really need to talk about the real issue—the same-sex blessing stuff and ordination and all that."

"Do you think homosexuals should be ordained?" somebody asked.

"I don't really know," one voice said.

"Why not?" another one said, "We're all God's children, right? And we're all sinners, too. So why shouldn't we ordain them? Why shouldn't we have a same-sex blessing rite?"

～

It's fully dark by the time we stop in Bennington for groceries. We wander around the supermarket in a little nervous daze. What are we doing, sneaking off like this? And do we even know each other?

Of course we do. A few years as colleagues. And we've been dating for months. It's not as if we've rushed into instant intimacy. We couldn't have even if we'd wanted to: He has kids. I have kids. He has a parish. I have a parish. Desire and restraint have been our modus operandi, though not restraint in any kind of imaginatively erotic fashion. We simply don't have the time or the place for privacy. So we have made out like teenagers on my living room sofa, my daughters asleep upstairs. We have stolen kisses in the basement of the manse where he showed me how he is rewiring the place. We have kissed and shifted awkwardly around in the front seat of his car and in the front seat of my car. We've kissed in each other's offices—though his is dusty and full of his father's books from his own decades in ministry, so sneezing, nose blowing, and looking out for the church secretary significantly lowered the passion quotient of those kisses.

But now here we are, standing in a supermarket with the unspoken, but transparent knowledge that the purpose of this trip is so that we can finally, finally make love.

∼

After a breakfast of French toast made from Wonder Bread—which greatly reduces the wonder factor—it seemed even clearer that the newly appointed chair of the Human Sexuality Task Force preferred *not* to talk about sexuality. It was left to the pastors, poker-faced (as is *de rigueur* in parish ministry) to approach and reapproach the subject.

Some clergy were clearly in support of same-sex blessings and ordination. Some opposed it. Either way, though, it seemed everybody kept saying "us" and "them."

"When people in our congregations ask us why the bishop would ordain one of *them*, what are we supposed to say?"

This speaker obviously was not big on gay rights.

"Says right there in 1 Timothy that a pastor *should be above reproach and the husband of one wife*. If we ordained gays and lesbians we wouldn't have to worry about how many times they had been married."

This was spoken by a supporter of gay rights. He was aiming for levity. But he was not playing to a very subtle crowd.

"Even joking, that's sloppy exegesis," somebody said, annoyed. "1 Timothy also says *I permit no woman to teach or have authority over a man*. And we've been ordaining women since 1970."

"And God bless *us*," said our female bishop, dryly.

"But he does have a point," said someone else, "Sloppy exegesis or not, people are going to come to us asking why—if the book of Romans condemns homosexuality or if Leviticus says it's 'an abomination'—why we're saying it's okay to have a blessing service for them? Or to ordain them?"

Them. Should *we* decide if we can let *them* into our club, the Christ Club? Not so long ago, this exact conversation had probably taken place about whether or not to ordain women. It would have been a bunch of men sitting together saying, "People are going to come to us asking why, if it says in 1 Timothy, *let a woman learn in silence, with full submission* and it says in I Corinthians, *As in all the churches of the saints, women are to keep silent . . . for they are not permitted to speak* are we saying it's okay to ordain them?"

At one time I had been one of *them*. Not now, though. Now I am one of *us*.

"Yes. Exactly. When we decided to ordain women we knew it was in stark violation of what the text says in several places . . ."

"Of course, of course," came a voice, "but . . ."

"Yes and *no*," came another.

Then a third voice, louder: "But that's not the issue. We're not biblical literalists. We believe in the grace of Christ . . ."

"Besides," interrupted somebody else, apparently not hearing what the last speaker said, "A woman doesn't *choose* to be a woman. She just is. . . ."

"That's not my point," said the third voice, as if used to being interrupted and misunderstood.

". . . and," continued the interrupter, "and as yet—am I right?—there is no incontrovertible evidence that says homosexuality is genetic. In spite of it being trendy to be gay, I continue to believe God made marriage to be between one man and one woman. If we have the inspired word of God singling out homosexuality out as a violation of natural law, then the church *ought* to have a big problem justifying blessing their unions or ordaining these people."

"Naw, you can't go there. It's a slippery slope," said the third voice again, sounding tired, "Because then you can't ignore the other areas we customarily ignore. What about all the gospel imperatives about the right use of our wealth to aid the poor? The basis for our entire economic system violates Jesus's words. You can't argue either for or against this question on the basis of what the Bible says in chapter so-and-so."

Someone quipped, "Maybe so. But the entire Christian Broadcasting Network was built and makes megabucks by doing just that."

~

M. and I buy too much food for two people and one night. Then we get back on Route 7, heading north toward Arlington in darkness. There is never much traffic on this road, and tonight is no different. M.'s rusty VW seems to have a little trouble on the steeper grades. The farther north we go the colder it feels; he cranks up the heat so high we can't hear the Miles Davis CD. The woods on either side of the highway are straight out of Robert Frost: lovely, dark, and deep.

Eventually we take the Arlington exit to pick up 7-A. It's the old scenic route, although now, because it is pitch-black, there is nothing we can see. But I know the road well. There are tilled fields and farm stands and Federal-style houses and blue-and-gold historic markers on either side of the road. And I know, also, that there is a convenience store just a bit ahead of us.

We haven't said much in some miles, so my voice sounds prim and formal when I nervously ask if we can use condoms.

I said *condoms*. *Condoms*. Growing up, we called them *rubbers* whether we needed them or not—whether we used them or not.

"Of course," he says. "Oh, don't worry. Of course, it's fine."

He had told me a while back that he's been "fixed." And I have things taken care of on my side, too. But it's not a matter of birth control. It's about what every middle and high school health teacher tells the students—safety.

M. pulls into the convenience store parking lot and says we need gas. He pumps it, then goes inside to pay. I wonder if he's buying condoms or if he had already packed some in his Dopp kit.

~

It was in that post beef barley soup and sandwich space after lunch that my mind began to wander. Somebody quoted something from Luther's writings, which bright Lutheran clergy are sometimes prone to do. This confuses the dimmer-bulb Lutheran clergy who know "A Mighty Fortress Is Our God" and a few of the bawdy lines in Luther's *Table Talk* but are otherwise ill equipped to quote the master. Sometimes, at large gatherings of pastors, I can envision the spread on seminary grades. You don't have to be a rocket scientist to serve Jesus, somebody once told me once. And God forgive my snooty self for thinking it, but there is plenty of evidence for that.

Still, as I drifted further away from the proceedings around me, I began to think that the same-sex marriage issue and the ordination issue were simply repackaged versions of a controversy on which Luther had taken a bold stand.

He had already booted out the practice of the priest receiving both bread and wine during Holy Communion while laypeople got only bread. He had used the same scripturally driven logic to condemn it that he did to condemn a celibate priesthood. What good was it for a man to be alone? Or a woman either? If what was good for the priests was good for the people when it came to Holy Communion, then what was good for the people was also good for the priests when it came to marriage.

In his personal letters, he rails over the tyranny of celibacy and of the God-given need for partnership. And eventually he began to play matchmaker with skillful German efficiency, drawing from an ample dating pool, pairing off monks with sisters as more and more of them left their monasteries and convents. To a friend he writes of nine nuns in particular who had escaped from a Cistercian convent in Saxony in April 1523:

> *Nine apostate nuns, a wretched group, have been brought to me by the honest citizens of Torgau. . . . I feel very sorry for them, but most of all for the many others who are perishing everywhere in their cursed and impure celibacy. This sex, which is so very weak by itself and which is joined by nature, or rather by God, to the other sex, perishes when so cruelly separated. O tyrants! O cruel parents and kinsmen in Germany! O pope and bishops, who can*

curse you as you deserve? Who can sufficiently execrate the blindness and madness which caused you to teach and enforce such things! But this is not the place to do it. You ask me what I shall do with the nuns. First I shall inform their relatives and ask them to take in the girls. If they are unwilling, then I shall have the girls provided for elsewhere . . . Whoever helps them serves Christ. They escaped from the cloister in a miraculous way.

—April 10, 1523, letter to George Spalatin

Within a few months, Luther was successful in finding husbands and dispatching the ex-nuns into new lives as married women. Finally, only one was left: Katherina von Bora. Marrying her himself was a logical next step.

If logic is what led him into marriage, it was love that sustained it. Nearly all his personal letters to friends and family are peppered with references to "my Katie"—sometimes "my lord Katie." His greeting in one letter says: "To my dear wife, Katherina Luther, doctor's spouse in Wittenberg, keeper of the pig market and gracious wife whom I am bound to serve hand and foot."

But when Martin's Katie became pregnant, speculation ran rampant. What kind of thwarted issue could emerge from the fornication of an ex-nun and an ex-priest, especially an ex-priest known to be a troublemaker and a rabble-rouser? She'd push out a wreck of a child—a two-headed monster. A spawn of Satan.

Yet when Katherina brought forth the first Luther child, all was intact. Ten fingers, ten toes, two arms, two legs. Only one head. And as if to restate the point, Katie and Martin had five more children, a minivan's worth of offspring, each of them equipped with the usual number of appendages.

So there were six Luther kids at play in the fields of the Lord at precisely the same time that the church considered marriage between monks and nuns to be both an offense against doctrine and a mockery of matrimony.

Was the question facing the task force really that much different?

It may have been the post-lunch lull, but discouragement set in like indigestion. Here we sat, a hot room full of pastors and most of them male, most of them married, most of them fathers. What did they know about being celibate and single? What did they know about solitary evenings or the fear of aging without a partner? What did they know of being denied the chance to have a family?

They were largely fat and satisfied. And all because Luther had broken rank with the church's teachings. All because he knew the value of companionship and sexual expression, having spent so many of his own years in solitude and celibacy.

～

We make the turn onto Route 313 and head west along the Battenkill. In daylight this is a beautiful drive. The river sparkles and dances. Mountains rise up on either side, brilliant with color in the fall, verdant in the summertime.

M. turns onto a hilly road I've never noticed before. It climbs steeply into a forested mountain. After a few miles, the macadam gives way to dirt and broken pavement. There is nothing around us for miles—no houses, no shops, no inns. It is as dark as a train tunnel.

Until, far off in the darkness, we see white Christmas lights twinkling in midair. I unroll my window a crack and hear rushing water. We pull into a bite-sized parking lot in front of a sprawling house with a well-lit sign that says "The Green River Inn."

The air is bitterly cold. Near us the river rushes loudly. We climb the porch steps, but before we can even ring the bell, the front door opens. A warm, maternal voice says, "So glad to see you've made it!"

The innkeeper reaches out and shakes each of our hands.

"Come inside and get yourselves warmed up. I'll show you around the place. Can I get you some hot cider or a little cup of tea?"

She manages to keep up an effortless patter, speaking to us as if it were normal and good for us to be here. I know she is a professional, well trained in the conventions of hospitality management, but her welcome makes me think that it *is* good to be here. That M. and I did not come to the Green River Inn only to violate church policy—we came to make what others argue over: love.

"Just let me show you your room. This way."

We follow her upstairs.

"Of course, there aren't many people in the inn tonight—no one, actually. It's mid-week, almost mud season. So you've picked a good time to get away. The room I've got set up for you is really the best one," she says, standing before a door at the end of the corridor.

She swings it open with a flourish, "Come on in and tell me what you think."

There is a fireplace, a sitting area, and a king-sized, canopied bed opposite the mirrored closet doors.

"Goose-down comforters," she says, giving the top of the bed a hearty press. "And here," she gestures, Vanna White revealing a vowel, "here is the corner fireplace. You just work it like this," she pushes a button and flames leap up. *Let there be light.*

"You've got a little balcony out here," she says, "I know it's too cold to sit out on it—maybe you'll come back in the summertime—but if you look out in the morning you'll get the most magnificent view of the river."

M. and I catch each other's eyes. Morning, waking in each other's warm arms. That long-delayed delight.

"Rocking chair with a hand-knit afghan, some homemade cookies and fruit," she says, pointing. She steps over to the closet and swings open the mirrored door, "and in here we have some very nice robes, which will come in handy because *in here*," she leads us into a huge bathroom, with a bathtub bigger than a banker's desk, "*here* is the Jacuzzi."

We marvel.

"Will you be needing anything else?" she asks.

We're fine, we assure her. This is more than just right.

"I put on the coffee pot right at dawn if you want a cup. But take your time. I don't usually get breakfast out until eight. I'll have fruit, my own muffins, fresh-squeezed juice. And tomorrow," she says enticingly, just before making her exit, "the hot dish is *strata!*"

Alone in the big room, alone with the gas fireplace and the canopy bed on either side of us, M. and I look at each other. Then he pulls me to him and I smell laundry soap and sweat. I slide my hands beneath his sweater, but not under his T-shirt. There will be time enough soon enough for skin.

"The hot dish is strata," I say, looking up at him.

He looks down at me, kisses the top of my head.

"The hot dish," he says, "is *you.*"

And so we settle in, shedding our shoes, opening the champagne, violating church policy, benefiting from the unfair double standard: gay pastors have been ousted from their parishes for coming out. But no straight, single pastor I know of was ever defrocked for quietly and discreetly making love.

~

I add my breath to your breath
that our days may be long on earth.

—Laguna Pueblo prayer

Unlike cars, we have all learned that marriages are only interesting when they break down.

Broken-down marriages are the stuff of movies and books, TV talk shows, and Hollywood celebrities. A *good* marriage is boring; everybody knows that.

But I get to look at the faces of each bride and groom every time I perform a wedding, and I believe that there has never been a bride or a groom who wanted anything other than that most boring of things: a *good* marriage. Their faces give it all away. There is just a moment—it's hard to describe—when naked hope seems to make their faces glow silvery and luminous.

It is a private moment, and I am a privileged witness. But getting that shining glimpse of palpable hope almost always makes up for all the taxing parts of getting a couple actually wed. Because, quite honestly, weddings are one of the most onerous parts of parish ministry. I'm not alone in this assessment. It makes us seem like cynics—and maybe my more conservative colleagues would disagree, if for no other reason than to ballast their staunchly held marriage-equals-one-man-and-one-woman platform—but clergy are not made happy when it comes to dealing with the vicissitudes and peculiarities of the affianced. And for a host of reasons: first, most clergy feel honor bound to go through some kind of premarital counseling with the moony-eyed couple in the pastor's office. Nobody wants to preside at a wedding that might end in divorce. So the counseling stuff is for their protection and our own peace of mind. Marriage is—need I say this?—a big step. Still, in doing the premarital work, I like to keep it simple. I always ask the couple to tell me their love story, which, with the reciprocal narcissism of the deeply in love, they are always more than happy to do.

They sit haunch by haunch on the couch in my office, well groomed and dressed—they're meeting with the pastor, so I guess they figure they ought to wear their Sunday best. Each of them takes turns narrating the story of how they met, how they courted, what speed bumps they hit, how he—or, more rarely, she—proposed.

Often there is a ring story. I love the ring stories. Grooms can be very inventive in the ways they present their diamonds. One of them proposed in a hansom cab in Central Park, though it didn't go quite according to his carefully detailed plan. Just as they were about to get into the hansom cab, the groom realized they had left the camera in the hotel room. He insisted they go back and get it. The bride was freezing. Why can't we just take the damn ride and forget about the camera, she wanted to know.

No, we need it. No, we don't. *Yes, we do*. So they went back to the hotel, then back once again to the hansom cab. By now the bride was not only freezing, but in a snit as well. It might not have been the best moment to propose, the groom told me, but he did it anyway. And he had the cab driver take a picture of them: by now the bride was happy and tearful but contrite too, sheepish that she'd been so cranky about going back to get the camera.

Another groom gave his girlfriend a gift certificate for a manicure a few days before he planned on surprising her with the ring. She was offended—what did he think was so bad about her nails just the way they were? He thought she needed to wear *nail polish*? She passed it along to a friend who actually enjoyed getting manicures.

Another groom proposed at the very top of Sacré-Coeur in Paris. Still another hid the ring inside a Plexiglas cube filled with Post-It notes on which he had written out his proposal.

So, all the while the couple is telling me their love stories and their ring stories, they are sitting close enough to lean in to each other, to rub each other's knees, little gestures that don't seem to them too inappropriate to do in front of a person of the cloth, who, no doubt, wouldn't understand the first thing about sexual desire.

When older people get married, they usually want less of the pageantry and folderol of a storybook wedding. But younger people often want all the garish accessories of the day: the sappy unity candle; the white paper carpet (somebody always trips); the famous trumpet voluntary or Pachelbel's Canon in D, played poorly—and only partially (nobody has that big a wedding party)—played; a bevy of bridesmaids wearing colors found only in bridal shops and gelato stands; groomsmen anxious for the open bar.

In the cases of these pageant weddings, there comes a time when, late in the game, one or the other of them has had it up to *here* with wedding details. The spiral notebook—or nowadays iPad—they have been using to track their progress is looking dog-eared. There is a problem with one or more of the relatives. Or the reception site or the transportation arrangements. Or all of the above.

It happened that way with my own wedding: Mere weeks before, the pastor who was to assist at the ceremony got caught groping a thirteen-year-old boy and was removed from his job. The friend who had offered to cater the reception ran a knife through her hand, severing a nerve only a week before the big day. My in-laws were in a train derailment coming up to Albany from their first (and last) visit to New York City. My mother became mysteriously ill and had to skip the rehearsal dinner, attending the wedding itself in a wheelchair.

There was a sleet storm on the day of the wedding. The reception was in a gallery hung with oil paintings of dismembered heads and other body parts rendered in a style to make Géricault proud. Not only that, but it had been a posthumously mounted show—in memory of the painter, who had committed suicide the year before. If omens mean anything, it should not be surprising that we divorced.

So I am generally sympathetic to all the little wedding details that can go awry. On top of that, I know that, one way or another, I'll get them married.

Of course, that can't happen before the nightmare known as the wedding rehearsal. This is another form of torture that older couples often skip. I can safely generalize that pastors are grateful to them beyond measure.

Because some awful things occur at wedding rehearsals. First, they would not be complete without the wedding-rehearsal-know-it-all. And unfortunately for my gender, it usually is a woman. Unfortunately, it is often the mother of the bride. Knowing that I am a woman and that I have daughters worries me: when wedding rehearsal day comes, how will I be able to avoid the dreadful trap of micromanaging the session? After all, I am a *genuine* wedding-rehearsal-know-it-all. Seasoned and savvy.

The wedding-rehearsal-know-it-all knows all the right ways to do things, and she will challenge anyone who challenges her. So there is usually some frosty discussion about the "groom's side" and the "bride's side," as if the church sanctuary were a gigantic bed. Seating the mothers always seems to elicit some conflict. How the bridal party gets down the aisle is reliably a headache.

"Step-together. Step-together," the wedding-rehearsal-know-it-all will say.

"No, that looks stupid," somebody else says.

Yes, I'm thinking. Yes, it really does.

"Go slow," the wedding-rehearsal-know-it-all says. "And smile!"

Then there is the question of blocking. Should the father raise the veil or should the bride? When does the maid of honor take the flowers? Should the bride's train be bustled up for when she lights the unity candle and then let down before the recessional?

Who the hell cares? I'm thinking. Why the hell does she have a train on her dress in the first place? This is not the antebellum South.

Wedding rehearsals take a lot longer than they ought to, but probably not as long as they might take, because fortunately there is always somebody itching to get it over with so they can go out and get a drink. Somebody besides me, that is.

Then, finally, the wedding day arrives, and with it unexpected glitches or surprises: the bride wakes up with a case of cystitis. Or the limousines get lost on the way to the church. The groom has a coughing fit. A little voice crows from the congregation, "Mommy, I have to pee!" The unity candle fails to light.

The unexpected is predictable.

But then the moment comes when the bride and the groom take each other's hands and turn their backs to the congregation and turn their shining faces toward me. I only hope my face can reflect some of that shine out onto the congregation. Because, in spite of all the tedium, irritation, and hassle of weddings, there is nothing quite like seeing the faces of the bride and groom as they stand together and say their vows.

It's one of the bravest things anybody can do—get up and *pledge* to love another person, come what may.

I know it's true that some of them won't love each other, come what may. I've been divorced. I know how it feels like to have love fail to do what, in love, was promised.

Yet right then, in that holy moment of love firmly pledged, hope is so real you could almost cut it like a wedding cake. And that hope goes a long way in making all the headaches of weddings worthwhile. Because when there isn't too much pageantry and there is a palpable sense of commitment, a wedding service is one of the strongest affirmations of life.

It might happen this way:

The bride and the groom have already been together for sixteen years. They have, unflappably, planned a fabulous hotel reception in Cooperstown, rented the chapel in the Farmer's Museum, and arranged for transportation for all the guests between the two places.

But they could not have foreseen the weather. Outside the church, a fierce November storm rages. The thin church walls can't keep out the wind, so the candles flicker. The orange glare of the portable heaters can't sufficiently warm the space, so the guests shiver. A wintry mix sluices the windows. Yet none of that even comes close to dampening the spirit of the event. The bride and the groom face each other in the Farmer's Museum church to make their vows. The groom reads from Psalm 143:

> *I remember the days of old,*
> *I think about all your deeds,*
> *I meditate on the work of your hands.*
> *I stretch out my hands to you;*
> *my soul thirsts for you like a parched land.*

Then they take each other's hands. The portable heaters rattle. The storm beats the clapboards. But their voices rise over the noise, and they promise to go the rest of the journey together, come rain or come shine.

～

Or maybe the wedding will go like this:

She had been a runaway bride before—not just once, but several times. This wedding was supposed to be a private ceremony, because "a little nervous" didn't even begin to describe how she felt about getting married. But she works in an independent bookstore with a bunch of middle-aged women determined to see her go through with this wedding. She's got a gem of a man this time, and they want to make sure to be there to support the couple. So they insist on attending. They sit close together in their black outfits and artsy jewelry, a coven of comrades.

The bride is wearing a stylish, short white dress. She stands at the back of the church. She has a friend on either side of her, and each of them is firmly holding one of her elbows. When the music starts and the maid of honor has already arrived at the front of the church, they help her make the mighty journey down the aisle. The handsome groom's eyes glaze with tears. The bride's knees are visibly shaking.

Then, when they make their vows to one another, all the women from the independent bookstore sniffle as one. The groom tries—and fails—to stifle a sob.

～

Or it may also happen this way:

The summit of Whiteface, one of the Adirondack high peaks, is accessible via a steeply graded, sharply winding road and then an old elevator shooting upward through the bowels of the mountain for the last couple of hundred feet. Most of the guests arrive that way.

But the bride and groom spent the early part of the day hiking it, changing into their wedding clothes just before finishing the climb to the summit. They chose the location—and their means of getting there—because they had already faced hard challenges together and wanted to signal their readiness to face those sure to come.

Now they stand together on a granite outcropping, waiting while guests spill from the elevator and make their way across the rocky summit. In the distance, other lakes and other mountains gleam in the sunshine. We can see for miles and miles.

Other hikers watch as the wedding party gathers. Some wish the bride and groom good luck and then go on their way. Still others are captivated by this man and this woman with their wind-whipped wedding wear and hopeful faces. Spontaneously they stand there as witnesses to the wedding, too. Some even join in singing the hymn the couple has picked:

Now thank we all our God,
with heart and hands and voices,
Who wondrous things has done,
in whom this world rejoices,
Who, from our mother's arms,
has blessed us on our way
With countless gifts of love,
and still is ours today.

⌒

Here is another way of wedding:

The living room is crowded with their two large families. Children gambol about the sofas and folding chairs. In the kitchen somebody is fussing with the cold poached salmon. Somebody else is setting out bottles of chilled champagne. Everything is running a little late, so the flutist and the guitarist are on their second round of "Sheep May Safely Graze," one of the groom's special choices.

At last the service begins, and a roomful of serious faces turn to look at the couple. No one had really expected anything like this to happen. No one makes a sound during the exchange of vows. No one stirs as they listen to the reading the couple has picked, a poem by John Cavenaugh. They have only been together as a couple for a few years, but they have already done much of what the poem describes:

I want to walk with you above the pines,
Scale mountains, leap rivers, speak to the sun and the moon.
And make wagers with the stars.
I want to roll laughing down lonely canyons . . .
And hear the music of coyotes resound across a moonless sky.

Then the groom turns to the musicians and nods. He has another special musical choice—this one for his bride. They begin to play "Bess, You Is My Woman Now" as the new wife gazes up at her tall and lanky husband. They kiss, we clap, and a little boy jumps up from his chair and wraps his arms joyfully around the groom's long legs.

"Is it okay if I call you Grandpa now?" he crows.

W. H. Auden wrote, "The choice to love is open till we die."

The groom is seventy-seven, the bride sixty-nine.

~

At another wedding, the bride is gaunt from chemotherapy and bald beneath her wig. She hadn't planned to be dying. She hadn't planned to be married either, though her partner had long hoped they would. Finally it became a question of the health insurance. His was better. So now, with death already beginning to part them, the groom slips a diamond ring along her bony finger.

Don't go, his face says.

Thank you for this ride, hers responds.

Then, another wedding, two years later:

On a sunshiny day a small wedding party gathers on a raft in the middle of a bright blue pond: the dead bride's husband, her mother, her son, a young woman radiant with the glow of pregnancy, and the young woman's parents. They are planning to name the baby after the groom's late mother, Miranda. It really is a story of life after death. So there can be no mournful tears today.

And I remember Shakespeare's quote, "Out of this nettle, danger, we pluck this flower, safety."

~

But some weddings, which look for all of the world just like weddings, don't even count, according to some people:

It was 2005. And I didn't ask my bishop for permission to do the blessing service of Barry and Ernie. Nor did I tell my bishop. I didn't ask my congregation. But I did tell my congregation. I asked the council if the ceremony could be in the church. And the council said of course. After all, we were the first Reconciling in Christ congregation in the Upstate New York Synod of the Evangelical Church in America. That had been one of my goals when I was called to Grace Lutheran Church—that we become the Lutheran equivalent of what other denominations regularly described themselves as—open, welcoming and affirming of persons of all sexual orientations. And after all, the whole congregation knew of my work with Schenectady Clergy for Sexual Inclusivity (our acronym was SCSI—pretty edgy sounding, yes?). My congregation knew where I stood on things. They stood there too.

I wasn't going to act as an agent of the state on the day of Ernie and Barry's union ceremony, as I do at every other wedding, because what I was doing wasn't legal. And I *was* violating the official policy on marriage that the national body of the ELCA—Evangelical Lutheran Church in America—endorsed, running the risk of being subjected to removal from the rosters of the national church for performing this wedding that neither church nor state would recognize.

But Ernie himself was an ELCA pastor, having been kicked out of the Lutheran Church-Missouri Synod when he had come out. And he wanted to get as close to getting married as he could in Grace Lutheran Church and in New York State. And if I had any misgivings about performing this ceremony, they were purely pastoral: Barry and Ernie had met on Epiphany and this was September. They hadn't known each other that long, and a part of me wanted them to take it slow. But I also figured that they were grown-ups, with children and with past lives; they knew what they were doing.

So on that September day, supportive members of Grace Lutheran Church filled the pews in lieu of Barry's and Ernie's families. Their families had chosen not to come. Did it cast a pall on an otherwise happy day? Of course it did. And as we gathered, it struck me as cruelly unfair that this ceremony, one that looked for all the world just like other weddings, wouldn't even count in some people's minds.

And indeed, it wasn't officially a "wedding," because in New York State the Marriage Equality Act did not pass until 2011. It would not be recognized by the laws of this state or authorized by my denomination or for that matter, most Christian denominations. The fight for all of that continues, slowly and steadily, with some denominations allowing clergy to perform same-sex marriages and more and more states recognizing them. Yet right then, on that day of Barry and Ernie's wedding, friends and church members gathered joyfully, a bit tremulously in the sanctuary at Grace. Speaking these words for the first time to a same-sex couple, I said to them:

"Barry and Ernie, you are meant, as children of God, to live lives of compassion, kindness, humility, and patience. Forbear each other; forgive each other. As God has forgiven you, you are asked to forgive, remembering that love binds everything together in perfect harmony. And now, because it is your intention to share your joys and sorrows and all that the years will bring, with your promises, I invite you to bind yourselves to each other in full and whole-hearted partnership."

And that is what they did.

Barry's voice choked with tears as he made his vows. Ernie wore that shaky smile of a man trying not to cry. (Now let me tell you that when, in particular, a groom cries at a wedding, I almost always come close to losing it. I cry at the drop of a hat. And I truly believe that women are suckers for men's tears. So imagine how hard I had to work to keep my voice steady. Because I had *two* weeping grooms!)

But we three got through the vows—and my nose didn't run and my mascara didn't run and I don't think my voice quavered too much. And then, when we had prayed and they had kissed and the Holy Spirit gave us all a distinct though invisible thumbs-up, we went to the home of one of the women of the church—a smart and generous-hearted older woman—who had prepared a wedding reception for them. There was delicious food. There were presents. And of course there was wedding cake.

7

Grievous Fault

I confess to God almighty, before the whole company of heaven, and to you, my brothers and sisters, that I have sinned in thought, word and deed by my fault, by my own fault, by my own most grievous fault wherefore I pray to God Almighty to have mercy on me, forgive me all my sins and bring me to everlasting life. Amen.

—Service of Prayer at the Close of the Day
Lutheran Book of Worship

The pastor's office is a private place. What I hear is confidential. I'm not there to judge, but to listen. People come into my office with problems. They come so I will listen. That's most of the reason why they come. And it's a reversal of the usual role, the liturgical role in which the pastor speaks and the people listen.

Without doubt, some of the most meaningful moments in my life have occurred when people have talked to me with opened hearts about what hurts them, enrages them, or scares them. It requires bravery to speak freely. It is their bravery that makes me trustworthy, not some kind of prescient, pastoral goodness of my own.

Because my office and the words said in it are private, I have learned to keep a neutral face when I see the person in the usual contexts of a church service or meeting or adult study class. Discretion is not simply advised. It's essential. Confidentiality is guaranteed.

The pastor's office is a kind of psychic quarantine in which people can package their problems in words, however imprecise, and then unpack them into the neutral chamber of the pastor's ears. I am a guesthouse for other people's pains and problems.

In Wim Wenders's intensely moving 1987 film *Wings of Desire*, two angels patrol the nooks and crannies of West Berlin. Played by Otto Sander and Bruno Ganz and dressed as ordinary men, these angels are invisible to everyone around them. But as they walk through the crowded streets, they are surrounded by a cacophony of human voices. They hear the thoughts of everyone around them—often mundane thoughts, though just as often the anguished thoughts and hopes of people going about their troubled lives. The angels don't speak back to any of the voices, even when those voices beg to be heard. They don't provide answers or solve problems. Sometimes you can see in the angels' faces the desire to touch or comfort or simply to be visible to those whom they supposedly guard. But though they are indistinguishable from the humans surrounding them, they are also invisible. The humans don't know that they are being listened to or cared about because the angels are not permitted to make contact.

I am not a romantic. I know that no such omniscience as that of the angels in *Wings of Desire* attaches itself to being a pastor. I'm clueless a lot of the time when people come to me with problems. Most of the time there *is* nothing I can do, so I am not in dereliction of my duty when I do nothing but listen.

But apart from the angels' omniscience, I sometimes do feel like them. When I walk among those I serve, I can hear more than what their voices are saying to one another. I remember what it is they have said to me, trusting in the quarantine of the pastoral office.

I have sat in my office with people who told me they were going to die from cruel diseases about which they clearly understood the terrible trajectory of its etiology. And I've been able to do nothing other than listen, perhaps hold them, or cry with them. I have sat with grown parents of sexually abused children whose abuser they have had to tolerate for years because it was another family member. I have sat equally with people devastated emotionally and financially by divorce and others who long to end their marriages, but cannot. I have sat with people unclear about their gender and about their sexual orientation. I have sat with parents who have had to grieve the loss of children.

So when, during the prayers of the church, we leave silence for individual prayer, it is not merely silent for me. My head is filled to brimming with the beseeching, private prayers of those whose problems I know. What answers are they given? Sometimes I think God is even less effective than I am in providing a meaningful response.

I am, though, no angel. Nor am I a limitless vessel into which heartaches can pour. Often there is spillage: I bring the heaviness home with me. I am harsh to my daughters. I complain about parishioners. I feel physically separated from the rest of my body, with only my ears and brain operational.

Nevertheless, hearing the sadness of others in the sanctity of the office is, though I hesitate to use such big words, holy work. There's a Danish proverb that claims "shared sorrow is halved sorrow" and while I don't believe that speaking out our sadnesses necessarily diminishes them, I do think it helps to know that the one they call pastor really is thinking, with tenderness, of their problems.

Of course, not everyone who comes to talk to a pastor is bringing a tale of sadness. Sometimes people come to talk about something they've done that makes them feel guilty. And more rarely, but most difficult of all, is when somebody confesses a serious crime.

And yet nothing said in a pastor's office is inexcusable—no matter how awful. Because the theology goes that wrongdoings confessed by sinners are pardoned by God's grace. We are told that is how it is supposed to work. We are also taught that God's grace extends even further, not merely to those who admit to wrongdoing, not only to those who confess. We are taught that God's grace is a blanket amnesty.

There is, in God, forgiveness-without-borders—for evil gone unacknowledged, for evildoers defending their rights to do evil, for evil cross-dressed as beneficial for the common good of all. All the cruelty and greed and lust and bloodlust you can imagine and more—apparently God can forgive it all. This is supposed to be good news. But if you're a pastor and you are already on shaky ground with the way you think

God is handling reality—if God exists as an external entity at all—then announcing God's forgiveness to someone whose deeds you find repugnant is hard work. Announcing God's forgiveness to someone who is telling you something *you* can't pardon is the toll the pastor pays because we stand for a theology that says God's grace is free for all. And if that's true, our liking or not liking it, our believing or not believing it, doesn't change a goddamn thing.

Several years ago, police arrested Dennis Rader of Wichita, Kansas, and charged him with murder in the deaths of ten people over the course of almost twenty years. This serial killer, unknown to police for so long, sent letters to police and local media outlets in which he described the details of the killings, using "BTK" as his signature for his method of first binding and torturing and, only after that, killing his victims.

The community was stunned. Dennis Rader had been married to his wife for over thirty years. He had been a Cub Scout leader. During the 1970s and 1980s he had worked installing home security systems, and at the time of his arrest he was a supervisor in the Compliance Department of Park City. He was a churchgoing man and had been elected president of the Church Council of Christ Lutheran Church in Wichita, of which he and his wife, Paula, had been charter members. No one in his church community, not in a month of Sundays, would have expected him capable of such cruelty and nihilism.

The shock was palpable. Neither his wife nor his two children visited Rader after his arrest, and the Sedgwick County judged waived the sixty-day waiting period so that Paula could have an immediate divorce from her husband.

For his part, Dennis did not contest the divorce and, beginning with his arrest, freely and unemotionally confessed to committing the murders, describing them in gruesome detail. He entered a guilty plea and again provided a graphic account of his crimes during his trial. After being convicted, he was sentenced to serve ten consecutive life sentences. Here was an undeniably evil man with a truly evil heart.

Yet even if he had an evil heart, he also had a pastor. And the pastor of Christ Lutheran Church, the Rev. Michael Clark, was left no choice but to minister to Rader. He *had* to lead his parishioners through this traumatic and mind-boggling experience. And he *had* to visit with, talk to, and pray for BTK.

In his Sunday sermon only three days after Rader's arrest, the Rev. Clark wrote:

> *As we continue on as a body of Christ, it is important that we show compassion and love towards Dennis. If what is claimed is true we should be about the business of asking for God's help in healing of heart and soul. As we travel from this day forward we should pray for all of Dennis Rader's family members. Bring them peace and comfort as they too wonder what each new day brings.*
>
> *As a body of Christ we can let the power of these events that come before us either destroy us, to overcome us, or these events can bind us up to a stronger body, to a stronger community in Christ. We have that choice. I propose that we choose to let this be a time of strengthening, of renewing and healing.*

And several months after Rader's arrest and confession, there was a short interview with the Rev. Clark in *The Lutheran* magazine. Of course he said the things that a pastor is supposed to say, things about pain and forgiveness and God's ways being unknown to us because God's capacity for forgiveness is so much greater than ours. He described the theology on which we have hung our shingles ever since Luther nailed the Ninety-Five Theses to the church door at Wittenberg: No one is beyond the reach of God's grace.

I believe that the Rev. Clark probably meant what he said. Or he was trying to. Sometimes merely saying words whose meaning seems warped or distorted by circumstances helps you believe in the truth of them in spite of yourself.

But it can't have been that simple to be Dennis Rader's pastor. As he himself observed, "They don't teach you how to deal with this in seminary." So in spite of what he might have said publicly about God's grace or about his personal belief that some evil spirit had been in possession of Rader, driving his actions, the fact remained: Dennis Rader now seemed to be a duplicitous, despicable man who had committed many murders with blood-loving and orderly cruelty. To declare that God could *forgive* him must have been excruciating pastoral work. No one wanted that no-longer-man-but-beast to be forgiven. But Pastor Clark was the one tasked with saying that he could be. That *God* could do it. And did he feel anger binding him just as tightly as Dennis Rader had bound his victims before their torture and death? Did he feel angry not simply at Rader and his staggering brutality, but also at the God who apparently extends such unjust grace?

I don't know. I can only speculate that he may have. Or that he must have. And yet that didn't alter the fact that it was his job to announce the availability of such unjust grace. It becomes part of the job for all pastors at their ordinations to administer what is called the Office of the Keys. There is a short passage in the gospel of Matthew where Jesus asserts what little he ever did about what his church would be like and what its pastors would do—though Jesus never speaks in terms of pastors and never once refers to ordaining them. But here is Jesus speaking to his disciple Peter after Peter has just confessed his belief that Jesus was "the Son of the living God." The writer of Matthew records these as Jesus's words.

> You are Peter, and on this rock I will build my church and the gates of Hades will not prevail against it. I will give you the keys of the kingdom of heaven, and whatever you bind on earth will be bound in heaven, and whatever you loose on earth will be loosed in heaven.

—Matthew 16:18–19

Whatever you may think of God or ministry, it is a weighty conferral to be told you are to administer the Office of the Keys. But that is part of what the pastor at his or her ordination promises to do. Announce forgiveness. As stewards of the mysteries of Christ, we are required not to bind by human judgment what divine mercy can pardon. Whether or not you are a pastor who continues to believe in the wisdom of human justice or distrusts the fairness of divine mercy, you are supposed to announce it.

Dennis Rader's pastor had to announce it for him.

I can't know what his pastor felt as he did that. But I can imagine it, however minor by comparison, my experience was with it.

During my internship year I had joined my supervising pastor on several of the monthly visits he paid to a congregational member serving time in a downstate women's prison. She had been convicted of drowning her little boy. She denied it, but the evidence had been overwhelming. During my visits with her I expected to feel some strong emotion—pity maybe, or repulsion—because my kids were close to the same age as her son was when he drowned.

But I felt oddly neutral about the whole experience, detached. Prisons didn't much bother me. I had written a manual on prison industry for the New York State Department of Corrections, so I had toured the nooks and crannies of a half-dozen different maximum-security facilities. And this woman was someone I did not know and would not know beyond the tenure of my internship. She probably *had* drowned her own son. Or maybe she hadn't and her sentence had been a terrible miscarriage of justice. I didn't believe that, but either way it did not affect me. I felt almost-but-not-quite guilty about my cool detachment.

It had to have been different for my supervising pastor. He had known her from before the child's death. The congregation had rallied around her and her husband when a fire had destroyed their apartment a few years ago. They had given the couple money, clothing, furniture, and prayers. When the little boy died and in all that followed—the trial, the conviction, the sentencing—the congregation kept her in the prayers of the church, in spite of the discomfort this caused some members.

Some people thought it a betrayal of themselves and of the dead little boy to pray for his mother each week in the Prayers of the People. But my supervisor insisted that her name be included because no one was beyond the reach of God's saving grace. Even more than a decade later, her name was among those on the prayer list in that congregation's monthly newsletter.

But it spite of the prayers, in spite of his loyal visits to bring her Communion, I believe my supervising pastor must have had complicated feelings of his own about having to deal with a convicted murderer as a congregational member. He never shared those feelings with me. When I was his intern, I never thought it right to ask. As his colleague, I have never expected him to disclose his feelings. Maybe he doesn't even know what they are himself.

So I wasn't prepared to deal with my own feelings when someone came to me to coolly confess to repeated instances of assault that were both illegal and taboo.

It happened a long time ago. And because the person was not denying the deeds, but rather claiming to repent for them and indeed cover them up, I was at first distracted by my own sense of shock. After that I became caught up in the pathos of the confession. I didn't feel sympathetic exactly, but I wanted to help in some way. If I am honest, I have to admit there was vanity involved too. I wanted to be the competent pastor dealing wisely with a peculiar and disturbing set of circumstances.

In seminary I once overheard somebody once say, "I don't really like her, but I can love her in Christ." I thought, what the hell does that mean, to love someone "in Christ?" Isn't that just a half-assed way to say you don't like them, but you recognize that you don't have to bother about that because for some reason God apparently does? And yet in the weeks following what I had heard within the confidential quarantine of my office I thought I began to understand that to love someone "in Christ" really did mean something. It meant I did not need to let my revulsion at this person's action get in the way of things.

I began to think that in spite of my horror at the confession I could go on loving this person "in Christ." And I guess I was a little proud of myself for that. I found I could laugh and smile and interact with this person no differently than I did with anyone else in the congregation. I could share Communion, be hugged, and hug back during the passing of the peace and remain publicly and visibly unconcerned among congregational members both because I was bound by confidentiality and because there was no apparent threat to any of them. And as I was busy feeling proud that I could love someone "in Christ" so successfully, I was almost able to forget the substance of what this person had told me and about the victims involved.

Almost, but not quite. Because, very slowly, the full significance of it started becoming more real to me. I started to feel ashamed of myself that I had been sympathetic to the perpetrator without ever really thinking compassionately of those affected. I felt used, as if I had been thrust into a position where it seemed I had no choice but to affirm a person whose deeds I despised. I was the puppet, this person the puppet master. Or was God the puppet master?

Over time I had more and more trouble as the intellectual exercise of loving a person "in Christ" ceded to my physical sense of repugnance. Whenever I was near this person, my body became tense. I tried to sidestep hugs. I tried to keep conversations brief. I willed myself to continue to remain a faithful pastor, available, if needed, for further talk with this person. I pastored, but I pastored hollowly. If I had ever truly believed that God could make all sinners innocent, now I came to doubt the wisdom of such a plan.

I tried to remind myself of the Walt Whitman poem "The Sleepers." In my final class before graduating from seminary, we had been required to write a paper outlining our understanding of ministry. I had used the "The Sleepers." It's a long, rangy poem that envisions a panorama of humans, all of them asleep. Like the angels who hear all human thoughts in *Wings of Desire*, the reader is given the omniscient vision of God to see the scores of individual people Whitman describes. Some are good and kind; others are horrible. But all of them are beautiful. All of them are innocent and shriven in their sleep.

Try as I might, I could no longer believe them all innocent and beautiful. I began to think that I had been naive to choose "The Sleepers" as a description of humanity and that Walt Whitman had been even more naive to write it. How can everyone be rendered innocent, even by God, when there are so many suffering victims?

⁓

In Fyodor Dostoyevsky's *The Brothers Karamazov*, the middle brother, Ivan, the one I like best, talks with his younger brother, the saintly monk Alyosha. Ivan explains why for him it isn't a matter of believing or not believing in God; it's a matter of accepting the terms of God's world. In Ivan's view, the suffering of the present world is not worth the promise of future harmony with God. He tells Alyosha that though there are endless examples of human cruelty, he will only cite a few, those having to do with the abuse of children.

To write this part of *The Brothers Karamazov*, Dostoyevsky researched newspaper reports and historical accounts of child abuse. And he has Ivan describe two instances of these to Alyosha. The first is the story of a five-year-old girl whose parents routinely beat her. On the last night of her life, she accidentally soiled her bed. Upon discovering what the little girl did, her mother flew into a rage, smearing the child's face with her feces and forcing her to eat some. Then, to teach her a further lesson, she locked the little girl in the icy outdoor privy for the night. Ivan envisions and describes the child's piteous cries for God—and God's complete silence—as she froze to death in the darkness.

The other story that Dostoyevsky finds for Ivan to tell is even darker and more cruel. He recounts it in a quiet, controlled voice, and the reader senses the mounting horror as the story unfolds:

There was a much-feared general who had two thousand people, most of them serfs, living on his grand estate. He kept hundreds of hunting dogs as well as many dog-boys to train them. But one day the eight-year-old son of one of the serfs threw a rock at the general's very favorite dog and injured its paw. The general found out who had hurt his dog and became enraged. He vowed revenge. He would make an example of the little boy. So he ordered him to be taken away from his mother and locked up overnight in the shack he used as a cell for wayward serfs.

The next morning, the general gathered all the serfs together. They were to witness the punishment to come. It would teach them a lesson, he explained, so that they would know what to expect if any of them ever again interfered with his property.

Then he ordered the boy to be brought out from his cell. He ordered someone to strip the boy naked, and it was done. As the boy stood there, pale and shivering with cold and terror, the general ordered that the mother be brought to stand right in the front, where she would have an unobstructed view of her son. And then the general had his dog-boys bring out all of the hounds.

Run! he ordered the little boy. *Run, I said!* And the boy began to run.

But where? And how? He was naked. The frozen ground burned his feet. Still, he ran. And as he did, the general gave another order: the dog-boys were to unleash the hounds, every one of them. At his command, the pack of dogs sprang forth to chase their prey, overtaking him in an instant. The stunned serfs and the disbelieving mother watched as the hounds, in a blur of teeth and claws, tore at the boy, puncturing the boy's white skin again and again until he was awash in his own blood; until he was no longer a boy but only shreds of bloody flesh, his dying screams drowned out by the growling of the frenzied throng of hounds.

Ivan tells Alyosha he understands that the love of God is boundless and that God can forgive any act of human cruelty, *any*. But Ivan also understands that retribution for the cruel deeds done is not part of God's forgiveness. And because deeds so cruel go unpunished by a God who can silently watch them and then forgive the perpetrators, Ivan rejects God. He tells Alyosha:

While there is still time, I hasten to protect myself, and so I renounce the higher harmony altogether. It's not worth the tears of that one tortured child who beat itself on the breast with its little fist and prayed in its stinking outhouse, with its unexpiated tears to "dear, kind God"! It's not worth it, because those tears are unatoned for. They must be atoned for, or there can be no harmony . . . too high a price is asked for harmony; it's beyond our means to pay so much to enter on it. And so I hasten to give back my entrance ticket, and if I am an honest man I am bound to give it back as soon as possible. And that I am doing. It's not God that I don't accept, Alyosha, only I most respectfully return him the ticket.

Ivan "gives back the ticket," as he puts it, to God's creation. It is not an order in which he can bear to live, however great the promise of future harmony. It is *because* he believes in God and in God's overarching forgiveness that Ivan must reject the life he has been given to live.

Dostoyevsky was a Christian of some sort, but Ivan's words are a resounding indictment of an all-forgiving God. I don't really know how Dostoyevsky was able to balance his belief against the potent logic in Ivan's argument against creation.

I know I have never been able to. People ask all the time, "Why is there evil in the world?" And of course no one ever has a satisfying answer. And they ask, "Where was God during this or that unspeakable horror?" No one ever has a satisfying answer to that question either. But it is rare when someone questions the indiscriminate forgiveness of God that is at the heart of Christianity at least.

In fact, most of the people I have talked to who are concerned about forgiveness are worried over their *own* lack of ability to forgive. They know they must forgive. They must pray for their enemy, whether it is their adulterous husband or his lover, whether it is their mother's murderer or their rapist. They find their inability to forgive a great failure of their willpower or a failure of their faith. Their guilt abrades their souls until the very person who has hurt them once becomes a source of new hurt. This time it is the painful recognition that they are failing to live as Jesus said to live, loving our neighbors, however unlovable, as ourselves.

For those most abraded by their inability to forgive, it is easier to hate themselves than to love their abuser.

But I want to know why that should be. Why should they forgive?

I could give you a pastoral care textbook of answers. But for me personally, I don't believe that humans can or are even expected to forgive every sling and error of outrageous fortune and other sundry miseries. If

God expects that, God asks of humans too high a price. And anyway, I don't think God does expect that.

Instead, I find myself with Ivan, unsatisfied by the lack of retribution. In theory, of course, I figure that if you're going to believe in God at all, an all-forgiving God is the only safe one to believe in—Ivan and I part company there. And I very much like the creation, so I have no desire to give back my ticket. But I don't think there is any way to deny that there is something fundamentally unjust in God's all-redeeming grace.

In what is surely one of the most moving stories in all the gospels, a woman—a sinner, naturally—anoints Jesus's feet with rich oil after she has washed them with her tears and dried them with her hair. Simon, Jesus's host at table, is shocked at both the woman's actions and that Jesus has permitted them.

"Simon, I have something to say to you," Jesus says.

"Teacher," he replied, "Speak."

"A certain creditor had two debtors; one owed five hundred denarii and the other fifty. When they could not pay, he canceled the debts for both of them. Now which of them will love the creditor more?"

Simon answered, "I suppose the one for whom he canceled the greater debt."

And Jesus said to him, "You have judged rightly."

—Mark 7:4–43

Such a moving story of the woman anointing Jesus's feet ends with a powerful parable on forgiveness. It is little wonder that this is a favorite Bible story for many—it is one of mine—as well as the subject of many paintings for its vivid image of the woman with loosened hair, kneeling in devotion at Jesus's feet, the men standing above and around her, glowering down at her crouched form.

The story closes with Jesus explaining to Simon the relationship between forgiveness and love.

"Therefore I tell you," he says, "her sins, which were many, have been forgiven; hence she has shown great love. But the one to whom little is forgiven loves little."

No doubt this is good news, in a general way, to the guilty and contrite sinner. But beneath its surface is an unsettling premise: greater sin leads to the need for greater forgiveness; greater forgiveness leads to more faithful love.

Does this mean that those mythic monsters we invoke when we want to epitomize extremes of human cruelty—Hitler, Stalin, Pol Pot, and many other icons of evil—will be capable of a greater love than those whose lives they destroyed? Jesus's words support that logic. But it is hard not to find the concept repugnant. So we tend to domesticate his words, tone them down so they only apply, really, to the small scale of personal drama. The cheating husband will be capable of a greater love now because he has been forgiven by his little-sinning wife. *O felix culpa!* Although even on the domestic level, this kind of forgiveness-and-love equation sticks in my craw.

Of course, it's easy to say that I am willfully as well as unfaithfully misreading these passages. That what they *really* mean is that those who think themselves so fine aren't really all that. Be humble. Remember the cracked goblet that refracts a more brilliant light.

That *is* a comfort to us everyday cracked goblets, we who try to be good and mourn our wrongdoings and failures. But what do we do with the seriously cracked ones? The sociopaths and mass murderers? What do we do with Dennis Rader? The woman who drowned her son? Those who violate children? At what point does our need for justice run head-on into our existential need for an all-loving God?

∼

Of course, even if I am troubled by all of this, and I am, I do not need to think about this: I have a shield and I hide behind it. All I must do is announce the forgiveness of God. At the end of the Brief Order for Confession and Forgiveness in *The Lutheran Book of Worship*, this is what the pastor says:

Almighty God, in his mercy, has given his Son to die for us and, for his sake, forgives us all our sins. As a called and ordained minister of the church of Christ, and by his authority, I therefore declare to you the entire forgiveness of all your sins; in the name of the Father and of the Son and of the Holy Spirit.

And then I mark the sign of the cross in the air in front of me, the cross that symbolizes forgiveness, blanket amnesty. No one in the sanctuary has spoken aloud the words describing sins for which I am announcing forgiveness. I am just announcing the scandal of God's grace. The people, shriven, respond, "Amen." And then we sing a hymn.

But when I announce the forgiveness of God, I do not always feel forgiven myself. Nor do I always feel like trying to follow God's lead and "forgive those who trespass against us" as it says to do in the Lord's Prayer. I have known too much hurt in my life. I'm good at getting hurt. I'm not as good at forgiving.

I know what it is to nurse grudges, to feel wronged without recompense, to have been betrayed in love and want to betray right back. I know what it is to hate others on behalf of others and not to want to stop hating them. I know what it is to live in a world that appears hell-bent on butchery and self-annihilation and to feel that what we need is something bigger than even radical forgiveness. I don't doubt for an instant its inestimable value. But sometimes I want nothing more than for God to come right here among us and help us sort this human chaos out.

8

Happy Christians

What Thou, my Lord, hast suffered, was all for sinners' gain;
Mine, mine was the transgression, but Thine the deadly pain.
Lo, here I fall, my Savior! 'Tis I deserve Thy place;
Look on me with Thy favor, vouchsafe to me Thy grace.

What language shall I borrow to thank Thee, dearest friend,
For this Thy dying sorrow, Thy pity without end?
O make me Thine forever, and should I fainting be,
Lord, let me never, never outlive my love to Thee.

— Paul Gerhardt, based on Bernard of Clairaux's
Salve caput cruentatum

I got to my daughter Linnea's concert early enough so that for once I'd be able to see the slide of her trombone. I chose two seats in the second row of chairs lining the gymnasium floor, one for me, the other for my older daughter, Madeleine, who was going to meet me at concert time.

I had brought stuff to read: a copy of the alternative newspaper I write for and Richard E. Rubenstein's book *When Jesus Became God*, background study for a series of adult classes I was leading on how political power brokering played into the development of the theology of the early church. I had not even cracked the book's spine to start reading about all this when a sturdy woman in a pink pantsuit juggling a bunch of flowers and an ample purse pointed to the vacant seat beside me.

"Is that taken?" she asked pleasantly.

Somehow forgetting it was Madeleine's seat, I shook my head.

"No," I said. "Sit right down."

Her handbag landed on the floor with a thud. She began to twist and wiggle her way out of her pink jacket. The bouquet rolled to the edge of her lap and threatened to fall, but she caught it just in time. Then she settled into her seat with a sigh.

"Sometimes just getting from point A to point B is such a challenge," she said.

I nodded. There was no disputing that.

"And now," she said, "we just sit here and wait. I'm always waiting for one or the other of my kids.

"Yes," I agreed. "Me, too. Now we wait."

"Is it your son or your daughter or your son-or-daughter and are they in the band or in the chorus?"

I had never considered the exponential confusion that might arise from having a son and a daughter or two sons or two daughters in perhaps either or both band or chorus. Multiple monthly instrument rental fees. Multiple concert attire. I had to think for a minute: how many musically gifted children did I have?

"It's just the one in the music programs," I said, "My younger daughter. She's in band and chorus."

"I've got two in each, a daughter and a son. Susan and Brian. Oboe and alto, trumpet and tenor. Your daughter?"

I was trying to sort out the instruments from the voices.

"Trombone," I said. "Soprano," forgetting that her chorus didn't sing in separate vocal parts yet. "She *might* be a soprano, eventually. But her name is Linnea."

The woman nodded, "Lovely name. Exotic," she commented, then paused. "Is your husband—well, Indian or something?"

It's a safe gamble, in this school district, to guess at ethnicity. My daughters and I live in the relatively frugal section of an otherwise affluent suburb filled with scientists whose ethnicities vary widely: Indians, Jews, Russians, Asians, Pacific Islanders, Iranians, and even your odd white European—you never know who you are talking to unless they are wearing some kind of identifying mark: hijab or sari or a Talbot's boiled wool jacket. And with the all-alike way the men dress, you can never be sure. Nevertheless, we're nothing exotic.

"It's a Swedish name," I told her.

My ex-husband used to boast about having a little Native American blood in him. He had skin several shades darker than mine and dark, straight hair. Both of us hoped there was something to his boasting. It would have spiced up his northern European ancestry, from which generations in the sand hills of Nebraska had leeched any ethnic distinction. It would have been cool if just the tiniest a part of him had been Native American, but we both figured his stock had been too morally repressed for a little miscegenation in the woodshed.

"Well, it's just a lovely name," the woman said.

I could feel her looking over at the newspaper. This week my name was featured on the front cover—I had written against invading Iraq. Casually I slid *When Jesus Became God* on top of the newspaper and covered up the headline with my name in it. But she was watching.

"What do you think of the book?" she asked.

"This? Have you read it?"

"No," she said, "But I just ordered a copy for my husband."

"I haven't even started it yet, so I don't know what to think."

"It sounds intriguing to me, though, you know? I mean, I don't believe Jesus was *God* or anything. I mean, I know he was God's *son*, but I guess they just decided at that Council that he was God. It's not like the Bible says he was. Just a bunch of men at a meeting. You *know*."

The Council of Nicea in 325—just a bunch of men at a meeting. I was surprised she even knew about it, that game-changing event called by the Emperor Constantine once he'd decided to Christianize the empire. I guess I'd have expected her to be more of a Jesus-is-my-personal-Lord-and-Savior Christian, based on the pastel pantsuit. But wasn't that catty of me—plus, what did I have against pastels? Maybe I was sitting next to an earnestly questioning Unitarian who happened to like shopping in the Coldwater Creek catalogue.

"Yeah, well, I think a lot of doctrine got handled that way," I said, "by people—for lots of different reasons—deciding what was most politically expedient and so on."

"I know," she said. "But if they would have just looked at scripture they wouldn't have had such a problem. With Jesus, you know? I mean, it's pretty clear if you read carefully."

I nodded. I wasn't used to bumping into Christians who claimed to read scripture *carefully*. Mostly I just seemed to bump into Christians who thought they read scripture *correctly*.

"I mean, how could *men* decide who Jesus was and wasn't?" she asked me, friendly enough, but with vigor. "What did they know?"

"I guess they thought the Holy Spirit was guiding them," I used finger quotation marks around "Holy Spirit," but I was just posturing. I felt a tiny tremor of shame. If I had one shred of orthodox faith left it me, it was that the Holy Spirit was real and breathing.

"Holy Spirit!" she said. "If any of them had just taken the time to read their Bibles, they wouldn't have needed the Holy Spirit!" she sighed. "It was all there, right in front of them. The scripture interprets itself."

Her comment took me aback. So much so that I didn't mention that there was no "regular" Bible back then; the development of the New Testament canon was just getting off the ground toward the end of the fourth century. Either she was a literary deconstructionist critic or a Christian literalist. Knowing that statistics greatly favored the later, I should have kept my mouth shut.

"Sure. Except where it contradicts itself."

"Oh, but no, it doesn't. You see, if you just read it carefully it all makes sense. My husband and I run a house Bible study once a week with other people from our church. And studying the word closely makes all the difference. God's plan for the world is so plain in the scriptures."

I nodded. I wasn't about to tell her that I make my living studying the word closely and carefully. I wasn't about to tell her that I didn't think God necessarily had a plan at all. I figured it was better for me to say nothing, so I just smiled.

"And people always muck around with what the Bible means. That's why there is so little unity among Christians."

I nodded again. This I agreed with.

She went on, "I like to think back to the first century of the church. It must have been a wonderful time. Everyone believed the same way; there was no division, no disputing. They were *happy* in the Lord."

I bit my tongue. I didn't bring up the early church heresies: docetism, ebionism, gnosticism, only three of the earliest little viruses that got into the hard drive of the early church and created havoc—hence the need for the Council of Nicea. I didn't mention that even in the New Testament book of Acts, people are quarreling over whether circumcision is good or bad, over whether or not to let the Gentiles join the Jesus club.

I didn't bring up Paul's anger at the Corinthians and the Galatians. Or the appearance of what was called "the household code" in five New Testament epistles, dictating, among other things, that women were to be submissive to their husbands and slaves were to honor their masters.

"I like that passage in Colossians," she was going on dreamily, "*with gratitude in your heart sing psalms, hymns and spiritual songs to God.* I like to imagine all those happy Christians singing."

At the moment I wasn't a happy Christian with gratitude in my heart. Also, I figured I knew what was coming next.

"Do you have a church you go to?" she asked.

"Yes," I said, "I do."

"Oh, great!" Now I was one less sinner she had to save. "Which one?"

"It's the Lutheran church, Grace, over there by the medical arts building."

"Oh. Lutheran." It seemed she wasn't at all assured of my salvation now. "I don't know much about them. Except we have Martin Luther to thank for getting the Protestants and the Catholics out of each other's hair. *That's* a good thing!"

I nodded, thinking about how many people were killed in the Thirty Years' War so that a prince could choose whether or not his subjects were to be Roman Catholics or Lutherans. *Cuius eius*—"his realm, his religion"—was the principle established by the Peace of Augsburg in

1555. By then, of course, millions of people had died from the protracted war and famine.

I was thinking back to how, in my family, my mother was the prince who'd chosen Lutheranism for her subjects. And I was thinking back to my Clinical Pastoral Education days—training for hospital chaplaincy—when I visited a youngish man in the Cardiac Care Unit who had had a massive heart attack. He was making a good recovery, perhaps in part because of the solicitousness of his wife. She fussed about him, holding his hand, stroking his brow, straightening his sheets.

He asked me what my denomination was; I told him. He went on to talk eagerly about his faith and about how and when he had gotten saved.

Then his wife patted the back of his hand lightly. "Honey, I don't think you need to go on about all that. Lutherans don't much care about salvation."

Apparently the status of the eternal souls of Lutherans was an unsettled question among self-identified Bible-believing Christians.

The woman next to me was still going on about the church.

"Well, anyway, the Lutherans sing all those good hymns," she said, then paused. "Is your pastor a Bible-believing Christian?"

It was more than I could stand. And I was stuck here, having given away my daughter's seat to a pastel pantsuited biblical literalist hell-bent on saving my unredeemed soul. I sent up a guerilla thought-prayer: Lord, just in case you *do* hear the prayers of Lutherans, have mercy.

"Yes, I hope so," I said and paused. "I'm the pastor."

"*You're* the—? Oh my goodness, that's wonderful. I guess I did know that the Lutherans had lady ministers, but I had forgotten. Now are you the youth minister, or are you and your husband both ministers at the church?"

"No, it's just me," I said, trying hard not to bristle. If you're a female pastor, it is regularly assumed that you work with children or that your husband is a pastor too.

"Well, I'll be, that's just marvelous. And you must be a very gifted minister or God would not have given you such a heavy burden—a whole church all by yourself."

I nodded, "I guess."

"And the men—they're okay with a lady minister? They don't, you know, feel threatened?"

"Not that I know of," I said. "I think they feel it's more about the word of God than the gender of the person speaking it."

"Well, that's true, isn't it. I mean, I know it says to keep silent in the churches, but I talk all the time. I lead the Bible study *with* my husband; it's not all him. I make sure my voice gets heard."

I'll bet you do, I thought. And I wondered how much time was left until the concert began.

But just at that moment my paltry little Lutheran prayer was answered. Because suddenly the woman turned away from me and frantically began waving her hand at somebody across the gymnasium. Then she stood up, left the flowers on the chair, picked up her purse, and began climbing over other people's feet to get to the aisle.

"Excuse me. I'll be right back," she said. "I see a friend over there and I've got to go talk to her about the bake sale."

Thank you, God, for the bake sale, I thought as I gathered up my books and purse and made my escape.

The concert was just about to start when I finally saw Madeleine. We ended up on the bleachers just as the fifth-grade boys' choir began to give a dolorous rendering of "Let There Be Peace on Earth."

"I guess the boys just aren't that into peace," I said to Madeleine. And for some reason we laughed so hard I thought a passing teacher would give us both a detention. Nevertheless, I guess you could say we were happy Christians.

~

I'm sure my pastel-pantsuited woman would agree with the majority of Christians who, when asked what Jesus did for humanity, would say, "He died for my sins" or some version of that. And though most world religions agree that there is sin or evil or misery galore in this life, Christians in particular see the need for a scapegoat to come along and wipe that sin away. Thus: "He died for my sins."

"Atonement" is what that's called. The church teaches that atonement is God's process for reconciling this miserable, fallen mess of a world and making it all Eden-clean. Given the state of humanity, does that strike you as hard to swallow? I think so, but I didn't invent this idea of atonement. I'm just a reporter.

Nevertheless, it came to be central to Christian doctrine, providing a framework for connecting human sin with Jesus's crucifixion. "Atonement" is necessary to imbue the horror of crucifixion with meaning. Even while it posits a humanity so far fallen from grace that it took the death of God to redeem it, it also oddly exonerates humankind. Otherwise we might have to admit to having killed—for no good reason—a man so pure that many people then and now thought he was God.

Across the centuries there have been many theories of atonement, and theologians still grapple with a concept that is both so endemic to and troubling about orthodox Christianity. But from a historical perspective, there are three Major League theories of atonement. As Lutheran seminarians, we were expected to learn them all thoroughly but champion one exclusively.

The first heavy-hitting atonement theory, the ransom theory, was developed by Origen (185–254). He was an early church polymath who by anyone's lights was an oddball, perhaps even certifiably nuts. I doubt any candidacy committee in the Lutheran church would have given the green light for his ordination. Fortunately for him, there were no Lutherans yet.

He held to some strange standards. For example, his commitment to teaching at the esteemed Catechetical School in Alexandria was only trumped by his concern that girls have equal access to it. The problem was, he just didn't see how he would be able to teach female students without being set aflame with passion. And if he couldn't teach the nubile young maidens of Alexandria without a telltale bulge beneath his robe, then the expedient thing to do would be to castrate himself.

The Roman historian Eusebius claims that Origen got the idea for that from Matthew 19:12: "For there are eunuchs who have been made eunuchs by others, and there are eunuchs who have made themselves eunuchs for the sake of the kingdom of heaven. Let anyone accept this who can."

And apparently Origen not only accepted it, but also did the deed himself. I pierced a third hole in one of my earlobes when I was in college. Even that was a messy and imprecise process. I don't have the stomach to think about how Origen managed self-castration. Yet the historical documents more support than dispute that he actually did it. That's a damn sight more Title IX—the federal law prohibiting discrimination on the basis of sex in education programs—than most women want, but apparently Origen thought he already had too much of what women want. (And maybe he did; we'll never know.)

In any case, he was a man of extremes, as is the atonement theory associated with his name.

The ransom theory posits a cagey God, a greedy Satan, and an unruly humanity. Once Adam and Evil ate the tasteless fruit of the Tree of the Knowledge of Good and Evil and were summarily expelled from Eden, the balance of power shifted to Satan. He had bested God. And until and unless God could pay some fabulously costly ransom, humankind remained in Satan's vice-grip claws.

God, either because of love for unruly humanity or simply not wanting to power share with the devil, struck a deal. God would send Satan the Son, the incarnation of God's own being. God would let the Son be killed in order that humanity might live, freed from sin.

The way Satan saw it, God could have the human chess pawns back if it meant he got the power of the chess king. And so Satan agreed.

Only he made a mistake in taking God's word for it. Because God had an entirely different plan in mind, a plan sure to infuriate Satan.

God pulled a bait and switch, the bait being the cross, the switch being the resurrection. After getting Satan to agree to release humanity upon the death of Christ, God allowed the crucifixion, along with the actual death of Christ, to proceed. Only just as Satan was getting set to gloat, just as Satan was about to crow about having gotten the cosmic equivalent of Monopoly's Park Place and Boardwalk, both with hotels, God resurrected Christ.

Christ wasn't dead anymore. He *had* been. But now he was alive again. A divine, as well as brilliantly realized, bait and switch. Humanity was saved and death hadn't triumphed.

Now, there are some problems with this theory mostly best left to scholars and armchair theologians who like to talk about stuff like this. But two are worth noting.

The first is that the ransom theory is kind of impersonal. It seems more a battle of wits between God and Satan than it does a concerted effort on God's part to redeem humanity. It's based not on divine compassion, but on divine trickery. And God knows all along that the trick will work. So is Christ's death really sacrifice? Subterfuge? Expediency? And what about humanity? Were we just mute pawns in a cosmic match?

The second problem, not surprisingly from a man who would castrate himself, is that the ransom theory is one of extremes. Origen's worldview was based on a radically polarized gulf between God and Satan. It leans heavily on the idea of dualism, of God and Satan as well-armed enemies locked in a Darth Vadar/Obi-Wan Kenobi struggle for the souls of humankind. But if God was truly omnipotent, wouldn't it always have been a pitched battle? And if that were the case, why all the cosmic drama? So I just never cottoned to the ransom theory, not that what I cotton to matters.

Theory number two—of which I also am not a big fan—the satisfaction theory, was developed by Anselm of Canterbury (1033–1109). It is almost as old as the Tower of London and far less fun to visit. Indeed, Anselm himself is probably more interesting than his theory, but it's his theory that people (who care) remember.

Anselm was a product of the high Middle Ages, a feudal culture in which a sense of honor carried infinite weight. So his theory, then, traffics heavily in the consequences of honor violated. Seen from the perspective of a feudal mind-set, when Adam and Eve had their fruity chew in the Garden of Eden, God's honor was besmirched. These days, besmirched honor is the stuff of reality TV shows and apparently is supposed to be entertaining. But the satisfaction theory is rooted in the notion that, at one time, very long ago, honor was a big deal. And the only right response to besmirched honor was vigorous recompense. At once and in full, like an American Express bill. There could be no minimum monthly payments.

And because it was *God's* honor that had been offended, no matter what recompense humanity were to offer, it would never be enough. It would always pale beside the enormity of the offense.

So God, the generous interloper, the Handsome Stranger, responded by coming to the aid of humanity. It was like the old vaudeville skit: the Merciless Landlord demands his rent from his penniless tenant, a Forlorn Lass. The Forlorn Lass then protests, in her highest, weakest voice: "But I *can't* pay the rent." The Merciless Landlord bellows, "But you *must* pay the rent." They go back and forth like this for a while. Then all of a sudden a Handsome Stranger with a well-waxed mustache dashes on stage. Opening his arms wide in a gesture of magnanimity, he declares, "*I'll* pay the rent."

According to the satisfaction theory, that is how God responded. The Son of God, condescending to human existence in the form of Jesus, becomes the Handsome Stranger. Jesus dashes onto the stage of human history and says, "I'll pay the rent."

But the rent is pretty high. Only God knows how high. Only the human death of the inhuman God will satisfy.

This is different from the way it works in the Ransom theory. In the ransom theory, God pays Satan. But in the satisfaction theory, God pays God-self. It's a closed circle, between God and humans. Satan isn't even a player. And because of that, the blame falls squarely on human shoulders. There is no Satan to take the heat. There is only us.

This is part of the reason why the satisfaction theory connects so well on an emotional plane. Humans stand alone, cowering with shame, imprisoned by guilt. The only useful way to transcend that guilt and shame is to feel that it is being transformed into a kind of frantic gratitude for all that God—and at such cost—has done for lousy and unworthy humankind.

Perhaps that is part of the reason why the Satisfaction theory is so remarkably abiding. It involves us on such a personal level; it challenges us so deeply. It forces us to regard ourselves as dreadful sinners—and who can resist such self-interested self-loathing? Then it forces us to accept our complicity in Christ's death—and who can resist such self-indictment? Then it forces us to grovel in thankfulness—and who can resist such self-abasement?

It goes without saying that it's a favorite among Lutherans.

Yet it has many critics, among them feminist, black, and other advocacy theologians who charge that it embraces a kind of divine child abuse. In addition, it is criticized as being quietistic because it doesn't require any ethical commitment on the part of humankind. In other words, a pious oppressor can well believe that his eternal salvation is guaranteed without regard to how he treats the oppressed. I don't like it because it seems like a vaudeville skit. But that's not a valid theological refutation.

Not too long after St. Anselm's satisfaction theory, but long before the Reformation, another theory came along, the moral influence theory. This was the work of the great medieval scholar Peter of Abelard (1079–1142). I really like the guy.

Permit me to air my bias, but Abelard is a tragic figure in the deepest sense of the phrase. Why Shakespeare didn't write a play about him had to have been because he didn't know about him. Abelard's woes make Othello and Desdemona's marital squabbles look like piffles. Abelard's righteous anguish turns moody Hamlet into a mama's boy. Compared with Abelard and Heloise, Romeo and Juliet are impatient, impulsive, immoderate horndogs. Compared with Peter of Abelard, they've got no right to sing the blues. But Abelard could have been born with a blues harp in his mouth and a bottle of Thunderbird by his side.

It all got started because he was one of those gifted, godly creatures who had as much brain as balls—the latter for a time anyway—and could outwit just about anybody.

In one of his early works, *Sic et Non* (Yes and No), he presented the contradictory responses of the early church fathers to the same theological questions. This certainly didn't flatter the church fathers. Or win Abelard any friends among his peers.

But his approach both aroused interest (because it promoted intellectual inquiry) and ruffled feathers (because it promoted intellectual inquiry). So from early on, Abelard was seen as a bright rogue, brilliantly challenging long-standing doctrine. And no one could deny Abelard's brilliance. Lionized as a teacher at several schools in Paris, he landed a plum teaching spot at the Cathedral School of Notre Dame, earning the title "Canon" within the first year.

Not that Paris isn't swell at any time (except maybe during the Reign of Terror), but twelfth-century Paris saw the rise of great cathedrals and universities. Europe was emerging from the Early Middle Ages—what used to be called the "Dark Ages"—when the great centers of scholarship and innovation were in Persia. As the High Middle Ages dawned, western Europe's medieval education and architecture were in full flower in Paris.

Because universities grew up alongside the cathedrals, there was no such thing as "a secular education." When Abelard went to Notre Dame, he did not need to go as a monk or a priest—nor did he want to. But voluntary celibacy was expected as part of the job and essential if he wanted to advance in his career. Marriage was out of the question.

However, while in Paris, Abelard boarded with Fulbert, canon of Notre Dame. And part of the terms of being Canon Fulbert's boarder was that he serve as the tutor to Heloise, the canon's illegitimate niece.

Heloise was a receptive student, Abelard a compelling teacher. You can guess the rest—love, more love, and then a love child. And because they couldn't live together openly as a married couple without Abelard losing his position at Notre Dame, they married in secret. They informed Fulbert of the marriage and arranged for Heloise to stay at a convent in Argenteuil, not far from Paris, where their son was born. They called him Astrolabe, naming him for the ancient instrument used to measure the location of stars and planets. Go figure.

But when Abelard moved Heloise to Argenteuil, Canon Fulbert was deeply troubled. Everybody knew Abelard was manipulative: as a student he had been as feisty as he had been brilliant. As a scholar he was as wily as he was insightful.

Now that Heloise was pregnant, Fulbert was certain Abelard would abandon her. What punishment for Abelard could Fulbert dream up that would preemptively fit the crime? He gathered together a bunch of his kinsmen and gave them their orders: break into Abelard's bedroom and castrate him.

Which they did. Poor Abelard. That will give you some blues rights.

Woke up one morning, my Baby's uncle's got a knife.
Woke up one morning, my Baby's uncle's got a bright and shiny knife.
My Baby's uncle did some carving
Made sure I was no husband; made sure I got no wife.

Castrating Abelard served nobody, of course. He recovered from his injuries, but his life was a real mess. Not only could he not function in bed, but he could not function in church either: canon law barred eunuchs from holding ecclesiastical office. From both legal and spiritual points of view, Abelard had no gender at all. His only option was to enter a monastery. He joined the Abbey St. Denis and then, out of misery, jealousy, piety, or some admixture of all three, he begged Heloise to forswear romantic love, give up their son, and join a convent. Out of misery, loyalty, piety or some admixture of all three, Heloise agreed. Abelard's sister raised Astrolabe.

In a lot of ways, the story only starts there. He was a great scholar, but everything he wrote seemed to rub somebody the wrong way. *Sic et Non* already had plenty of detractors, chief among them the famous and powerful monk Bernard of Clairvaux. When Abelard's book on the Trinity, called *Theologia*, came out, he ran into a mess of trouble. Critics of his book thought he was denying the absolute nature of God while at the same time hinting that if anyone was as smart as Abelard himself was, they, too, would come to that same conclusion.

So his church colleagues, in a kind of medieval equivalent of denying him tenure, brought in a papal legate who condemned *Theologia* not on the basis of its content, but on the fact that Abelard had circulated it without first submitting it for peer review.

Abelard was personally and publicly forced to throw his book into the fire, a castration of intellect this time.

> *Woke up this morning, a burning book for a hand,*
> *Woke up this morning, a burning, bloody book for a hand.*
> *I put that book down in the flaming fire*
> *And now I'm a bleeding, broken man.*

Monastery life was hard for Abelard—and for those around his prickly, argumentative personality. Soon he found comfort in teaching again; as before, students flocked in droves to hear him at the Oratory of the Paraclete, a kind of desert outpost of the Abbey. But he remained controversial and he knew he would again face persecution, so he left Abbey St. Denis and went to serve as the director of order and discipline at a monastery in Brittany.

It was the ideal setting in which to write his autobiography, *Historia Calamitatam* (*The Story of My Troubles*). Brittany was cold, dreary, and remote. And the brothers in his charge resented him for being a far stricter disciplinarian than they had been expecting. In fact, they tried to poison him—three times. Once they tried to strangle him.

In the meantime, he had arranged for Heloise, now a gifted nun and administrator, along with the sisters of her order, to take up residence at the Oratory of the Paraclete where he had stayed. Many of Abelard and Heloise's famous letters were exchanged when he was in Brittany and she at the Oratory. Even though he was a castrated monk, his visits to her there still stirred up controversy. He never seemed able to outrun trouble.

If there were anybody able to put the screws to Abelard, it was his arch-enemy, Bernard of Clairvaux. He hated Abelard—for his *Sic et Non*, for his rationalism, for his (former) sexual hi-jinx. So Bernard summoned Abelard to a conference at Sens in 1141. Once again, his work was to be condemned; once again, he would be dishonored and disgraced.

Only this time Abelard saw the writing on the wall. Rather than try to tackle Bernard at Sens, he decided to go directly to Rome to make his appeal. During the journey, however, he fell ill and was brought to a monastery outside Paris. There he lingered at death's door for weeks before dying. Initially he was buried there at the monastery. But not long after, his body was exhumed and his remains were brought to Heloise at the Oratory of the Paraclete.

Today, Heloise and Peter Abelard are buried in the same coffin in Pere Lachaise cemetery in Paris. Or at the very least, their tomb there claims that they are.

Woke up one morning, bones by my Baby's side.
Woke up one morning, moldy, broken bones by my Baby's side.
Been so long since I kissed my baby,
It's a stinking, rotten, mercy that I died.

~

The theory associated with Abelard is the moral influence theory, and there is simply no way that it is as interesting as the man.

Unlike the highly intellectualized, objective theories set forth by Origen (the voluntary castrato) and Anselm, Abelard's theory is subjective and ethics based. Nothing gets done by the crucifixion that doesn't have directly to do with us. In other words, no debt is paid to God, no ransom to the devil. No divine book-keeping is going on. It's just God coming to us in Christ, showing us that the effect of our sin is so great that it kills. It even kills God's own child.

So how then are we to live? The moral influence theory asks—and answers—that question. It says that in the cross we see the magnitude of divine love. It's that love that saves us from fear and produces in us a loving response, a response that helps us put aside selfishness and sin. So we are to live lives of selfless love, as Jesus did. Christ's power is redemptive precisely because his life is the exemplary one. Therefore we are called to be followers and imitators of it.

Abelard's own hymn encapsulates the whole thing:

Our sins, not thine, thou bearest, Lord; make us thy sorrow feel,
Till through our pity and our shame love answers love's appeal.

But for all its simplicity and clarity, the moral influence theory has an enormous number of critics. Some say it outright ignores the guilt of our sin. Others say it gives short shrift to the idea of God's holiness and the divine propitiation that Christ's crucifixion accomplishes. Still others ask if God's justice can be met simply through the rekindling of love in the sinner.

As a seminary student, I was taught that it was an anthropocentric rather than christocentric theory. In other words, the emphasis is on what *we* can do in response to the crucifixion rather than what *God* did. But Lutheran theology is grounded in the idea that nothing humans do is good and nothing humans can do has even the slightest capacity to be soul saving. We are that depraved. The only way for humans to be good is for them to be declared good: forensic justification by grace through faith. And that only happens through Christ.

Now Abelard's theory does not come right out and say that through good works humans earn their salvation. It only says that Christ's example inspires good work. But the moral influence theory, looked at through the lens of Lutheran doctrine, is easy to spurn.

As I age, I'm beginning to see more and more that I am less and less a Lutheran with twenty-twenty doctrinal vision.

If we have to be burdened with atonement theories at all, Abelard's is the only one that makes any kind of sense to me. It's the one that's most real, most relevant.

Still, even Abelard's theory only describes the *how* of crucifixion and resurrection.

None of the atonement theories answers the *why* of the crucifixion and resurrection.

Why is divine death good news in a world that is still chock-full of bad news?

Even as a kid I never understood why it was good news any more than I understood why Good Friday was good. Sure, good came was supposed to have come out of it, but why was it necessary in the first place?

I still have no answer as to the why of the crucifixion. And I can't take comfort in the complex intellectualizing of the atonement theories formulated to explain how Christians are saved from eternal damnation.

Eternal damnation, for that matter, raises another massive question. Why would a loving God consign anybody to eternal damnation? I mean, okay, maybe a *little* damnation. Twenty-four hours in a juice box–sized jail cell, maybe. Two or three years in a very big time-out chair with little in the way of tasty foods to eat. But eternal damnation? You can't convince me that a loving, parental sort of God would invent and then use such an extreme form of punishment.

As I see it, rather than clarifying the nature of God's relationship with the world, the basic Christian doctrine of Christ's atonement muddies the relationship. Apparently, God went to great lengths to save us from the rotten fruit of Eden that it was God's idea to let dangle, eye-level with the innocents, in the first place. But why? Was the whole arboretum of Eden merely God's lab for gauging the human proclivity to disobey and the insatiable human capacity for guilt?

Never have I hated a mythological fruit like the fruit Adam and Eve ate. Give me golden apples or Dionysian grapes. But keep the fruit of the Tree of the Knowledge of Good and Evil. I don't want to eat it. And yet the spoiled pit still sticks in my throat. I can't swallow it or expel it. I can only try to breathe around it.

At my worst moments I think that is at the heart of Christian theology: choking for breath. Breathing through guilt. And that doesn't feel like redemption. It feels like emphysema.

9

God Is a Man's Name

It is the unbroken tradition of the Catholic Church that women have never been admitted to Holy Orders. . . . The apostolic Church faithfully carried out this exclusion of women from priesthood that was instituted by Christ. Moreover, it should be also said that the maleness of the priest reflects the sacramental mystery of Christ and the Church. As representatives of the Head of the Church, the bride-groom, the priest must be male. There must be a "natural resemblance" between the priest and Christ. For Christ himself was and remains a male.

—Vatican Declaration on Women's Ordination, 1976

The pastor stands in the pulpit preaching in a commanding voice. His words are not artful, but they are doctrinally correct. He does not make jokes because he is not joking. He does not need the microphone. But it's on, and the amplification makes his voice punishingly loud. It would not surprise me if he were to bang the pulpit. He declaims in harsh iambics, stressing the syllables in some words in the way only male preachers ever do.

He is preaching from what I have come to think of as "my" pulpit. After all, I have been preaching here at Grace most Sundays for years. The microphone level is set for my voice, and that's why his already booming voice booms more aggressively.

But he is in the pulpit at my request. He is, after all, a member of this congregation, on leave from parish work while he finishes a graduate degree. I have asked him to preach. I have asked him to preside at

165

Communion. I am assisting in the worship by doing the parts designated for lay ministers. Second fiddle certainly, but by my own choice.

I have always liked this man. Though I knew we differed somewhat theologically, I never thought he would use the pulpit to "correct" the theology of the pastor loci—me. Or maybe he isn't really doing that, and I am simply insecure about the strength of my identity in the mostly male world of priests and pastors.

I am finding the service nerve-racking. He speaks with unwavering conviction and preacherly affectation. He says "Jay-*sus*" with a stress on the second syllable and a sibilant that would make a televangelist proud. I am fearful my congregational members will prefer his style to mine. I promise myself to never, ever let a guest pastor both preach and preside at the same service if I am present to do one or the other. Don't give such power away, I'm saying to myself, even as I have myself convinced I don't have what it takes to do the job right—which is a penis, I guess.

So with every "He" and "His" and "our heavenly Father," I shrink farther down in my seat. His doctrinally top-heavy sermon seems aimed at my theological shortcomings: I do not talk enough about the divinity of Christ, Christ's salvific work, and our worthlessness as sinners. This pastor's words chasten me. He is a man preaching with authority. I am a woman, which makes me a bad excuse for a pastor.

At the end of the service, he and I recess, him bowing deeply and conspicuously in front of the altar, also something I never do, before we make our way up the aisle. We stand side by side at the door of the sanctuary and shake hands with people as they come out of the sanctuary and toward the coffee and cookies set up in the foyer. Many, many people tell him what a powerful preacher he is, how they have enjoyed listening to him. I wonder if what they are really saying is that they miss a man in the pulpit.

Then it is my sister's turn to shake hands with me; she pulls me to her in an unaccustomed hug and whispers in my ear, "It's because of pastors like that that I stayed *away* from church for so many years."

"He scared me," I whisper back.

"I don't want to come to church to be scared," she tells me. Then she pulls back, applies a friendly smile to her face and moves on to shakes the other pastor's hand.

I am momentarily comforted.

But for the next week I wonder if what I really am is a doctrine-diluting pastoral fraud, a woman wearing a man's collar, a feminist blaspheming the Father-God.

I do baptize "in the name of the Father, and of the Son and of the Holy Spirit." But I have always taken pains not to use male pronouns for God. I don't speak of "Father God," though if the word "Father" appears in a part of the liturgy, I don't change it.

I don't use female pronouns for God, either. It seems to me to limit the vastness of what is supposed to be an illimitable divine presence if you narrowly tie the concept of God to gender.

I don't believe that God *has* a gender. But actually, neither do many theologians who insist on the use of "Father" language. They agree that God transcends gender but also assert that calling God by the patriarchal title does not connote maleness. As I see it, that's more a matter of wishful thinking than sound logic.

But whether or not God is called by patriarchal or matriarchal titles, the default pronoun for the divine is "he." You really almost never hear anything else when people talk about God. In fact, sometimes you hear it even when it isn't being said. If there is anything truly omnipresent about God, it appears to be the use of the masculine pronoun.

A couple of years ago I served on a panel with four other female clergy: a Unitarian Universalist, a Pentecostalist, a United Methodist, and a Reform rabbi. The audience was almost exclusively women, and at least half were lesbians. Our topic was "Women and Spirituality in the Twenty-First Century." Each of us was allowed five minutes to articulate a vision for women in the new millennium—I guess the event planner trusted we could be brilliantly succinct on such a wide-ranging topic.

As we each described our views on faith, I started to think that our individual fashion choices seemed to embody our theologies. Clothes might not make the man, but tonight they seemed to be telling stories on the clergywomen.

The Unitarian-Universalist—straight, I guessed, but unmarried—wore a simple, tasteful dress that looked as if it had come from Talbots or Ann Taylor. She wore comfortable pumps, and, instead of a cross around her neck, she wore the UUA insignia (a double circle surrounding a flame rising from a chalice). She spoke a lot about the need for understanding one another. She talked about the need to honor the diversity of ways we can experience God or, if we don't believe in God, the diversity of ways we can experience a *presence* like God's presence might be if there *were* a God.

The United Methodist pastor was a fair-trade fashionista. She wore a mélange of ethnic separates—a woven vest that looked to be from Guatemala; silver-and-stone earrings, possibly Bangladeshi made; and a batik wrap skirt that might have been Indonesian. She could have been a spokeswoman for the not-for-profit shops that cater to American consumers who want to shop responsibly. She was dressed responsibly. Not surprisingly, she talked about the need for justice and social responsibility.

The Pentecostalist was dressed to the nines, including high heels, serious coiffure, plenty of jewelry, and a wedding ring. She had inch-long lacquered nails that she waved around a lot as she issued bromides about how, if we just hard try enough and if we just pray hard enough to the Father, we will just succeed at whatever it is we try because all you just have to do is just believe in yourself and just pray, pray, pray to the Almighty Father. And our Almighty Father will just work a blessing in your life.

The rabbi wore chinos, a turtleneck, and a wedding ring. Her partner was home with their child. She talked about what it meant to live faithfully, as a lesbian, according to Hebraic law. She had a cogent theology. In five minutes she helped me understand more about Shabbat observance than I had in three years of working side by side with an Orthodox rabbi in the interfaith center at the university.

After our presentations, the audience was invited to raise questions. They were, for most part, as vast and vague as the panel title itself.

Because I listen for this kind of thing, I noted that only the rabbi and I never once referred to God by a masculine pronoun. I felt an unspoken kinship with her. So it came as a surprise when a woman in the audience rose to her feet and said, heatedly, that as a woman she could not get past the omnipresent insistence on the maleness of God.

"I noticed that every single one of you, even though you're women, called God 'he.'"

The rabbi and I responded in immediate unison, "No, I did not!"

But the woman went on, saying that yes, we had all called God "he."

Again, the rabbi and I, an impromptu chorus, said, "No, I don't call God 'he.'"

"Well," the woman in the audience challenged, "I sat here and I listened closely and I assure you you did. And if we play the videotape of this back," she motioned toward the camera, "I'm sure you'll discover that you did call God 'he.' And as long as women have to be subjected to a masculine concept of God"—she made quotation marks in the air with her fingers—"will remain the obstacle I can't get around. I can't have faith in a male-gendered deity."

The argument went back and forth, but not with any rhetorical craftsmanship: *No, we didn't say "he,"* we said. *Yes, you did say "he,"* she said. The woman in the audience kept shrugging away our words. It's always hard work arguing with a believer.

But she was wrong. I had listened closely too. The rabbi had spoken carefully, with no gender reference to God. I had done the same. We had both been speaking carefully in this way for many years. The woman in the audience had heard something neither the rabbi nor I had said.

But that isn't surprising. We are so culturally hardwired with the sense of God's gender that it is hard to hear the absence of the masculine when we talk about God.

Years ago, when Madeleine was four and I was still a seminary student, conscientiously trying to instill in my daughter the concept of a genderless divinity, I was surprised to hear how often she called God "he."

"Why do you do that?" I asked her. "Call God 'he'?"

She hadn't learned such things at my knee, that was for sure.

"Because God's a man, Mommy," she said.

"Well, sweetie, how do you know that God is a man?" I asked her.

Madeleine's eyes reflected real surprise that I, a pastor in training, would ask so stupid a question. The nice thing about children is that until they reach a certain age they believe that, when they answer *your* questions, they are really teaching you something you don't already know. And this time she was.

"Mommy, it's because 'God' is a *man's* name!"

~

I came of age as an English major reading Andrea Dworkin, Adrienne Rich, and Margaret Atwood. I knew all about Sylvia Plath with her head in the oven and Ted Hughes with his hand in someone else's panties. I learned how Simone de Beauvoir fetched playmates for Sartre when that cad's passion for her cooled. Colette's wicked Willy kept her in the attic and made her write, then claimed her work as his own. Pauline Reage, in fear of losing the attention of her lover, penned *The Story of O.*

Later, when I went to seminary, I discovered that things were every bit as bad for women in church history as they were for women in literary history. In fact, it seemed that the church played an enthusiastic role in the diminishment of woman as human beings. Contemporary feminist writers articulated the need to redress the historic wrongs of patriarchy.

Rosemary Radford Ruether's groundbreaking book *Womanchurch* tried to do that in a liturgical fashion, proposing the development of home churches where women could participate in rites observing the mostly overlooked events in women's lives. There was a service for welcoming the start of menstruation, another for its cessation at menopause. There were services mourning the abuse and victimization of women.

There was a service for purging misogyny from religious thought. She included quotations from writings as diverse as the *Malleus Malificarum*, that medieval go-to guide for routing out witches, and the towering twentieth-century giant of Protestant theology, Karl Barth. In volume III of his *Church Dogmatics*, he wrote:

> *The covenant of creation dictates a certain order, a relation of priority and posteriority, of A and B. Just as God rules over creation in the covenant of creation, so man rules over woman. He must be A; he must be first. She is B; she must be second. He must stay in his place. She must stay in hers. She must accept this order as the right nature of things through which she is saved, even if she is abused and wronged by the man.*

Barth's quote is particularly interesting considering that his own domestic arrangement included not simply one but two B's—his wife, Nelly, as well as his live-in mistress, Charlotte Von Kirschbaum. In addition to being Barth's mistress, Von Kirschbaum was his secretary and an erstwhile theologian whose own writing took an early feminist approach to theology. Somehow this makes her home life with Barth and Nelly all the more ironic. Or maybe just even more sad.

At the Lutheran Seminary in Philadelphia, where I did the bulk of my studies, there was little real attention paid to women's concerns—there had been more of that where I had begun my studies three years earlier at the United Methodist Seminary in Denver, Iliff School of Theology. In a strange way, it was a relief not to have to think about patriarchy. The more I learned about the historic plight of women, the more disempowered I felt. Not only that, but it was also falling out of fashion in the mainstream church and in popular culture to talk much about women's issues. Weren't American women at least doing all right for themselves? So why were they still whining so humorlessly?

For a long time I chose the path of least resistance. I was a straight woman in a largely male professional field. If I wanted credibility among my colleagues, I had to adopt a diluted feminism in my thinking. I got so I didn't talk as much about women and oppression and abuse and the evil ways of men. It got too burdensome and lugubrious.

I don't think this is uncommon for female clergy. Decades ago, when women were first being ordained, a slight androgyny in dress and attitude seemed a requirement; it was the best way to be taken seriously. But now there are clergy shirts with puffed sleeves in pastel lavender, blue, and pink polyester if you want to soft look. Younger clergywomen, as often as not tatted and pierced, opt for casual. And a dozen years ago I got tired of showing up at wedding receptions, having doffed the white alb I wear to lead worship, only to be wearing a dog collar and a workaday skirt. So I bought a coral silk shantung number with spaghetti straps and a fitted silhouette—my Yes Dress. I've been in ministry and practiced yoga long enough to show some shoulder.

Yet even as I intellectualized and distanced myself from all I knew about the historical and ongoing mistreatment of women, I also knew that intellectual defensiveness is the worst kind of quietism. You can put your head in the sand, but pretty soon the tide will shift and take the sand away.

Sadly, the more I have learned, the more I have come to believe that religions are irredeemably patriarchal. And if you are of even moderate intelligence, there is no way to dodge the fact: it is in the sacred texts of world religions that we find the most ardent support for injustices against women. It is true—and worthwhile—that feminist scholars have developed literary critical approaches to scripture in the hope of reclaiming and reappropriating the narratives for contemporary women. But not all the reclaiming and reappropriating in the world can root out where the problem begins. It begins with the Bible itself and the relentless anonymity of the women portrayed in both the Hebrew and Greek testaments.

Even apart from the stories in which women are abused or belittled, it's by virtue of their namelessness that the women in these stories are easy to marginalize or forget.

And in some of the stories—stories not fit for Sunday School—they are painful to remember.

Jephthah's daughter, for example, is largely forgotten. Maybe she is forgotten because she had no name. But it may also be that her story is just too sad.

Of course, Jephthah's daughter's story is not as gruesome as that of the Levite's concubine—also unnamed for reasons having to do with her insignificance. Her story, as well as that of Jephthah's daughter, is in the Hebrew book of Judges.

The Levite's concubine's story goes like this: A Levite living far off in the hill country of Ephraim has taken a concubine from Bethlehem. Concubines were legal wives but of inferior status, used chiefly for sexual pleasure. After a while and for reasons unknown, the Levite's concubine runs away from him and returns to her father's house. One translation says merely that she becomes angry with her husband, another says she "prostitute[s] herself against" him and that is why she left him, perhaps to avoid the punishment, which, according to Mosaic law, would have been death, perhaps by stoning or burning.

In any case, the Levite, loathe to lose his valuable property, travels to her father's house, where he and his concubine achieve some kind of peace. They remain with the father a few days, leaving to go home in the afternoon of the fifth day. But they only make it as far as Gibeah before night falls.

A hospitable old man returning from his work in the fields offers to look after their every need, and so they accompany him to his house.

It's at this point that trouble begins. The townsmen, "a perverse lot," come to the old man's house demanding that he send the Levite out to them so that they may have their way with him. The old man is determined to protect the Levite at all costs.

Being a generous man, he offers the crowd his virgin daughter to do with as they please. He also offers them the Levite's concubine. Two women ought to be the equal of one man.

But apparently they are not, for the townsmen refuse the old man's offer. Perhaps they are only hungry for the Levite's fair flesh.

Finally, in a last-ditch effort to save his own skin from sexual assault, the Levite himself casts his concubine into the street. Because the concubine is, first and foremost, a piece of property and a sexual object, it may not have troubled him that she will be subjected to gang anal and vaginal rape. Perhaps it seemed logical to him that she might satisfy the lusts of the crowd because she has been serving his own lust. And indeed, though she may be a poor substitute for the male flesh of the Levite, the townsmen decide she is better than nothing.

They wantonly raped her and abused her all through the night until the morning, the ancient text reads.

They let her go at sunrise, beaten and torn. With what strength she still has, she crawls back to the house of her host and collapses at the front door, clutching the threshold with her hands.

Sometime later, when day has fully broken, the Levite awakens and determines it is high time to head home. But as he opens the door to leave, he finds his concubine lying in a dirty heap at his feet.

"Get up," he says, "we are going."

But she doesn't move a muscle. She cannot obey him. Nor could she defy him even if she wanted to. Even his commands cannot awaken her. Because she is dead.

Angered at the loss of his property, the Levite slings his concubine's ruined body across his donkey and starts his journey home. As he rides, he tries to figure out the best course of action to take. *Something* has to be done. He has had a close call with the unnaturally lustful townsmen of Gibeah. The only way to spare *himself* was to appease *them*. He was more than generous in giving them his concubine. But look at what they did! How they insulted him! Of what use is his concubine to him now?

He returns to the hill country of Ephraim, an outraged man with an outrageous plan—a plan that makes *The Godfather's* severed horse's head look tame.

When he had entered his house, there he took a knife and grasping his concubine he cut her into twelve pieces limb by limb and sent her throughout all the territory of Israel.

Then he commanded the men whom he sent saying "has such a thing ever happened since the day the Israelites came up from Egypt until this day? Consider it and take counsel and speak out."

—Judges 19:29–30

That's exactly what the Israelites do. His hatchet job produces the effect he desires. War ensues.

The eighteenth-century Calvinist Matthew Henry writes of this story in *Commentary on the Whole Bible:*

In the miserable end of this woman, we may see the righteous hand of God punishing her for her former uncleanness, when she played the whore against her husband. Though her father had countenanced her, her husband had forgiven her, and the fault was forgotten now that the quarrel was made up, yet God remembered it against her when he suffered these wicked men thus wretchedly to abuse her; how unrighteous soever they were in their treatment of her, in permitting it the Lord was righteous. Her punishment answered her sin, . . . Lust was her sin, and lust was her punishment. By the law of Moses she was to have been put to death for her adultery. She escaped that punishment from men, yet vengeance pursued her; for, if there was no king in Israel, yet there was a God in Israel, a God that judgeth in the earth.

~

Being turned into a pillar of salt seems a mild outcome in comparison. That's what happened to Lot's wife, who also doesn't have a name. The reason she was turned into a pillar of salt is that she disobeyed God. In defiance of God's command, she turned back to look at the burning city of Sodom, their home, from which God had granted them permission to flee—Lot, his wife, and their two daughters.

They had been given this dispensation by God because, among all the men in Sodom, Lot was the only good guy. Why do we know he was a good guy? Because of the following story in Genesis, which is supposed to convince of his radical hospitality to visitors:

Two visitors, "angels," the text says, arrive in Sodom. Lot opens his house to them so they will not have to spend the night in the town square, prey to the rapacious instincts of the townsmen. Anyway, then Lot—though probably not Lot *himself*—prepares an ample feast for them, and they eat and drink. But before they can even get to the brandy and cigars, the townsmen, just like the townsmen from Gibeah, surround Lot's house. They bang at his door. *Bring the men out to us that we may know them*, they cry. And it's all Lot can do to squeeze out the front door and entreat them to consider a possible alternative: his virgin daughters. He says:

I beg you, my brothers, do not act so wickedly. Look, I have two daughters who have not known a man; let me bring them out to you and do to them as you please; only do nothing to these men for they have come under the shelter of my roof.

—Genesis 19:7–8

Apparently there wasn't much in the way of shelter beneath Lot's roof for Lot's daughters, though. They only escape being gang-raped because the townsmen don't want them. Maybe the daughters were just real Plain Janes—in any case, describing them this way, however demeaning, is as much of a name as they have ever had.

~

In the New Testament, you hear it said all the time that women played large roles in the ministry of Jesus. And yet if we really think about these women, an awful lot of them do not have names. We know some of them, of course: there's Mary, Jesus's mother, more lauded for being a virgin than for being one of the bravest of her son's followers, going all the way to the foot of the cross with him even after the disciples fled in fear. There's Mary's cousin Elizabeth, who gave birth to John the Baptist and gave companionship and support to Mary during her pregnancy.

There are Martha and Mary, the two women we routinely stereotype—Martha as the household drudge resentfully doing all the housework and Mary as the faithful, and probably prettier, one because she sits at Jesus's feet. In Hollywood, they might be played by Kathy Bates and Scarlett Johansson, respectively.

And there's Mary Magdalene. She is always assumed to be the woman taken in adultery. But there's no scriptural support for that. Not a shred. In fact, it was Pope Gregory the Great, in a famous sixth-century sermon, who allowed as to how Mary Magdalene *might* have been that morally impure "city woman" in Luke who is described as "a sinner." But the blame cannot be laid on Pope Gregory alone. Even though there is not an iota of textual evidence for the idea that Mary Magdalene gained her reputation in the streets of the city, people have long associated her with either this story or the woman taken in adultery in the gospel of John. You see, it was simply easier to believe that Mary Magdalene was a whore than to believe that she was a partner in Jesus's ministry—that she was in fact another disciple and, not incidentally, the first witness to the story of the resurrection (which the disciples, we are told in the gospel of Luke, thought was an "idle tale").

In addition to these named women, there are a few others—Anna, the widowed prophet who spends all her time serving at the temple; Salome, who stood at the foot of the cross with Mary; and Tabitha, whom Peter raised from her deathbed.

But many of the significant women in Jesus's ministry are merely nameless. As a Sunday School student, I had to learn all the names of the disciples, including their alternate names—Nathanael, who was also Bartholomew; Jude, who was also Thaddeus; Simon, who became Peter or Cephas. When I was in high school, I taught Sunday School. Just as I had had to learn the disciples' names, I insisted that my young charges did too. But even though it was easy enough to think of many women who played significant roles in Jesus's ministry, there was no way to memorize their names. They simply didn't have any.

For example, there's the aforementioned "city woman" who appears in gospels of both Mark and Luke. We're told she's a sinner and that she enters the house where Jesus is eating with some Pharisees, religiously observant Jews. Coming into the room, she kneels at Jesus's feet, bathing his feet with her tears, drying them with her hair, and anointing them with oil. The Pharisees are outraged, but in Luke's gospel, Jesus tells them:

> *Do you see this woman? I entered your house; you gave me no water for my feet, but she has bathed my feet with her tears and dried them with her hair. You gave me no kiss, but from the time I came in she has not stopped kissing my feet. You did not anoint my head with oil, but she has anointed my feet with ointment. Therefore, I tell you, her sins, which were many have been forgiven; hence she has shown great love. But the one to whom little is forgiven loves little.*

—Luke 7:44–47

Stories similar to that of the sinful woman in Luke appear in Matthew, Mark, and John. And in both Mark and Matthew's versions, Jesus is so moved by her humble tenderness that he issues a prophetic declaration. "Truly I tell you, wherever the good news is proclaimed in the whole world, what she has done will be told in remembrance of her."

This woman of great love and humility whose presence gave the occasion for one of Jesus's strongest statements should surely be worthy of a feast day! But we don't even have a name by which to remember her.

Nor can we name the Samaritan woman at the well in John's gospel. She has come to draw water at a time of day when women were permitted to go to the well. It was there that she saw Jesus. He wasn't supposed to talk to her—she was both a woman *and* a Samaritan, making her doubly unclean. But he does talk to her. He tells her to go get her husband, and he will give her living water, presumably meaning the water of baptism.

I have no husband, she tells him.

Jesus insists otherwise, telling her what she already knows: that she has had five husbands. "And the one you have now is *not* your husband," Jesus adds. Or perhaps he says, "The one you have now is not *your* husband." Either sentence is laden with judgment.

But her shame is trumped by her astonishment at his knowledge. If he can know such things about her, then he is no mere man—and nothing at all like the five husbands she herself has known. She is astonished, but she thinks she knows who he might be. So she rushes off to invite the people of the city: "Come and see a man who told me everything I have ever done! He cannot be the Messiah, can he?" And, we are told, many in the city believe because of her testimony. And yet the one who called others cannot be called by name.

The Syrophoenician woman who appears in both Matthew and Mark's gospels also has no name. Not only her gender but her religion too bespeak her unworthiness. Her people are infidels, enemies of the Jews. It is they who, a hundred years earlier, sacrificed a pig on the Jewish high altar.

So this woman is some crazy combination of brave and foolish when she kneels at Jesus's feet and begs him to heal her little daughter. His response is harsh, sarcastic. *It is unfair to take the children's food and throw it to the dogs*, he says—"dogs" a racial slur for her kind of people. He's making it clear that the good news Jesus brings is for the worthy children of Israel, not for infidel Syrophoenicians.

But the woman will not be silenced. On her knees at Jesus's feet, she ventures to argue with the master. Why does she act so brazenly? Or is she simply desperate to help her daughter? Is she aggrieved enough to correct Christ? Absolutely. She loves her child. I can completely understand her boldness.

"Even dogs under the table eat the children's crumbs that fall to them," she says to him pointedly, maybe even a little archly. And with that, Jesus is persuaded. "'Woman, great is your faith!' he says, 'Let it be done for you as you wish.' And her daughter was healed instantly."

But there is no name for this woman, who, with her words, widened the mind of Christ.

~

Now we come back at last to Jephthah's daughter, probably the most forgotten woman in both Hebrew and Greek scripture. And while the Levite's concubine's story is compellingly brutal, Jephthah's daughter's story is wrenchingly sad.

Jephthah himself ended up as a mighty warrior for the Lord. But it hadn't always been like that. He had had a troubled childhood. He was his father's son by a harlot, and he skipped town after his half-brothers stole his inheritance. He joined with a band of outlaws and earned his reputation as a bad-ass dude raiding the countryside. Word got around of his willingness to take on anybody. So when the Ammonites threatened war on Israel, Jephthah's half-brothers came calling, promising to make him their leader if he would just come and help them fight.

The stakes were high: Jephthah had an old family score to settle. So, just like the old hymn advises, Jephthah takes it to the Lord in prayer.

And Jephthah made a vow to the Lord, *and said, "If you will give the Ammonites into my hand, then whoever comes out of the doors of my house to meet me, when I return victorious from the Ammonites, shall be the* Lord's, *to be offered up by me as a burnt-offering."*

—Judges 11:30–31

Jephthah's vow exemplifies the maxim "Be careful what you ask for."

Because of course Jephthah defeats the Ammonites, and word of his success spreads throughout the area. And as the victorious warrior returns home from battle, the very first person he sees is his daughter. She is rushing out to meet him, her brave warrior father. She is playing music with her finger cymbals and dancing for joy. Father is home from the war!

But just as she grips him in a welcome-home hug, Jephthah remembers his vow to the Lord. Suddenly be begins to tear at his clothing and to shout at his daughter:

Alas, my daughter! You have brought me very low; you have become the cause of great trouble to me. For I have opened my mouth to the Lord and I cannot take back my vow.

—Judges 11:35b

I imagine the look of fear and confusion on Jephthah's daughter's face. I imagine that her mother, following her down the road to greet her husband, hears his words and falls to her knees. I imagine that, contrary to what the story tells us next, horror and heartbreak follow.

But the story goes on mildly, as if a death sentence hasn't just been issued:

She said to him, "My father, if you have opened your mouth to the Lord, do to me according to what has gone out of your mouth, now that the Lord has given you vengeance against your enemies, the Ammonites."

And she said to her Father, "Let this thing be done for me: grant me two months so that I may go and wander on the mountains and bewail my virginity, my companions and I."

"Go," he said and sent her away for two months. So she departed, she and her companions, and bewailed her virginity on the mountains.

At the end of two months she returned to her father, who did with her according to the vow he had made. She had never slept with a man.

—Judges 11:36–39a

That last line haunts me. Because this is the climax of the story, it becomes clear to us that our takeaway from the story is not supposed to be that Jephthah's nameless daughter died a martyr to her father's vanity, a martyr without the legacy of her own name. Rather, what we are told makes this story a tragedy is that she had never slept with a man.

But the chilling fact that she—and so many other biblical women— had no name to be remembered by?

That is of no importance.

⁓

But of course it is of vital importance. Particularly because there continue to be so many nameless and marginalized women in our contemporary world: nameless mothers who have no food to give their children or access to pre- or postnatal care, nameless women denied contraception, nameless women who have lost their husbands and sons in civil warfare and religious warfare and guerrilla warfare in country after country, nameless women and girls sold in the sex trade or sexually abused and then shunned by their communities for no longer being pure, nameless girls denied education, forced into early and abusive marriages, nameless women within our own communities who live with abusive partners.

Several years ago my sister Jackie discovered Woman to Woman International, which, among other things, creates sponsorships between first-world women and women in Iraq and other countries, helping them to become more financially self-sufficient. As my Christmas present that year, Jackie sponsored an Iraqi woman in my name. Only shortly after that, the organization sent word that letters were not to be exchanged. The sponsor was not to know the address of the Iraqi woman. The sponsor could not even know her *name*. It would not be safe for her if she were known by name. And so the woman my sister paid to sponsor remains nameless and unknown by the one in whose name she was being supported. Which means I never knew how or even *if* she was supported. I never knew her fate. I never knew anything about her.

Names provide both identity and power. In the second version of the creation story in Genesis, God brings all the creatures of creation before Adam:

So out of the ground the Lord God formed every animal of the field and every bird of the air, and brought them to the man to see what he would call them; and whatever the man called each living creature, that was its name. The man gave names to all cattle, and to the birds of the air, and to every animal of the field.

—Genesis 2:19–20a

It is a naive fancy on my part to want to go back to the Hebrew and Greek scriptures and identify that half of humanity so routinely denied identity even as they form the stories that comprise Judeo-Christian mythology. But it keeps me mindful that there are other women, women living now, whose needs must be made known and met and whose names must be learned and spoken.

10

Press Junket Christians

Stand up, stand up for Jesus, the trumpet call obey;
Forth to the mighty conflict, in this His glorious day.
Ye that are brave now serve Him against unnumbered foes;
Let courage rise with danger, and strength to strength oppose.

—George Duffield Jr. (1818–1888)

At the airport newsstand, I pick up a bottle of water and a copy of *Newsweek*. There's a US flag–wrapped cross on its cover and articles on politics and Christianity inside. My kind of reading material, I think to myself grimly. I bring them to the counter and set them in front of the cashier, who rings them up.

"You *sure* that's all you want?" he asks me with a playful smile.

"Yeah," I say, "You got the water, right?"

"Yeah," he says, "But—you *sure* that's all you want?"

"That's all!" I force a little smile.

"So you're *really* ready to have me ring you up?"

"I am." I keep my smile on. He doesn't seem like a creep. But I don't understand his playfulness. What's so funny?

"O-*kay!*" he pushes a button and the total, six dollars and sixty-six cents, appears on the LED screen. "You owe me six-six-six!" he says and chuckles, "The mark of the Beast!"

Glad he has a sense of humor, I thought. That beats a self-proclaimed end-times prophet by a damn sight. I handed him a twenty.

"And I owe you . . . *thirteen* dollars and thirty-four cents." He hands me my change.

"*Great,*" I say, chuckling with him.

"Hey, don't worry," he says. "I'm only playing around. After all, you're only going to *fly* in a *plane* on *Election Day!*"

"Lucky me," I say to him.

And to some extent I am lucky. Because it may be Election Day 2006, and I may be about to fly in a plane—not my favorite activity—into Washington, DC. But I've gotten an upgrade to first class for both my trip down to help a friend's elderly mother in Florida and for the trip back, so I'm feeling a little bit excited about the prospect of air travel. During my maiden voyage among the privileged, I discovered the real reason to like first-class flying. It's not the roomier seats or the pillow and blankets. It's not even the tasty snacks, although I ate more than my share of high-end potato chips on the way down. It's the wine. They let you have a glass before takeoff. And just before that sexy/scary moment when the plane rattles down the runway so fast you think you'll either have an orgasm or a panic attack, they come and take away your empty plastic cup so nothing will fly around and stain your business suits.

But then a few minutes later, right after you've finished saying your frantic prayers—*please God, let us not crash on takeoff*—and the plane has reached cruising altitude, those angels of mercy return. *Chardonnay, wasn't it? Yes, thank you. Thanks so much.* It's snacks and wine the whole way, which is a very fine thing for a fearful flyer like me.

Boarding begins. Everybody files into the plane and stows their carry-ons. Normally when I fly I'm on the lookout for terrorists. Now that I've been upgraded, I'm on the lookout for celebrities. Terrorists don't fly first class.

And soon enough I see one. It's not George Clooney, but it will have to do.

It's Charles Colson, and he is speaking to one of the flight attendants in a resonant voice. He's tall, and she is smiling up at him. His wife is tall too. She's white-haired and bulky, kind of masculine. She wears a bright red jacket with a large pin of the American flag on the lapel.

He wears an American flag lapel pin too. Charles Colson. One of the Watergate Seven, Nixon's hatchet man. He was a hawk, a staunch supporter of the Vietnam War and of Richard Nixon. He authorized the firebombing of Daniel Ellsberg's psychiatrist's office and the theft of the Pentagon Papers. Even I had heard about all that, although I was still reading Nancy Drew mysteries when Watergate stories were flooding the media. Chuck Colson was the man Hunter S. Thompson described as "the guiding light behind Nixon's whole arsenal of illegal, immoral, unethical 'dirty tricks' department."

Then, shortly after he was convicted, Chuck Colson found Jesus. People made fun of him, saying he had converted because he thought he would get a lighter sentence. And sure enough, he only served seven months.

But now we are preparing for takeoff. Now the airline attendant is demonstrating proper oxygen mask usage. I watch with trepidation, always certain that, should I ever need to use one, I'll be unable to make it work. I'm just not good at handicraft. Next she's showing us where the flotation devices and emergency exits are. And soon we're rumbling and bumping down the runway, my heart pumping along with the speed of it all. Then the landing gear thuds into place and we're off the ground and climbing. I don't like the climbing part. I rifle through articles in *Newsweek* but mostly focus on the pictures. There's a two-page spread showing a spectrum of American conservative evangelical leaders, their male faces lined up side by side in a left-page-to-right-page progression from less conservative to most conservative. And lo and behold, there is Chuck Colson's smiling face far to the right on the right-hand page.

Just then the plane gives a serious jolt, and the pilot comes over the loudspeaker giving us details about the weather here and at our destination. She tells us it will be a pretty bumpy ride for most of the flight. There are storms along the coastline all the way to Washington. Now that I am supplied with that information, I don't hesitate when the flight attendant comes by at cruising altitude. I order some white wine. White wine at midday seems less of a commitment to alcoholic degeneration than red wine does.

I get to thinking about Jesus, which is something I do a lot on planes because I tend to pray a lot on them. The truth is, I don't like a lot of his followers. Maybe we are all laboring in the same vineyard, but it's a vineyard of varying microclimates, and we are harvesting different kinds of grapes. And that's me being metaphorically generous.

Take Chuck Colson, for example.

Apparently he really had been serious about turning his life over to God. When he got out of prison he started an advocacy ministry for inmates, and he donated all of his profits from lectures and books to the prison ministry. But politics must have been his first love because he couldn't keep his religion out of it. In his columns for the conservative journal *Christianity Today* and in his public speaking, he inveighed against same-sex marriage, evolution, and abortion and advocated moral absolutism and intelligent design. He was one of the drafters of the Manhattan Declaration, wherein he called for evangelicals, Catholics, and Orthodox Christians to oppose with vigor rules and laws permitting abortion, same-sex marriage, and other matters that go against their religious consciences. In October 2002, he was a cosigner, along with four other prominent evangelical leaders, of a letter sent to President George Bush outlining their support for a preemptive invasion of Iraq.

Charles Colson understood himself to be a man of God. And yet I can't square that resumé of political action with love of God, even though I know that the language of war pervades sermons and hymns. George Duffeld's bathetic nineteenth-century hymn is a potent example:

> *Stand up, stand up for Jesus, ye soldiers of the cross*
> *Lift high his royal banner; it must not suffer loss.*
> *From victr'y unto victr'y his army shall he leadeth,*
> *Till every foe is vanquished and Christ is Lord indeed.*

And it occurs to me that Charles Colson, flying into DC on Election Day wearing his American flag lapel pin, is probably going there to give some kind of speech about something. Somebody will write an article about it. There will be photo opportunities, maybe a television or radio interview. He's yet another news-making Christian. I look down at my magazine and at the smiling male faces of the conservative evangelical leaders aligned across the pages.

~

I wonder all the time about how people get their news. There's lots of news to get, after all, lots of sources telling us the stories of the world. And in the last thirty years, conservative evangelical Christians have been more and more making news, telling us what they believe, what we should believe, how we should vote, and what politicians, programs and points of view we should endorse and which we should eschew.

Conservative historian Bruce Shelley has written a serviceable and readable one-volume book titled *Church History In Plain Language*. But when he discusses the last few decades of Christianity, his approbation of the political rise of the religious right bleeds through:

> *The passion of the Religious Right lay in their perception that the United States was falling under the influence of secular humanism and that traditional family values were under attack in the media and the public schools. . . . To counter the agenda of the cultural left, the Religious Right preached, promoted, and marched against abortion, the Equal Rights Amendment, homosexuality, pornography, and the increased government involvement in education and welfare.* (p. 477)

From the Moral Majority to Promise Keepers, from the Christian Coalition to faith-based initiatives, it's pretty clear that the religious right is at home with political activism. Organized, well funded, and well connected, most of these efforts have had success with at least some, if not all of their goals. But all the organized political activism in the world wouldn't make a difference without a strong media presence to advance the cause. With the rise of the religious right has come a concomitant growth in Christian media outlets. Conservative evangelicals know that they have to be news makers if they're to spread the word about their convictions. So it is little wonder that they have built and continue to proliferate a media empire, seizing on all the different avenues for furthering their missionary reach. Advances in Web technology have provided yet another mission tool and only continue to further outreach with the growth of social media.

The Christian Broadcasting Network alone, founded in 1960 by Pat Robertson, is an evangelical Christian television network with programs and content translated into 42 languages and broadcast to 136 countries. *It garners nearly $300,000 in revenues.* Its mission statement is indicative: "CBN is a global, nonprofit ministry preparing the nations of the world for the second coming of Jesus Christ through media, prayer partnering, and humanitarian aid." And a visit to its Web site reveals the many ways that its programs, blogs, ministries, merchandise, and opportunities for giving advance this mission.

The use of media by religious groups is a growing phenomenon but scarcely a new trend. There is a long tradition in this country of fringe Christian fundamentalists using media to articulate their positions, to warn their adherents of the earthly dangers surrounding them, to name their enemies, and to mobilize them for defense.

A chilling example is *The Defender Magazine*, founded in 1926 by anti-Semitic and Christian fundamentalist preacher Gerald Winrod. The magazine was an outgrowth of his anti-evolutionary group, Defenders of the Christian Faith, and a venue for Winrod's racist and anti-Semitic views. Winrod himself believed that the "Jewish menace" to the American way of life was pandemic and that we might do well to look to abroad to Germany for guidance in dealing with it. By 1934—a year after Hindenburg named Adolf Hitler chancellor of Germany—*The Defender* had a subscription base of well over a hundred thousand readers.

Fellow Christian patriot—if we want to call him that—Lewis Ulrey wrote this for Winrod's *The Defender*:

Into this bedlam and chaos in Germany Adolf Hitler injected himself as a new messiah to lead orderly Germany from political confu-

sion to systematic unity. Hitler put it up to the Germans to decide between the Jewish ownership and domination of the country or domination and ownership by the ninety nine percent of the German population. Human nature being what it is, it is not strange that the Germans decided against the Jews and in favor of Hitler.

Carl McIntyre came along a little later in the century. A preacher who had seceded from mainline Presbyterianism to form the Bible Presbyterian Church, he later joined forces with Joseph McCarthy's anti-communist crusade. And, like Winrod, MacIntyre founded a magazine, *The Christian Beacon*, and was tireless in his prolific production of books, pamphlets, sermons, and tracts.

In the 1950s he started a daily, thirty-minute radio program called *The Twentieth Century Reformation Hour*. During this program he disseminated his militant fundamentalism, attacking communism, socialized medicine, fluoridation of water, and sex education. He took a hard—which is to say, damning—line against all Christians who did not subscribe to his theology. Liberal clergy were a particular focus. Though these men (they were all men then) might have seemed like your average Christian Joe, they were in truth "atheistic, communistic, Bible-ridiculing, blood-despising, name-calling, sex-manacled sons of green-eyed monsters."

Imagine that!

Luckily—providentially?—a kinder, gentler form of outreach was just around the corner. As technology developed, so did the opportunity to reach out to the scattered flock through better and better broadcast media. And so the more fanatic right-wing fringe gave way to a more reasoned and reasonable Christian polemic.

Oral Roberts, Billy Graham, and Rex Hubbard were pioneers in the 1950s, featuring Sunday broadcasts of a more or less traditional church format. By the 1970s there were actual Christian networks with programming expanded well beyond that of televised church services. Jim Bakker's PTL (Praise the Lord) network and Pat Robertson's Christian Broadcasting Network created a loyal viewing audience. After the sexual and financial scandals of the televangelists in the 1980s, viewership declined, but not terrifically so.

The offspring of these pioneering televangelists are alive and well, I hear, on Sunday mornings. Because on Sunday mornings I am usually in church, I do not get—or am maybe spared—the chance to hear them.

Christian radio seems unavoidable, though. Twist up and down your dial no matter where you are driving, and you'll find Southwest Radio Church with Dr. N. W. Hutchings's genuinely grating voice, *The Bible Answer Man* with Hank Hanegraaf, *Let My People Think* with Ravi Zacharias, *Renewing Your Mind* with R. C. Sproul, or that perennial gold standard of Christian programming, *Focus on the Family*, founded by Dr. James Dobson.

There are hundreds of radio stations and Web sites with a range of formats: Christian newscasts, talk shows, call-in shows, and music programming that runs the gamut from oldtimey hymns to heavy metal, with a lot of white-bread praise music in between.

The production values vary a lot. The theologies not so much: God is a male presence who demands our total commitment and obedience. Because we are incapable of fulfilling that requirement, we have to rely solely on the saving work of Jesus recorded in the Bible, the writings of which are ably opened up for our spiritual edification and sanctification by knowledgeable pastors. So it is often pastors who use the Bible in the service of promoting political activism. And perhaps what is most stunning is the certainty on the part of many religious leaders on the right. They are certain in their opposition to abortion, the funding of birth control, and the unquestionable sinfulness of homosexuality. They are certain in their views on marriage, creationism, and the need to support Israel, no matter what. I sometimes wonder if they ever remember that even the disciples had questions. They weren't so certain of everything. They had fears. They had doubts. None had answers.

But answers can be marketed, can be turned into political movements. Answers force people to action even when both the answer and the action it elicits are, to many progressive Christian views, incompatible with Jesus's very teachings.

Chris Hedges, author of *American Fascists: The Religious Right and the War on America,* recounts how, a quarter-century ago, his Harvard Divinity School professor, Dr. James Luther Adams predicted that fascism would return not wearing brown shirts and arm bands but cloaked in the language of the Bible, carrying crosses and chanting the Pledge of Allegiance.

It's a chilling image, perhaps an extreme one. But over the years, the public perception of what it means to be Christian has changed, and from my perspective as a Christian progressive, it has changed in frightening ways.

∼

When I was growing up or at least going through my adolescence, it was not *cool* to be Christian. To be Christian meant being nerdy, unstylish, judgmental. I *was* Christian—I remained active in the church until I went away to college. I'd never felt that I was having anything that could vaguely have been termed a "faith crisis," but I was always a little embarrassed about my Christianity.

Because, like everybody else my age, I wanted to be cool. And even though he had a beard and wore sandals just like the Beatniks my older sister—and therefore, I—loved, Jesus never struck me as particularly cool or even particularly memorable apart from the appalling horrors of Holy Week. The Jesus I met in church was sort of like my pastor, affably chuckling at potluck suppers, eating his way through years of ham and scalloped potatoes, and telling little girls they couldn't become pastors.

But by the time I got to seminary I was developing a whole different understanding of what it meant to be Christian. Christians still weren't cool, but they *were* compassionate.

The ones I knew—and I was one of them—were concerned about social justice. We protested apartheid in Namibia, boycotted diamonds from South Africa. We talked about ways of promoting economic justice and inclusiveness for women, people of color, and the disabled—gay rights was not yet even on the table for discussion. We studied liberation theology and feminist theology and what it meant to say that the gospel was good news particularly tailored for those who lived in poverty. It was "the preferential option for the poor." We believed in the need for dialogue among religious traditions, divestment as a tool for social change, diplomatic alternatives to warfare and violence, and better stewardship of creation.

And we tried to live simply and with integrity, staying aware of political and economic realities that affected all strata of society.

This way of being a Christian was more about being full of compassion and conviction and less about being mired in the status quo and conventional thinking. So in a sense I came to feel that it was as cool to be a socially engaged Christian as it was also to be a socially engaged Jew, as many of my friends were (and are). After all, I learned from my Jewish friends and not from the Lutheran church of my childhood the Hebrew phrase *tikkun olam*—which means to try to heal the world.

This has been more or less my view of things for the last twenty-odd years. But the truth is that in the latter part of the last century, one very public expression of Christianity has been morphing, changing into something that I often don't recognize. Certainly there has been an increasing prolapse of evangelical Christianity and conservative politics so that more and more they come to be seen as one and the same.

And that leads to significant repercussions for two very significant sections of our culture. For those who are politically conservative but not Christian, this can be confusing because it violates one of the most fundamental aspects of a conservative political outlook: that religious affiliation and conviction has no place infiltrating governmental structures and beginning to dictate a public religiously inflected morality. The free market includes the free market of ideas as well, and for political conservatism to become inextricably linked to Christianity is to hamstring that very sense of a free market.

And for progressive Christians, to see Christianity being co-opted into a right-wing political ideology is to watch the evisceration of Jesus's central teaching of compassion and action-based witness on behalf of those less fortunate. For progressive Christians—and that term certainly describes the congregations I've served over the years—trying to figure out what kind of Christians we are has grown to be an important undertaking. Just in the course of my lifetime, as the religious right has become a greater presence in American life and culture, identifying oneself as Christian becomes increasingly problematic. And so progressive Christians need more and more to find a more prominent media voice, a more public way of advancing an identity of "Christian" that isn't some version of a conservative political agenda.

And we don't really do that very well. It sometimes seems that Christian progressives have trouble even *identifying* goals. Sure, we serve soup at the soup kitchens. We vote to be welcoming and inclusive to persons of all sexual orientations. We send student groups to help out after hurricanes. We fight malaria and drink shade-grown, fairly traded coffee.

But we don't do a lot of the kind of organized political lobbying for gay rights, reproductive rights, economic justice, and all the other worthy concerns we end up mostly paying lip service to. We hew to the separation of church and state. And we don't make waves in the news.

And thanks to our country's commitment to the separation of church and state, freedom of religion is our private right and not a mandated civil imperative, of course. But the increased use of the media by religious groups and the corollary response by the media to this phenomenon make clear that, while church and state may maintain their separation, the free market doesn't have to. Religion is news now; it's public discourse. Covering religiously driven political events and entertainments no longer remains a sectarian enterprise; such coverage has become central to what people believe Christianity is all about. Progressive Christians just don't have the media presence that evangelicals do.

When I started writing a column for an alternative newsweekly twenty years ago, I did so because I wanted to see a progressive, openly religious voice in an independent media outlet. And I'm pretty sure that not every alternative newspaper would have taken on a Christian as a columnist—and maybe with some good reason. I'm grateful that my editor had the wisdom to do so. And my express aim in writing the Reckonings columns was to thwart some stereotypical-but-with-grounds views of Christians as judgmental Bible thumpers, right-wing moralists, pro-war wags, or government infiltrators.

Because I know that what we hear and see and read about the world will almost always come to us secondhand, from some kind of reporter's perspective, and filtered through some kind of bias. (That is, after all, how we get the stories about Jesus in the gospels—secondhand told by writers, each of whom was advancing a slightly different agenda for faith in Christ.) I wanted to have whatever small voice I could in making sure that conservative evangelical voices were not the only ones in the public discourse on what it means to live as a person of faith.

And here's a little vignette about why progressive Christians need to be both more public and more aware of how Christianity is portrayed in the media.

I have always complained about how, when the local media want to get an "official Christian" opinion on something, they always contact the more conservative churches. I guess I must have written about this in a Reckonings column at one point because in 2005 I got an e-mail from a reporter, Tanisha Mallet, at my local ABC affiliate informing me that the next time an issue came up, she would be happy to interview me or some other more progressive Christian clergy in order to feature a more diverse—and therefore more accurate—picture of what differing Christians believe.

"Great," I wrote back. "Thank you."

Then, a few months later, I got a phone call. Massachusetts had just legalized same-sex marriage. Would I be willing to have a reporter and a photographer come to my house and talk with me about that momentous event?

"Certainly," I said.

Like any press-junket Christian spokesperson, I immediately started planning what to wear.

Well, the reporter and the photographer came out to my house on a gorgeous May day. We went into my backyard, where we set up a couple of chairs in front of what passes as my garden, and Tanisha began the interview. She asked intelligent questions; she appeared to be genuinely interested, and she certainly was well prepared. I felt very good about the experience. I have been interviewed before and have been asked stupid questions. I have been misquoted before. But I felt I was in good hands with Tanisha Mallet.

So that night my oldest daughter and I sat down to watch my moment in the sun. As the 11:00 news began, we heard a teaser about upcoming news stories: "Support for gay marriage from an unlikely source!"

"Hey, that's you, Mom!" Madeleine said.

"No, I don't think so, sweetheart," I said, "I don't think they would unilaterally characterize churches as unlikely sources for support of gay marriage. Or at least they wouldn't say that about me or about Grace Lutheran Church."

I wasn't just saying that for my daughter's benefit. I believed it. I guess it's astonishing how naive a grown woman can be.

The thing is, the interview started out brilliantly. Tanisha did a fine job throughout. She knew her stuff. The editing was smooth. Nothing I said was taken out of context. Even the yard looked sort of okay. But then, just as the interview was coming to a close, the camera pulled back from my face, dropped down, and panned in closely on the ring I was wearing.

It's a ring I still wear. It's a pretty ring—blue topaz with little pavé diamonds on either side of it. When I wear it, I put it on my right hand. It's something I bought for myself after my divorce. If you don't have a husband, you ought to at least be able to have a little jewelry, was my reasoning when I made the purchase. It wasn't a splurge, but it was a consolation.

But as Tanisha and I talked about gay marriage, the camera zoomed in on this ring that obviously was not your usual wedding ring setup— the marquise-cut-diamond-and-thin-gold band thing. Nevertheless, pictures being worth a thousand words and all that, the TV screen–sized image of that ring seemed to imply that it had some kind of "official meaning." Like maybe it was the kind of wedding ring a lesbian might choose to wear if she couldn't be legally married. I mean, what other reason could the cameraman have had for showing my ring? If you could see my hands, you'd know I'd never have made it as a hand model. And besides, this wasn't the home-shopping network!

Shortly after that gratuitous shot of my ring, the interview ended. And I felt, frankly, betrayed.

I am a heterosexual clergywoman who supports gay marriage, and I have performed and will perform both blessings and weddings of same-sex couples, even though there was not then, nor is there yet, an officially designated rite for such by the Evangelical Lutheran Church in America into which I was ordained. But by showing my ring, by the camera's subtle or maybe not-so-subtle hint was that I, myself, might be partnered in a same-sex union, and so why wouldn't I support a cause in which I had a personal stake? Tanisha Mallet's good work, my own stance as a heterosexual committed to gay rights, was misrepresented and its impact lessoned by virtue of a cameraman's choice to show rather than tell.

"Damn the media" is what I said to my daughter when the segment ended. "Damn them all."

But, just like conservative evangelicals, progressive Christians really need the media too.

11

Leaving the Body

Angels (they say) don't know whether it is the living
they are moving among or the dead.

—Rilke, *Duino Elegies*

The sheer incongruity between Miranda and the idea of "illness" was almost assurance enough that there couldn't be any serious concerns. Miranda, my massage therapist, was one of the most alive and embodied people I had ever known. She was petite, but she was a powerhouse with healing in her hands, an infectious smile, and boundless curiosity, all directed in the service of making life better for as many people as she could. Though I could only afford the occasional massage, I treated it as a kind of pilgrimage when I drove the ten or so miles to her house where she had her studio, a tranquil room with candles and crystal and greenery and a softly splashing fountain.

And over the years I was her client, Miranda had come to know my body well, the way a conscientious massage therapist does. Her fingers bore into my thick, clenched muscle and seemed to loosen its anxious hold on the bone. She knew how to work with my scoliotic spine, how to unknot the rhomboids deep beneath my scapulae. I yielded beneath the pressure. As she cradled my head in her hands for craniosacral rebalancing, my chattering mind fell silent.

So when her partner, later to be her husband, called to tell me that she'd had surgery, that she was in the hospital and would like me to visit, I was surprised. I was her client, not her pastor. Of course I would visit, I said. I thought I was going to see her as I would go see a friend.

Most people after surgery, look wan and wrung out. But I found Miranda sitting up in her hospital bed talking animatedly to her mother and her partner about this strange new odyssey of illness. It was another topic to explore, another terrain to traverse with attention to its landmarks. And when she saw me standing in the doorway, she called me over to hug her—her grip was strong and there was color in her face. Yet the surgery had only been two days earlier.

She explained what was going on: She'd had gas pains off and on for a while—nothing troubling, but no fun either. Then, inexplicably, she developed a bulging lower belly. She was fine boned and thin, very physically active. The potbelly didn't make any sense. That was when she called her doctor—reluctantly. She didn't have great health insurance and as a rule preferred homeopathic therapies. But he insisted on an immediate hysterectomy. As she put it, she had gone through menopause in the mere twinkling of an eye, just shy of age fifty. No more pesky perimenopause. How lucky is that?

Of course, Miranda didn't look sick. Instead, she looked as if she had jury-rigged a fake IV, put on one of those silly, ass-revealing gowns, and gone to sit in a hospital bed because somebody had dared her to do it. Any minute now, a doctor would come in and accuse her of fraudulently representing herself as a sick person. Then legal consequences would follow in short order. The Albany *Times Union* would run the story: "Massage Therapist Impersonates Cancer Patient."

Nevertheless, she went on with the real story.

It was ovarian cancer, she explained, and then the brightness faded from her eyes a little. Back then, I didn't know that ovarian cancer is one of the "bad" ones—as if there are any "good" ones. The statistics weren't great, she said. But both she and her doctor believed that her relative youth, her strength, her fitness, and the inner resources that those who loved her counted on would aid in what she seemed optimistic would be a full recovery. I had no reason to doubt her enthusiasm. She was a healer. She would be healed herself. I wasn't worried.

Miranda's mother and partner were beaming at her proudly. If anybody could beat this thing, she could. And for now, at least, the tumor and most of its terrors were out of her body. No more potbelly. No more periods.

～

Just six weeks after I had been called to serve Grace Lutheran Church, my mother died. She had been ill, but death itself had come suddenly and unexpectedly. What my sisters and I assumed was another short, routine hospitalization for a woman with emphysema turned out to be her final hospitalization. I had left her on a Tuesday night to go to a church council meeting, having had a wonderful conversation with her in which she was fully lucid and some blend of annoyed at being in the hospital and flattered by the attention of the male nurses—the prednisone she was taking making her, as it usually did when she required it, an amorous, redheaded seventy-nine-year-old.

By Wednesday morning her condition had changed. She lay silent and small in her hospital bed, fumbling and plucking out the oxygen tubes, which my sister Jackie and I would replace as we took turns sitting with her throughout the day. She was dying, we were told, even though just the day before a discharge planner had met with Jackie to discuss transferring her to a skilled nursing facility. But now she was dying. Throughout the day the family came to say good-bye. Jackie's husband, Alan, brought our sister Leslie to see her. Leslie, who'd lived with and relied on my mother for everything, would have a whole new, unknown life without my mother there to care for her.

Jackie's children came to say good-bye: the firstborn grandson, Jeffrey, her golden boy; then came Rachel, the first granddaughter on whom, as the mother of daughters, she doted; then came Christian, who, as the potentially last grandkid (my girls were born later), had been the recipient of my mother's great capacity to delight her young grandchildren.

Then my family came to say good-bye: my ex-husband, Joe, stood stoically at her bedside. I knew how much he feared hospitals and also how much he loved my mother. For her part, she never failed to let me know how much she regretted our divorce, which we often did ourselves. Our daughters, Madeleine and Linnea, then thirteen and nine, bravely leaned over the hospital bedrail to kiss Grammy good-bye, confused and hurt by the sorrow of death, knowing but unable to fully grasp, its finality.

Finally, as night fell, Jackie and I were alone with our mother. Alone, that is, except for my mother's pastor, who had been there all evening. We thought Steve would never leave. He had been a conscientious and caring pastor, and I think she had also served as his confidante in personal matters. Eventually we insisted he go home to his own family. We didn't say this to him, but we needed this private vigil. The nurse called housekeeping to bring us cots to sleep on, and as we each bedded down on either side of her bed, we wondered how many days and nights we would be there, midwives to our mother's death.

I woke early the next morning, seeing through the bedrails my mother's soft belly rising and falling, her belly in which I had lived and been formed and against which I had been cuddled as a child. She had not died while we were asleep. But now that we were awake, now that we stood next to her, holding her hands, stroking her face, telling her we loved her, she did. There were tears in her blue eyes as she died, and I like to think it was just a biological phenomenon of death and not sorrow that I was seeing. But I will never know. I wanted her to have a happy death as much as I had always wanted her to have a happy life, and I have never been sure of either.

～

When Jackie and I left the hospital later that morning, I knew what I had to do next: I had to plan my mother's funeral. I knew just how to do that. And I had to get back to work. I figured the congregation would give me support and sympathy while I mourned the loss of my mother—and they did. But I was following a long-term, much-beloved male pastor. I didn't feel there was any margin for error. I figured as a divorced, single-mother, female pastor, I had too many strikes against me to let grief over my mother's death slow me down.

I crafted my response to her loss with what I thought was an admirable sense of detachment and a levelheaded acceptance of the facts, keeping at bay the hurtful knowledge that all of what remained of the woman who had carried me into life was a cardboard box of ashes I kept on a shelf in my closet. So I grieved, but not immoderately. I cried, but not overmuch. I didn't miss a single Sunday's preaching. I had to show the congregation that I had very broad shoulders. That I could carry on, that I could carry it all.

Soon I was proud of the no-nonsense expediency with which I had handled the grief. All anybody needs is a good day planner and a will to soldier on, I thought. But for months afterward, each time I went for a massage something happened that I could not understand and could not control. Once I had climbed beneath the blankets on the warm massage table, Miranda would place a little pillow filled with lavender across my eyes. And within moments I would start to cry. These were silent tears—no little hiccoughs, no shaking shoulders. I just lay there and wept into the eye pillow in the perfectly private darkness of my well-suppressed mourning. I don't think Miranda ever even knew I was crying unless afterward she noticed that the eye pillow was wet. And I didn't know *why* I was crying. The losses I'd had in the past few years—the divorce, my mother's death—hadn't really been surprising. God shuts windows and then open doors and all of that crap I thought I should believe but didn't. So in one way the tears were a great mystery to me.

In another way, though, I knew what they were about. My brain had refused to give my sorrow shelter. It just didn't fit into the demands of my life, that sorrow. So my body had taken it into itself, stashing it in its secret safe boxes for existential hurt. Miranda's hands were releasing all that sorrow. My husband, who had once loved my body, was gone. My mother, who had known my body as no one else had, was gone. Miranda gave me the only kind of healing I needed, the touch that assured me my body still mattered.

And she knew my body the way a mother knows her child's body, which is such a different way from how a lover knows his lover's body.

The lover's hands are site specific and goal oriented. His eyes are selective. Breasts and belly and bottom and vulva—all destinations. A lover's touch is always aiming for the moment, the culmination, *la petite mort* of orgasm. And after that the lover's hands are less urgent. They no longer seek. They withdraw and fall to stillness. They are content with emptiness.

The lover doesn't linger over his lover's body. Not in the way a mother lingers over her child's body, knowing every fold of skin, the feel of every bone—having knitted them together within her own body. The mother knows the smooth swell of her child's calves, the velvety softness of her child's ear, the birthmark beneath the hair on the back of her child's neck. And all of it is dear to her. She has bathed and soothed and kissed all of it, and not one inch is more special than any other inch.

When she touches her child, she seeks nothing in return, no reciprocal gratification. Touch is its own reward. No one spot will feel better than another. She touches because for her the child's body is not the sum of contiguous parts but a whole wonder, the élan vital. Certainly that is how I felt about my children's bodies. And when I see images of the pietà—the Virgin Mother cradling the body of the crucified Christ—or the *Stabat Mater*—Mary standing at the foot of the cross—I am always so moved. It is as though the crucifixion were mirrored in her own body and magnified in her sorrow: because Jesus's body was one she knew the way only a mother can know the child's body.

And that was always how I felt when my body lay still beneath Miranda's knowing hands.

~

Miranda responded well to chemotherapy. She soon was able to go back to seeing clients and teaching at the massage school where she had trained. She traveled to Thailand to learn new massage techniques. She began to massage cancer patients. That was her real calling, she told me, to massage the bodies of people whose bodies were being stolen out from under them by cancer. Maybe that explained why she herself had developed cancer, she posited—to make this discovery. She wanted to find a reason. Or maybe she thought the universe—she didn't speak much in terms of God—really had given her cancer, that it was part of her intended journey and that she had much to learn from it. I never doubted that she would learn much from it. I just don't think God or the universe intends for us to suffer. Or, as Jesus is recorded as saying in Matthew, "Tomorrow will bring worries of its own."

Months passed, then a full year. I went for two or three massages. Sometimes I thought Miranda's touch was lighter than I remembered, as if she had lost some strength. But finally I decided it was my imagination.

Then one day after a massage she handed me the usual post-massage glass of ice water and mentioned that her doctor had discovered more cancer cells. It still wasn't that worrisome, she said, but she was going to need additional treatment. Her tone was light. She seemed concerned, but not worried. She explained that she trusted her oncologist; he was supportive of a variety of therapies, not just chemo and radiation. And she had a lot of support from her mother, her partner, and her sons. The bad thing was that she would have to stop teaching and giving massages for a while. Being sick was awfully time consuming, she told me. That alone was almost reason enough for kicking this thing.

More time passed, but I didn't see Miranda. I like to tell myself that it never even occurred to me to visit her, but that's not true. I thought about it, but I feared seeing her. So I rationalized reasons not to: we weren't social friends; I wasn't her pastor. It was *she* who ministered to me. The truth, of course, was much uglier than that. I didn't want to see her. It frightened me to see her so sick. It frightened me that she could die. It frightened me that she was only a few years older than I and she still had so much she wanted to do. If something like this could happen to her, could it also happen to me? So I didn't visit and didn't call out a sheer sense of cowardice.

Then one day she called me. She had some things she wanted to talk about. She wanted to come to my office.

I offered to drive out to her house, but she insisted on driving the forty-five minutes to the church. She said it felt good to drive. So when we next saw each other it was not in her studio—with me naked and grateful beneath my eye pillow and warm sheets—but in my office. She had never seen it before. There had never been any reason for her to.

I watched her walk from her car to my office door. She looked beautiful, not sick. She was too thin, but what woman doesn't want to be too thin? Her face was carefully made up and she had on a shining red wig. She was wearing some beautiful jewelry she had bought in Thailand and lovely flowing clothes. But as she carefully settled into my office sofa, moving slowly, as if she were sore from some kind of beating, her demeanor made it pretty clear she wasn't here for small talk. She had no time for wasted words. There wasn't a trace of a smile on her face. I'm not sure I had ever seen her when she wasn't smiling.

"Everybody thinks I can beat this thing," she said. "But I know I can't."

"I don't have the right spirit to beat it," she went on. "People say I'm strong and positive and a fighter. But I'm not. Not really. I fake my strength. I fake all this positivity. The truth is, I have learned to expect the worst. I have never seen a reason not to expect the worst. My ex-husband drank himself to death. I found his body days later. When I was eight and we were on vacation, my father drowned swimming off a beach on Martha's Vineyard. At first my mother and the priest told me he was just sick. When they couldn't figure out how to hide the truth from me anymore, they told me he was dead."

"I know I'm not going to beat this," she went on. "I don't have faith. I don't believe in God. And if I did believe in God, I still wouldn't believe that God could do anything about this cancer. It's just a random, meaningless curse."

She talked softly and with conviction. She was telling me her truth, not asking me or expecting me to be able to make it into something different. I understood that, and I respected her. But I despised hearing this. I wanted to stopper my ears and shake my head and tell her no, no, no, what you are saying is not true. The cancer is making you lie, the chemo is ransacking your common sense. You have to be strong because I cannot take it if you are not strong. I wanted to close my eyes on the image of her sitting on the sofa in my office, a small woman in a splendid red wig.

Let it not be so. Let it not be so. My heart beat with a prayer meant more for me than for her. I wanted to cry the way a baby does in the forsaken lost-ness of a moment it believes cannot end except in abandonment. It would not do for her to need *me.*

She did, though. She needed me. So I listened.

She couldn't tell this to anybody else, she said. Her sons, her mother, and her partner would not let her say what she knew to be true. In their view, it was essential that she remain positive, always fighting, praying, visualizing health. "But it doesn't matter," she said, "I'm not going to make it."

And I knew that if I disagreed with her, I would be denying the deepest truth of a dying woman. I held her hand. "I understand," I said.

∾

The cancer returned again. The chemo started up again. Miranda got thinner, weaker, smaller. Months passed and she fought and fought, knowing the outcome, keeping quiet about what she knew about the outcome.

She and her partner decided to get married. It made sense. He had better health insurance. Miranda hadn't wanted to marry. It wasn't that she didn't love her partner—she did. She explained to me that from the very first moment she saw him, she knew there was something terribly important that she needed to learn from him. But she hadn't known that it would be how to die.

They were married at Grace after the morning church service on a rainy Sunday three days before Halloween. Miranda wanted only the most minimal of rituals, so the service lasted ten minutes at most. She wasn't conventionally religious, and this was not to be a conventional marriage. But she *had* wanted a ring, and her partner had found her an exceptional one. It was studded all the way around with best-quality, perfectly cut diamonds. It made a brilliant ring of sparkles around her bony finger.

"*Miranda*, I take you to be my wife," her partner said, tears in his eyes, repeating after me, "to join with you and to share all that is to come, to give and to receive, to speak and to listen, to inspire and to respond, to forgive and to strengthen, and in all circumstances of our lives together to be loyal to you as long as we both shall live."

And she responded with the same words, her small hands, the hands that had touched so many, cradled in his.

~

A few months later, her husband called and asked me to come over to their house. I just assumed Miranda had wanted him to call. But once I got there I found out that she hadn't even known I was coming.

Her mother met me at the door and led me into the kitchen where she began to fix a tray of food for Miranda. She was beside herself with worry, she said.

Miranda had not been a good Catholic for a very, very long time. She would not pray.

She would not make her confession or receive the sacrament.

Years had passed since Miranda had gone to Mass. It frightened her to think that Miranda had turned her back on the church in this way. Would I talk to her? *She* had talked until she was blue in the face. And now all she wanted was for her daughter to go to heaven. But Miranda would not meet God even halfway.

Then Miranda's husband came into the kitchen. He led me gently by my elbow into the living room as Miranda's mother brought the tray down the hallway into the bedroom.

Her husband spoke softly so that her mother would not hear. He wasn't worried about Miranda not being a good Catholic, he said. He respected his mother-in-law's Catholicism, but he and Miranda shared a different kind of spirituality, one no less deep and no less valid than

Catholicism. I nodded. I understood what he meant. But, he said, he was worried because Miranda saw death as the end of everything. She would not accept the possibility of a God who could give her shelter. It broke his heart to see her refuse God. He needed her to believe, as he did, that there was a divine presence encompassing her.

He wanted me to talk to her about life after death, about hope, about the God she did not see and in which she would not believe.

I didn't understand his faith in my power to persuade her into believing what he wanted her to believe. Nor did I think it was fair to Miranda to try to persuade her away from her own experience and beliefs about life and death.

Finally he led me down the hall into the darkened bedroom where Miranda lay. She had changed radically since the day of the wedding. Frail, with sunken hollows in her cheeks and around her eyes, she spoke with effort in a voice so hoarse and low I could barely hear her. I was afraid to sit on the bed, afraid of snapping her fragile, brittle hold on life. But she made me sit close. She wanted to talk.

She couldn't sleep through the night, she told me. She would wake up and need to go to the bathroom. She couldn't do that alone anymore, so she would have to wake up her husband. It never bothered him, she said. He just wanted them to be together. After finishing up in the bathroom, they would come back to the bed and lie side by side, talking. As they lay there, they talked of everything. She had never felt as close to him as she had these recent nights. She knew how deeply he loved her, how deeply she loved him. She had never experienced, with him or with anybody else, this profound kind of intimacy, she told me. Then she paused. She was silent for a long time. I thought perhaps she was tired. Perhaps I should leave.

But the she began to talk again. In spite of that, she would give up these middle-of-the-night talks. She would give up anything if she could give up everything. If she could only give up the fight.

Her husband and her mother and her sons all wanted her to keep on going. Her doctor had said her body would be able withstand another round of chemo but that it would not change the final outcome of anything, just prolong her life a little longer. And that was what her family wanted. She didn't. The chemo was death in life to her. She didn't want to suffer through it anymore. She didn't want to suffer at all anymore, even for them.

It was time to die.

"Yes," I said. "I see that. I believe you."

~

I saw her a week later when her husband called to tell me she had entered the hospice unit at a local hospital. Years of ministry have pretty much taken away the shock of seeing the dying. But when I went into Miranda's room, I knew this was a different and worse kind of dying than I had ever seen. She lay on the bed in a feeble shroud of skin, her whole body shrunken to the size of a large Raggedy Ann doll. And like Raggedly Ann, her legs were splayed out in front of her, thickly bound in white gauze strips—to prevent swelling or to provide cushioning, I couldn't tell. Her scalp was covered in random patches of colorless hair, making her look old and unsexed. She sat in bed unmoving, unspeaking. In spite of all the dying I had seen, I did not understand how someone already so much a part of death could still be alive. It was if she had no reason for being here—nor any clear way to leave, her body unwilling to let her go.

She gazed downward, at nothing I could see. Except for her shallow respirations, she looked like a mannequin of a dying woman. She gave no sign of being aware of anyone's presence, though her husband and both sons were there. Her mother was there, still whispering to me sotto voce that she wished Miranda had prayed more.

Not long after I arrived, a friend of Miranda's came in carrying a toolbox of oils and a big handful of flowers. She pulled up a chair as close to Miranda as she could get. Then she began to anoint Miranda, speaking softly, touching her gently. She placed flowers in the scattered wisps of Miranda's hair. Though she had no strength to hold them, her friend placed flowers in Miranda's hands. She lay flowers across her chest.

I thought vaguely and fearfully of the baskets and sprays the funeral directors heap on the coffins of the dead before they are lowered into the earth. After the family leaves, the flowers are taken away. Then, without further ritual, the cemetery groundsmen lower the coffin and lay the dead in the grave. I had a colleague who made a point of staying until he could see the casket lowered into the grave. He didn't know why he did it, he told me. Out of superstition, maybe. Or fear.

Everybody in the room was silent, watching.

Her mother's brow was furrowed. She had labored to bring Miranda into the world. Now she was watching in helpless horror as her daughter slowly took leave of it.

I felt I knew what she was thinking: What good would all this oil and all these flowers do? This wasn't a Catholic rite; it wasn't even *Christian*. It was just plain pagan.

She was afraid to tender her daughter into the hands of a lesser god than the one she had been taught to fear and dread. It was the God of fear and dread who must be placated—no pagan god could get her into heaven.

It wasn't clear what this ritual might mean to Miranda either. Perhaps she could still smell the oils. Perhaps she could still hear. I didn't know. I could never remember in what order the senses failed before the dying one was made to give leave of all five.

Miranda's friend continued with her ritual, touching the husk of a body we all loved, speaking softly as if no one else were in the room and nothing out of the ordinary was happening. This dying was a part of life; that was all. It was as important for Miranda to be garlanded and perfumed for her death as it was for any bride to be gowned and coiffed for her wedding.

I did not know if the woman was a charlatan or a shaman. I did not know whether she was seducing the dying into the crossing or the living into hoping for Miranda's safe passage. But I was certain she was wise to touch with ease and affection the body that still belonged, however marginally, to Miranda.

Then the shaman's voice fell silent. She retrieved the flowers from Miranda's chest and brow and hands. She held them beneath Miranda's nose for a moment. If Miranda smelled them, she didn't, or couldn't, say. Then she gathered up the little bottles of oil and carefully placed them into the plastic slots in her toolbox. Before leaving, she leaned in closely to gently hug Miranda's fragrant and barely living body.

"Go in peace," she whispered to her. And then she left.

Once she was gone I felt a rush of relief. Now it would be okay if I left too. I could go without it seeming that what I was really doing was fleeing. But I was. I had served my time on the deathwatch. I didn't have to stay here. Outside the hospice were a sunshiny sky and a world brimming with blessings. I had daughters I needed to cook for or lose to in a chess game, daughters I could nag about the laundry or flossing. They were convinced of the uselessness of either, I of the necessities for both. I had a parish full of querulous parishioners, anxious to carp or query or, most wonderfully, laugh. I had *life*. And I could go into the world of the living and try to forget that in the world of the dying, the woman who had been minister to my sorry flesh was now rendering up her own. Maybe, if Miranda died soon, I would never have to come back to witness more of that.

I made my good-byes to the family, explaining that I had to go home to my daughters—an excuse I am able to use less and less now that they are grown. Then I stepped closer to Miranda, afraid to hug her, not like her shaman friend who had touched her body with such sureness and ease. But I had known Miranda to massage my body with the calm authority of one who knows beyond argument that touch is the most basic sacrament. I would not let myself be horrified by Miranda's body now. I leaned down and put my hands gently on her shoulders. Her bones felt as brittle as dry cornflakes.

I brought my face close to hers. All I had to do was say a last good-bye. I had said a last good-bye before—to my own mother, whose eyes by then were tearful, perhaps unseeing; my own mother, who had seemed, as Miranda did now, as if her body were simply a casing of flesh.

But I could not say good-bye to Miranda. Speaking was beyond me as I tried hard not to cry. So I said nothing. I just leaned closer to her, perhaps even to kiss her—vainly trying to demonstrate to those assembled that Miranda's dying flesh didn't frighten me.

But just then Miranda moved her hand into mine like a snail seeking a borrowed shell. She turned her wisp-tufted head to my ear and in a small voice whispered softly the only words I heard her speak that day, *I'll say hi to God for you.*

I lifted my head an inch and looked at her dying face. She had thought of herself as a pessimist and a doubter. Maybe she had been. But she was also a healer, healing still.

12

Ash Wednesday,
Maundy Thursday

Here is my servant, whom I uphold,
my chosen, in whom my soul delights;
I have put my spirit upon him;
He will bring forth justice to the nations.
He will not cry or lift up his voice,
or make it heard in the street;
a bruised reed he will not break,
and a dimly burning wick he will not quench.

—Isaiah 42:1–3

2008—Ash Wednesday, Grace Lutheran Church, Niskayuna, New York

Everything is quiet now that the people have gone home. I am sitting in my office, lingering after the evening Ash Wednesday service. My office opens directly into the chancel, and I have left the side spotlights on in there so that when I go out I won't be stumbling around in the darkness. Plus, it's strangely creepy to walk alone through a big empty church sanctuary at night. I've done it plenty of times, but having a light is far more comforting.

The Altar Guild women have finished up and gone home too. They have cleaned the Communion ware and taken home the linens to soak out the wine stains and to wash and press the corporal and purificators, fancy church names for what are essentially expensive embroidered linen towels. They have emptied the cut-glass dish of remaining ashes, pouring them back into the jam jar labeled "Ashes for Ash Wednesday." They have set the jar back on the shelf in the sacristy so we can use them again next year. My first year as the pastor at Grace Lutheran Church there weren't any ashes, so I created some by burning the accumulated matchsticks I found in the bottom of a coffee can in the sacristy and mixing in a drop of vegetable oil. This worked well enough, though not all of the matchsticks burned completely and I was afraid I might end up thumbing a piece of matchstick onto someone's sweaty brow, where it would undoubtedly stick. *That* would be a problem.

Lent has come. It is an early Lent, still cold outside, the ground still snow covered. So it will be an early Easter, which in upstate New York means you can most likely count on having to wear a winter coat over your new Easter finery. Today has been a bitterly cold day, and this evening the wind really started up. It howled during the service and made the overhanging eaves creak and groan. The roof at Grace is steeply pitched and asymmetrical in the way of 1960s church design. When it is windy, it sounds as if the building is crying out in anguish. For several years we had a cleaner who wouldn't go into the sanctuary when it was very windy because the moaning of the wind beneath the eaves reminded him, he said, of restless souls in anguish. If you were able to hear what I'm talking about, his fearfulness wouldn't strike you as far-fetched.

I need to start gathering up my things and getting ready to head for home. I promised my daughter Linnea I would make a Caesar salad for dinner. It's just the two of us at home now, her sister away at college, and I'd like to eat sometime before ten o'clock so she can get to bed at a decent hour. It's going on eight-thirty already. But right now my body feels heavy and sluggish. The Ash Wednesday services always get to me. In a way, the moaning of the building—the sound of restless, anguished souls—was appropriate. Ash Wednesday is a reliably sad service.

And things were a little askew tonight. Just little things. I got the pages of my sermon mixed up. One of the hymn numbers in the bulletin was different from the one on the hymn board. I took chalice pall and purificator off the chalice, and a fat fly dive-bombed into it, paddling his way to a happy, drunken death in the sweet kosher wine. These things happen. Especially the kamikaze flies—they happen a lot. An Altar Guild woman quickly took the chalice into the sacristy, dumped out the corpse and the wine, and refilled it from the Manischewitz bottle in the cupboard.

My own image for Ash Wednesday is that of a doorway leading into the dark season of Lent. Historically, Lent and Advent were both penitential seasons. They were the "closed" times of the year in which joyful events and rites of passage were not observed. No weddings were permitted; no confirmations or baptisms were allowed. It was important to maintain the solemnity of the season. And the Ash Wednesday service inaugurated this time of repentance and reflection, the ashes themselves a reflection of the fleeting aspect of our human lives.

Lenten disciplines, the proverbial "giving up of something," were also designed to put people in a penitential frame of mind. I don't know of anyone who tried to give up bigotry or prejudice, self-righteousness or sadness for Lent. But I think that would be more greatly pleasing to God than giving up Chardonnay or cheeseburgers.

As a pastor, I've always had mixed feelings about these penitential seasons. Many of us don't need to be further self-critical. Many of us don't need to dwell any more heavily than we already do on our failures or our sinfulness. For others, a dose of humility or self-reflection is probably a good thing—especially if that introspection bears compassionate fruits. But I'm not sure a season in the church year is the best way to facilitate that.

But Lent arrives each year, and we sing all these songs about blood, sacrifice, and human unworthiness. Some people do still give something up for Lent. I have always thought that a kind of a dumb thing to do. But I suppose it can be a convenient time to go on a diet—piety and vanity aren't really such an odd combination. But why get your knickers in a knot over the unseemly amount of beer you consume or curse words you use or chocolates you chew when children are starving and soldiers are dying and intelligent people are having to argue against intelligent design ("ID" writ large)?

Have mercy on me, O God, according to your steadfast love;
   according to your abundant mercy
   blot out my transgressions.
Wash me thoroughly from my iniquity
   and cleanse me from my sin.
For I know my transgressions and my sin is ever before me.

—Psalm 51:1–3

It seems to me that if Good Friday is about collectively mourning the death of Jesus, Ash Wednesday is about preemptively mourning our own. In Ingmar Bergman's movie *The Seventh Seal*, Death plays chess with a medieval knight. The knight is an able player, and Death even gives him some tactical advice. Still, there is no way for the knight to win. And with the services of Ash Wednesday, we begin Lent by acknowledging our inevitable journey to—quoting Hamlet—"that undiscovered country" by which Shakespeare means not Papua New Guinea, but death.

Ash Wednesday is the one time in the church year when we can't avoid talking about our mortality, our mutability. The ashes we wear remind us that we will die. And that's not the happiest of thoughts. And the cross Christians treasure as the means of salvation is also the symbol that tells us Jesus died, just as we will, too.

For twentieth-century televangelist Robert Schuller, the cross was just a bridge too far. When he was working in the late 1970s with the architect Philip Johnson to build the Crystal Cathedral in Orange County, California, he made it abundantly clear that there were to be no crosses visible anywhere on the outside or the inside of that massive building, the largest glass structure in the world. Perhaps for Schuller, with his theology of positivity, the cross was just too negative, a symbol of failure. And I read somewhere of a choral conductor who had been invited to bring her choir to the Crystal Cathedral. They were told they could sing anything they wanted, provided nothing was in a minor key.

So there were to be no crosses visible, nothing sung in a minor key, nothing that admitted of suffering and death in that pavilion of positive thinking. Danish theologian Soren Kierkegaard characterized the kind of Christianity that can't look at death and denies human suffering as, simply, "honking geese at feeding time." (And indeed, Crystal Cathedral Ministries filed for bankruptcy in 2010. The building was sold to the Roman Catholic Diocese of Orange County, which is opening a Catholic television station in the former cathedral. Kierkegaard may have been right on target.)

This avoidance of the cross doesn't just obscure death, though. It obscures life as well. Like it or not, we are mutable. Our bodies are not permanent. Death is part of our existence. Whether or not you buy into the idea of resurrection, we all must die first. The resurrection doesn't take place on the last day of Lent. The last day of Lent ends with the brutal murder of the savior. Ash Wednesday is a stark reminder that there is no way we are going to come out of life alive.

Nevertheless, each year when I plan the service, I try to find some way to soft-pedal the message and make the service less *sad*. Not that I succeed.

> *Against you, you alone have I sinned*
> *and done what is evil in your sight,*
> *so that you are justified in your sentence*
> *and blameless when you pass judgment.*
> *Indeed, I was born guilty,*
> *a sinner when my mother conceived me.*

> —Psalm 51:4–5

Same as always, the hymns tonight were sad. The choir's haunting anthem was called "Dust and Ashes Choke Our Face." The readings were about turning, repenting, acknowledging what little miseries we all are. The readings are always the same for Ash Wednesday, ever reminding us of sin. The same psalm—Psalm 51—is said each year. And then there is the imposition.

When I was a girl, all the Catholic kids went to church on Ash Wednesday so that the priest could place an ashy smudge on each of their foreheads. I always thought it was really cool, and I wanted to have a smudge on my forehead too. But we didn't do ashes in the Lutheran church. Then somehow, as liturgical styles evolved, Lutherans started imposing ashes too. It wasn't until I was an adult that I received ashes for the first time.

"Remember you are dust and to dust you shall return," the pastor said to me and marked a small cross with his thumb on my forehead. I wasn't prepared for how it felt to wear the ash and to know it symbolized my own death. I wasn't prepared to hear the words that so starkly reminded me of its inevitability. The ashes were not cool; they were *cold*.

Yet the ashes are a powerful symbol for so many people of faith, a way to mark the passage into Lent. Old Testament scholar Walter Bruggemann, in his poem "Marked By Ashes," summons our awareness to the ephemerality of all human existence:

> . . . *we begin this day with that taste of ash in our mouth:*
> *of failed hope and broken promises,*
> *of forgotten children and frightened women,*
> *we ourselves are ashes to ashes, dust to dust;*
> *we can taste our mortality as we roll the ash around on our tongues*

Ashes symbolized sorrow and powerlessness, as today they symbolize the unrest in our souls—some would say the sinfulness of our souls. But they're weighty and solemn symbols, these dark smudges I wipe onto my parishioner's brows. They're emblems of grief and mourning—in the Hebrew Scriptures, mourners and penitents alike dressed in sackcloth and ashes—as well as signs of our own mortality. Still, I secretly ponder what good it does for us to be reminded of our impermanence.

So each year I struggle a little over the ashes. But it is an important tradition for the people of Grace. Nearly everybody in the congregation decides to come forward to receive their cross of ash, mostly on their brows, sometimes on the backs of their hands. They form a line down the center aisle of the nave and one by one come to stand before me. One by one I carefully place my thumb on the brow of the person in front of me, and I remind them that they will die. I say, "Remember you are dust and to dust you shall return."

Remember you are dust and to dust you shall return.

I must have said it fifty times tonight. Same as every year, I focused on their brow when I made the cross of ash. I can't look right into their faces. It's too hard, too sad. When I distribute the bread during Communion, we share what feels to me like a sublimely intimate gaze. Our hands touch; our eyes lock onto each other's. Some people smile; some tear up. But I can't look into their faces when I mark their foreheads. I would cry if I did. As it is, I always get that burning feeling in the back of my throat from trying not to become tearful.

I would cry because I know there is a good chance I will bury a couple of these people in the course of the coming year. They will become a statistic I will record in the big, leather-bound Parish Register ("Funeral at Grace; interment in Vale Cemetery").

I might cry because the people my own age who bow their heads to me are thinking about their deaths. And that makes me think about mine.

Or I might cry because tall men, not yet stooped with age, are bending forward for my touch. Not for *my* touch, really. But it is through my touch that I am saying something to them about God. And so they bow their heads to the five-foot-three of me, and I say to them, "Remember you are dust and to dust you shall return."

And the hardest part is when my daughters come forward. Imagine saying to your kids "Remember you are dust and to dust you shall return?" I'd rather shoot off a toe than say that to my darlings. But it is what I have to do. I am their pastor. I am marking every face that stands before me with the sign of their mortality, the reminder of their inevitable deaths.

"Remember you are dust and to dust you shall return."

I never want to say this to my children. But I have said it to them for as many Ash Wednesdays as I can remember. I can't very well say that to everybody else in the congregation and then, when they come before me, say, "and you will never, ever be dust, my darlings."

For that would not be true. It will never be true. Besides, I am their mother first and foremost, much more than I am their pastor, and I cannot lie to them. Not about important things, anyway. And knowing that life is finite, contained within dates that one day will be chiseled into granite or brass and noted in a Parish Register someplace, is an important reminder for me to give them.

"Don't forget your lunch money." And "Remember you are dust and to dust you shall return."

"Please call me when you get there. I mean it." And "Remember you are dust and to dust you shall return."

> *You desire truth in the inward being*
> *therefore teach me wisdom in my secret heart.*
> *Purge me with hyssop and I shall be clean,*
> *wash me, and I shall be whiter than snow.*
> *Let me hear of joy and gladness*
> *let the bones that you have crushed rejoice.*

—Psalm 51:6–8

Tonight I tried to leaven the somberness of the service, reminding everyone that, just as the ashes remind of our created-ness, our mortality, and yes, our eventual deaths, they also remind us of our cleansing in the waters of baptism, of our being made to be a blessing to one another. And I read the words of promise from Ephesians:

> *For by grace you have been saved through faith, and this is not your own doing; it is the gift of God—not the result of works, that no one may boast. For we are what he has made us to be, created in Christ Jesus for good works, which God prepared beforehand to be our way of life.*

—Ephesians 2:8–10

Still, there is no avoiding the hollow, lonesome feeling that hangs in the air as we speak Psalm 51 together or sing in a haunting, minor key *Lord Jesus, think on me/And purge away my sin;/From earth-born passions set me free/And make me pure within* or see each other's wrinkled brows marked with ashes.

But now it's time for me to at last go home. I half hope Linnea will have washed her face so I don't have to see the mark I made on her brow. It's time for me to shake off this lethargy and sadness. I push myself up from the chair and put on my coat, scarf, and gloves, bundling up tightly against the cold wind. I pick up my pocketbook and tote bag. I glance into the mirror on the back of the bathroom door. There is a dark stain on my brow. It doesn't look like a cross to me, but it is one.

Besides all the carefully reasoned factors that have gone into my desire to leave the parish, the largest one is this: I can't go on much longer marking foreheads with the sign of death. I can't go on much longer talking freely about our sin and offering up the broken body and blood of Christ. What used to feel like such a privilege and an honor has comes to seem a brutal invasion. Why is it necessary that I always—and always in potent ritual—remind people of sin and suffering and death? It's clear from the world around us that we are big into suffering and death, and many of us are painfully aware of the sinful mess we have made. Wars and poverty and cruelty and neglect are the ashes marked all over the earth, not in a cruciform, but in willy-nilly hieroglyphs of human anguish.

I remember watching the shaman who anointed my dying friend Miranda with scented oils. She spoke softly to Miranda and put flowers in her hair and hands and on her chest right over her heart. I never offer those to the people of this congregation, so many of whom I love most dearly. I never offer blooms, but ashes; not scented oils, but the broken body of Christ. And when I baptize babies, the liturgical imagery is of death by drowning, only after which can they be raised to new life in Christ. Christian ritual is ringed round with anguish.

O Lord, open my lips and my mouth will declare your praise,
for you have no delight in sacrifice;
if I were to give a burnt offering,
you would not be pleased
The sacrifice acceptable to God is a broken spirit,
a broken and contrite heart, O God, you will not despise.

—Psalm 51:15–17

I close my office door behind me and walk across the front of the chancel. The heels on my boots are loud on the stone floor, then silent as I walk up the carpeted aisle. I turn around to look at the spot-lit back wall before I leave the sanctuary.

Behind the altar there is a massive wooden cross. Its standing beam goes from the flagstone floor all the way to the apex of the sharply pitched ceiling—a distance of maybe forty feet. The crossbeam is placed very high up on the standing beam. Both are very narrow, just a few inches in width, making them disproportionately thin in relation to the cross' imposing height. The whole effect is a little odd. It almost doesn't look like what it is. When you are walking down the church aisle, you don't even really notice it. And when you stand in the chancel, you can easily forget that you are standing beneath a towering wooden cross.

That is what it is like in the daytime, anyway. But it is different at night. Because if you stand at the entrance to the church nave when only the side spots are lit and the rest of the sanctuary is in darkness, what you can see is a thin, pitch-black shadow of the cross in bold relief on the far wall. You can't see the cross itself very well. But you can see its shadow. I have come to like the cross best this way. On those nights I have worked late or have had a meeting, as I'm on my way out of the church, I usually turn on the side spots and turn off the rest of the lights. I stand for a moment in the darkness and look at the spot-lit cross that isn't there. I am more aware of the presence of its shadow than I am of its floor-to-ceiling wooden beams.

And so this is what I do on my way out tonight after the Ash Wednesday service. I stand for a while, seeing the shadow more clearly than the cross itself. Then I switch off the lights so that all that remains lit is the red "exit" sign over the front door. And then I open that door and I go out.

~

My personal religious observances run the usual Judeo-Christian gamut with the occasional Hindu celebration thrown in (you know how we do, dear Ganesha, Remover of Obstacles, Lord of Beginnings). But there are two days that have a special spiritual resonance for me. One is Maundy Thursday, the first of the three days, "the Triduum," that lead to Easter Sunday. And the other is Yom Kippur, the day of atonement and the holiest day in the Jewish calendar.

It's on Yom Kippur that observant and even not-so-observant Jews fast and pray, with the awareness that along with the acknowledgement of failing to keep the *mitzvot*—the commandments—of Hebrew scriptures also comes the opportunity to perform greater *chassadim,* acts to promote human kindness.

It might seem odd for a Lutheran pastor to have such an affection for Yom Kippur, particularly because I haven't fasted during it since my college roommate and I did thinking we could kill two birds with one stone: be holy and get thin in one fell swoop. Neither worked, of course.

On Yom Kippur, I don't attend prayer services—the *shiksa* in the clerical collar—nor have I even heard the words of the Kol Nidre, the traditional opening prayer, except on YouTube. Yet I'm always aware of Yom Kippur. I'm aware of it as a day set apart, a day to take seriously our fallen world, our part in its brokenness, and the opportunities we also have to be part of the healing of it—in other words, our own call to *tikkun olam*—to try to heal the world.

What Maundy Thursday shares in common with Yom Kippur is that it, too, is a day when we are called to remember what we must do to heal the world. "Maundy"—the unwieldy word that, as a child I thought was "Monday," signaling to me early on that a religious world is one of contradictions, because how in hell could Monday also be Thursday?—derives from the old French *mande*, meaning "mandate." I'm probably going to really lose you when I tell you that "mandate" really means commandment. That's right, like *mitzvot*. Apart from being full of contradictions, religions are also full of etymological alphabet soup.

But at that mythic Last Supper that Maundy Thursday commemorates (think Leonardo da Vinci; think *The Da Vinci Code*; think paint by numbers; think black velvet), whoever wrote the Gospel of John reported that Jesus said, "I give you a new commandment, that you love one another. Just as I have loved you, you should love one another."

He may not have actually said it. We don't know. The room wasn't bugged. But somebody who thought he said it wrote it down. And either Jesus—or the guy who thought he said it—wasn't just whistling "Dixie."

And so we come back to it: *tikkun olam*. And the *mitzvot* we've inherited: Love one another. And remember how broken and sinful we are. Not what you'd see inside a Hallmark card. (But who shops for cards anymore anyway when you can send an e-card on Rattlebox?) The point that both Yom Kippur and Maundy Thursday make for us is that we've got our work cut out for us. Nobody said it would be pretty. Or that we'd do it perfectly. But it's our job. Our common human job: to love one another. Come hell or high water. And as Dante and the recent movie *Noah* make clear, there's plenty of imaginative invention to suggest that we know enough of both hell and high water.

My combined professional and/or personal view of things is that I don't frankly care about anybody's religious affiliations, disaffection for, or view of religion in general. *Ça m'est egal*, like the French say. Nevertheless, you can still take a serious page from Yom Kippur and Maundy Thursday. Trust me. We can love our neighbors better. And it's a long shot, but not a bad idea: try to heal the world.

~

2013—Maundy Thursday, Emmanuel-Friedens Church, Schenectady, New York

In 1529 the Swiss reformer Ulrich Zwingli met with Martin Luther in Marburg, Germany. This was more than a scholarly conference with keynote speakers and continental breakfasts. Instead, it was an attempt brokered by the German Landgrave Philip of Hesse to form a united Protestant theology. This would, Philip hoped, simultaneously crystalize a unified Reformation doctrine while at the same time strengthening the German Protestant states in an alliance against their Roman Catholic counterparts.

Well, it didn't go so well at the Marburg Colloquy. Though Luther and Zwingli agreed on many points, Luther wouldn't budge on the question of Holy Communion. *Hoc est corpus meum* is what he scrawled on the table in a bold hand. This *is* my body. While it is true that Luther rejected the Roman Catholic doctrine of transubstantiation, which taught that the bread and wine, in becoming Christ's body and blood, are no longer what they formerly were, namely bread and wine (Luther rejected the notion that the "accidents" would no longer be what they actually looked like), he did believe in the real and literal presence of Christ in the elements of the sacrament. Zwingli disagreed. For him, Holy Communion was a memorial supper that only symbolized the body and blood of Christ.

Luther would have none of it. Not at all. For Luther, what "is" meant was not up for dispute. So if Jesus said, "This is my body," then that was what he meant. And legend has it that Luther pounded the table in frustration where he had scrawled the Latin words and heatedly insisted to Zwingli: "*Hoc est corpus meum!*" What is historically verified, though, is that when they parted company, Luther pointedly refused to shake Zwingli's hand, sending larger Christendom a potent message. And we have enough of Luther's letters and writings to know that's just the kind of guy he was.

And I'm enough of a Lutheran geek that I was thinking about the Marburg Colloquy during my first Communion service at the federated United Church of Christ and American Baptist Church where I have been called as one of the interim pastors.

It's Maundy Thursday, and, as is their tradition, we are having a joint service with the United Methodist Church just down the hill. They have an interim minister too, a kindly retired Chinese man with a soft voice and a gentle demeanor. The two of us are distributing Communion.

The people come forward one by one, and Pastor Dan holds out a loaf of bread so that each one of them can break off a bit to eat. As they do, he says with a smile, "See how much Jesus loves you!"

Then they step over to me where I hold the chalice of grape juice (hey, it's a Baptist church). And I say, "The blood of Christ is shed for you." Over and over I hear myself say it, and I keep reminding myself I'm in a church that has its roots in a different Reformation tradition. It's a memorial supper here; there's a different theology determining the meaning of Holy Communion in these three denominations gathered together tonight—the UCCs, the ABCs, and the UMCs. I should be saying "The cup of salvation!" or "drink and be thankful" or maybe "God's good Gatorade" or some such thing. Maybe I should just do what Pastor Dan is doing and say, "See how much Jesus loves you!"

But I don't. It's as if I simply can't. It's as if Martin Luther and Ulrich Zwingli are duking it out in my brain, the centuries between Marburg and the new millennia dissolved like a Communion wafer in wine. In my head, Luther is slamming his fist on the table: "*Hoc est corpus meum!* The phrase "real presence" careens around my consciousness like an errant pinball. And the muscles in my cheeks involuntarily refuse to move in such a way that might allow anything flowery or metaphorical or twenty-first-century–esque to come out of my mouth. I just stand there, holding out the grape juice and saying over and over in my solemn Lutheran way, "The blood of Christ is shed for you." "The blood of Christ is shed for you." I do, however, remind myself to smile.

~

2014—Maundy Thursday, First United Methodist Church, Schenectady, New York

I'm mere weeks away from finishing up my sixteen-month stint as one of two interim pastors at Emmanuel-Friedens. For this year's Maundy Thursday service, the United Methodist Church now has a settled pastor, Sara, and we will be leading worship at her church tonight.

David, my co-pastor, is the same age as I am. Each of us celebrated our thirtieth (David) and twentieth (me) anniversary of our ordination date earlier this year. These were especially meaningful observances for each of us. For David, this was because when he came out, he was forced to leave his parish, his parsonage, and the American Baptist denomination. After some years of exile, he was able to return to ministry in the United Church of Christ, a much more progressive denomination. My anniversary was meaningful to me because, though I have wrestled plenty with my identity as a pastor, I am aware that I am still not be able to be a pastor in the branch of the Lutheran church in which I was raised because they continue to forbid the ordination of women. What this means is that between David and me, we have fifty years of parish ministry experience. We have buried, married, baptized, prayed for, and counseled hundreds and hundreds of people. Yet in the eyes of many Christians, neither of us is worthy to lead them as pastors, David because he's gay, me because I'm a woman.

Maybe it's because we'd be pariahs in some Christian communities or maybe it's because we have similar senses of humor and like to send each other goofy texts during boring meetings or maybe it's some combination of those things, but we have had a great year in ministry together. Leading worship with a friend is a lot of fun. This Maundy Thursday service was going to be one of the last times we would do so.

Earlier in the week, Sara had e-mailed us an order of worship. Frankly, it looked confusing. David and I were talking about it as we walked down the hill to the church.

"Do you understand any of this?" I asked David, indicating the bulletin, "There's going to be Holy Communion, foot washing, and anointing all going on at once? It's going to be like a three-ring circus!"

"A sacramental extravaganza," he quipped, "And it could be a hot mess."

"I know," I said, "and I hate foot washing."

"I do, too," he said, "Eeeww!"

"And what's with the anointing? I don't know anything about anointing."

Sara had asked us to arrive a half-hour early so we could figure out who was doing what. It was a warm spring night—Easter was coming late this year—so it wasn't too troubling that the door to the fellowship hall was locked. We traipsed around the huge building to the front and tried to enter that way. The front door was locked too. By now it was getting close to showtime. We needed to get inside and get our Sacramental Extravaganza jam on.

By the time we made it back to the fellowship hall door, somebody had unlocked it, and we went searching through the cavernous building for Sara.

We found her in the sanctuary, sitting on the floor in the main aisle looking up at the stained glass windows where the sun was pouring in and sending the vitreous colors bleeding all over the pews and walls. It was lovely.

"Oh, hi," she said, "have a seat. I'm just enjoying the view."

So we did, getting down on the floor next to her.

"I'm so glad we're doing this together," she said, finally.

We nodded.

"The order of worship?" I asked, "Can we talk about that?"

"Oh, yeah. It's one I used to use at the church I served in Hollywood. It's kind of fun. People liked it. I just figured we'd tweak it for the three of us. Here," she said, getting up. "Let's go over what each of us is doing."

Then she went off to get some supplies we'd need for the service, and David leaned into me, "You know," he said, "I think maybe younger pastors are a little more relaxed in their approach than you and I are."

"Yeah," I said, "I think so."

Sara came back with a washbasin and water, some towels, and a dish of oil. The Communion elements were already laid out on the altar. It was indeed going to be a kind of liturgical three-ring circus. Sara explained that we'd each in turn describe the significance of these ritual actions. Then David would preside at Communion, assisted by a layperson. At the same time, she was going to be over on *that* side—she pointed—of the sanctuary doing foot washing. (I gave an inward sigh of relief). Meanwhile, I was going to be over there on *that* side—she pointed in the other direction—doing the anointing. Worshippers could come forward and partake of any one or all three of the experiences.

Anointing? I wanted to know. Anointing how?

"Oh, well, when somebody comes up to you, what I do is I ask if they have any special thing they want me to pray about for them. And if they do, I make up a prayer about that, and if they don't I just say a more general prayer of blessing. And I put some oil on their foreheads and that's that."

"Sara," I said, "I'm a terrible pray-er. I don't do well with spontaneous praying. Not at all."

"Oh, I'm not good at that, either," she said blithely, "but something always comes out. It'll be fine."

So she handed me the oil and a towel on which to wipe my hands between prayers. I wasn't persuaded in the least. I began to try to think of canned prayers I knew by heart. The prayer that started "Lord God, you have called your servants to ventures of which we cannot see the ending, by paths as yet untrodden, through perils unknown . . ." was a good one. The only problem was that I didn't know the rest of it, so that wouldn't really do. There was my favorite prayer attributed to St. Augustine that went

> *Watch thou, dear Lord,*
> *with those who wake, or watch, or weep tonight,*
> *and give thine angels charge over those who sleep.*
> *Tend thy sick ones, Lord Christ.*
> *Rest thy weary ones.*
> *Bless thy dying ones.*
> *Soothe thy suffering ones.*
> *Pity thine afflicted ones.*
> *Shield thy joyous ones.*
> *And all, for thy love's sake. Amen,*

But I thought that seemed kind of long. And besides, parishioners were already arriving in the sanctuary, Sara was directing David and me to chairs in the chancel, and I had to find the hymn numbers in the hymnbook and try to figure out which passages in the worship order I was supposed to read. I really hoped this wasn't all going to be a dog's breakfast, to use the phrase the Emmanuel-Friedens organist uses whenever I choose a hymn he doesn't think the congregation can sing.

Here's the thing about worship services: they can be awful. They can be kitschy or poorly planned or boring or too long or too wordy. They can include very bad praise bands, where the drummer can't keep time and the lyrics are so trite and so saturated with male imagery for God you want to vomit. They can include so much incense that you really need to whip out the albuterol inhaler and take a puff before you try to sing the next hymn. They can include frightening liturgical dance or clowns (or worse, that breed of excess scariness known as "climes," which are clown mimes). I'm not kidding: worship services can be many unpleasant things.

But they can also be quiet moments of alchemical serendipity.

Sara stood up to welcome the combined congregations from the two churches. Then she said that, after some hymns and some readings, everybody was invited to come forward as they wished to experience whatever they wished—the receiving of Communion, the foot washing, or a prayer with anointing. She said that there was no particular order to where you chose to go. Nor did you have to come up at all if it felt better just to remain seated. As she spoke, I guessed that there would be a lot of people opting for Communion—there's comfort in the familiar. I figured there would be a few brave souls willing to test the waters with foot washing—or hand washing, if they were wearing socks or pantyhose. But I didn't figure many would come forward for a personal time of one-on-one prayer and anointing. And that was just fine with me.

So I stood there stiffly as people moved up to the Communion rail and David began to serve them. And sure enough, a few people began to head over toward Sara's station, where she sat, barefoot herself, on a pew across the way.

But then suddenly there was someone standing before me, a familiar face, someone from Emmanuel-Friedens. She smiled shyly.

"Is there anything you want me to pray about?" I asked, also feeling shy.

She shrugged a little. I thought she was going to say *no, nothing in particular,* and then I would just come up with some kind of generic prayer. But instead she leaned in and whispered what was on her mind.

"Okay," I said, and I dipped my finger into the oil. Marking a cross on her forehead and holding my hand there, I closed my eyes and I began to pray. I said her name and asked God to bless her. And I prayed for her with a keen awareness that she was trusting that somewhere, somehow, there was a God who was hearing me raise up her concerns. I prayed as if I believed that too. Because sometimes—okay, more than sometimes—I really think I do.

I opened my eyes again as I said "Amen," and we looked at each other.

"Thank you," she said.

"It was my pleasure," I said. And, strangely enough, it was.

For the next ten minutes I held the anointed forehead of each man or each woman who had formed a queue in front of me. Some were the faces of strangers—those were the members of the United Methodist congregation. Other faces were those I'd seen in worship on most Sundays at Emmanuel-Friedens, black faces and white faces, old faces and young faces, men and women. I knew many of their stories. Some wanted me to pray for something specific—for a sister or a spouse or for healing from an illness. Others only seemed to want to feel my touch and hear words of care addressed to their God. These public moments were of such an intimacy that though I had spent more than a year as their pastor, I felt, during my second Maundy Thursday service with them, that I had come to know them in a new and closer way.

Soon David came to stand before me. Both of us knew our time together at Emmanuel-Friedens was drawing to a close. We were ready to leave, but we were not sure what was going to come next. David was going to be married in June, and he would be serving a newly planted church in the Hudson Valley. I had plans to travel for a few weeks, but after that it wasn't clear where or even if I would continue to serve as a pastor.

I put my hand on his forehead and I realized I'd never touched David before. Sure, we'd hugged hello and good-bye at Christmas and Easter or whenever. I'm sure we'd congratulated each other on our ordination anniversaries and hugged then. But I had never put my hand on his forehead or looked closely into his eyes and really thought of him as someone who needed or wanted to hear my words raised to God on his behalf. It was a strangely sweet and strangely strong moment. And in my prayer, I felt I was praying for both of us, asking for discernment in our vocations and also for traveling mercies as we parted as fellow pastors serving together and moved forward separately into our lives.

Then, finally, Sara stood before me, she who had given me the dish of oil just a few minutes before. I dipped my thumb in and I marked a cross in oil on her forehead. Then I prayed for her, inwardly also thanking God for her, realizing that I'd learned something this Maundy Thursday, something trustworthy and real in this sacramental extravagance.

After that I handed her the dish of anointing oil, wiped my fingers on the towel I still held. And then I asked her to pray for me.